Andri Gerber, Oya Atalay Franck, Michael Mieskes (eds.)
Architectural Intelligence in the Age of Artificial Intelligence

Architecture | 93

Andri Gerber (Prof. Dr.) is co-head of the Institute of Constructive Design at the School of Architecture, Design and Civil Engineering in Winterhur, ZHAW Zurich University of Applied Sciences in Switzerland.

Oya Atalay Franck (Prof. Dr.) is dean of the School of Architecture, Design, and Civil Engineering, ZHAW Zurich University of Applied Sciences in Switzerland.

Michael Mieskes is a self-employed artist and lecturer at the School of Architecture, Design and Civil Engineering, ZHAW Zurich University of Applied Sciences in Switzerland.

Andri Gerber, Oya Atalay Franck, Michael Mieskes (eds.)

Architectural Intelligence in the Age of Artificial Intelligence

[transcript]

Bibliographic information published by the Deutsche Nationalbibliothek

The Deutsche Nationalbibliothek lists this publication in the Deutsche Nationalbibliografie; detailed bibliographic data are available in the Internet at https://dnb.dn b.de

2025 © Andri Gerber, Oya Atalay Franck, Michael Mieskes (eds.)

transcript Verlag | Hermannstraße 26 | D-33602 Bielefeld | live@transcript-verlag.de

Cover concept: Kordula Röckenhaus
Printing: Druckhaus Bechstein GmbH, Wetzlar
Proofread: Tim Flight
https://doi.org/10.14361/9783839430699
Print-ISBN: 978-3-8376-7905-2 | PDF-ISBN: 978-3-8394-3069-9
ISSN of series: 2702-8070 | eISSN of series: 2702-8089

Printed on permanent acid-free text paper.

Contents

Part 1: Introduction

Architectural Intelligence in the Age of Artificial Intelligence
Andri Gerber, Oya Atalay Franck 11

Part 2: Fundamentals

AI for Architects
Elena Gavagnin 29

AI Creativity and Chance Operations
Dieter Mersch 37

The Simulation of Intelligence and Creativity: On the Foundations of Machine Learning
Christian Georg Martin 53

Baking and Building: Reflections on Architecture and Artificial Intelligence
Michael Mieskes 71

Part 3: Interviews

The Classical Tradition of Artificial Intelligence
Andri Gerber in Conversation with Mario Carpo, February 11, 2025 (online) 85

Learning from Images
Andri Gerber in Conversation with Philipp Schaerer, Zurich, February 5, 2025 95

Part 4: Essays

A: Data

What can a Multidimensional Language Model Tell Us about Architecture?
Julia Krasselt 113

From Data-Driven to Design-Informed: A Socio-Technical Dialogue on AI, Context, and Design Futures
Bige Tunçer, Cem Ataman 125

Beyond Machine Perception: AI Urban Imagination
Darío Negueruela del Castillo, Iacopo Neri 141

B: Media and Representation

Projections: On the Design Process in AI Architecture
Roberto Bottazzi.. 157

Open Media and Experimental Intelligence
Lidia Gasperoni 167

C: Practice

Architectural Practice and Artificial Intelligence
Stefan Kurath 187

Beyond Disruption: Digital Intelligence and Human Intuition in Architectural Practice
Adam Kiryk..195

The Generative AI Paradigm: Architectural Praxis Reshaped?
Christoph Geiger, Clemens Lindner 205

D: Teaching in times of AI

The Power of Interpretation: A Reflection on the Application of Parametric
Programs and Artificial Intelligence (AI) in Teaching
Giulio Bettini, Ron Edelaar 219

AI Architecture Studio Without Architects
Immanuel Koh 227

Annex

Authors 243

Image Copyrights 255

Part 1: Introduction

Architectural Intelligence in the Age of Artificial Intelligence

Andri Gerber, Oya Atalay Franck

> ARCHITECTES: Tous imbéciles. Ou-
> blient toujours l'escalier des mai-
> sons.[1]—Gustave Flaubert

The surface of depth

It is no surprise that the recent rise of Generative AI tools has been enthusiastically received by the public. Tools such as Midjourney and Dall-E have opened
the possibilities for almost everyone—the digital divide notwithstanding—to
create worlds and to visualize ideas and concepts. Meanwhile, ChatGPT and
other tools based on large language models (LLMs) have introduced new ways
to express and conceptualize complex discourses. At first glance, these new
possibilities seem extremely democratic, as such tools were formerly restricted
to specialists like architects and writers. Not least because of these new possibilities to create three-dimensional worlds, architects, like many other professions, have seen their expertise jeopardized. However, there is much more
going on beneath the surface of these tools that concerns not just architects.

It might not be a coincidence that the metaphor of "depth" appears so
often in this context, as evidenced by the name of the latest tool to attract
public attention, Deep Seek AI, which goes along with the already existing
DeepL, DeepAI, and the notions of Deep Neuronal Networks (DNN) and Deep
Learning. As a metaphor, "depth," standing for the incommensurable, has a
long tradition. One could refer for example to Honoré de Balzac's comparison

---

1   "Architects: all idiots. Always forget the stairs." Gustave Flaubert, *Dictionnaire des idées
     reçues* (Éditions Conard, 1913), 6.

of nineteenth-century Paris with an ocean, whose depths are inscrutable.[2] This obsession with depth in the context of AI is symptomatic of a desire to leave certain things in the shadows and to suggest that "intelligence" is not just simulated but "real." Before the emergence of AI, the discourse around the world wide web was similarly accompanied by metaphors of depth and obscurity, as for example in the terms "deep web" or "dark net"; intriguingly, AI tools are dependent on the web, predating it massively for data along with all types of databases. While AI is often conceptualized through biological metaphors—the brain, neuronal networks, etc.—the metaphor of depth is a spatial metaphor that helps to conceptualize the shady side of AI, which has less to do with the tools themselves than how they are used to create, in the words of Matteo Pasquinelli, a "planetary business of surveillance and forecasting."[3] Again Pasquinelli warns us that "the problem of AI has nothing to do with intelligence per se but with the manner in which it is applied to the governance of society and labor via statistical models—ones that should be transparent and exposed to public scrutiny."[4]

The opacity of depth resonates with the pretended transparency or even invisibility of technology, creating an interesting chasm between what we do not see because it is so pervasive—transparent—and what we do not see because it is overtly complex—the depth. Martin Heidegger warned us as long ago as 1953 that technology should not be considered a means, and that both accepting or negating it would make us its slaves, while considering it as something transparent would make things even worse.[5] The transparency, or even invisibility, of technology is only dissolved when the technology is not working and we cannot perform our tasks, at which point it becomes visible. This transparency is often a consequence of the narratives of efficiency surrounding AI. And invisibility, as Eduard Kaeser suggests, is a signum of power.[6]

---

2   "Mais Paris est un véritable océan. Jetez-y la sonde, vous n'en connaîtrez jamais la profondeur." Honoré de Balzac, *Le Père Goriot* (Revue de Paris, 1834–5), ch. 3, 14.

3   Matteo Pasquinelli, *The Eye of the Master: A Social History of Artificial Intelligence* (Verso, 2023), 12.

4   Matteo Pasquinelli, "How a machine learns and fails: A grammar of error for artificial intelligence," in "Spectres of AI," ed. spheres Editorial Collective, Maya Indira Ganesh, and Stina Lohmüller, special issue, spheres, Journal for digital cultures, no. 5 (2019): 3.

5   Martin Heidegger, "Die Frage nach der Technik," in *Die Technik und die Kehre* (1953; Klett-Cotta, 2002), 5.

6   Eduard Kaeser, *Trojanische Pferde unserer Zeit. Kritische Essays zur Digitalisierung* (Schwabe Verlag, 2018), 28.

Alongside the "conceptual" depth of AI, there is also a "physical" depth we should not forget: the whole infrastructure of AI and the corresponding energy demand, carbon emissions, and water for cooling data centers, which are often overlooked. The invisibility of technology often makes its relation to the "ground" equally invisible.

Before talking about intelligence in the context of AI—and architecture—it should be made clear that this is not primarily a technological problem, but a social and a political issue—and here we have the first connection with architecture, a social and political discipline par excellence. But to understand this extended dimension, we must also comprehend the technological dimension which makes any reflection about AI so challenging, as most of us cannot understand what is going on from a technical point of view.

In order to describe the all-encompassing nature of modern technology the term "technocene"[7] has been coined, adding to the existing monikers "anthropocene"[8] and "capitalocene."[9] AI comes with a promise of totality and a model of knowledge that is contained and finite because it is computable, but as architectural historian Werner Oechslin has underscored, science is never finite and deals with the unknown, not with the known.[10] This all-encompassing nature of AI is very problematic, because it bridges everything through data—science, society, politics, economy—and at the same time flattens all differences and frictions. It is from this perspective that the abhorrent term "generative management" emerged, an oxymoron that aptly captures the paradoxes of our time. In this context, Orit Halpern and Robert Mitchell have introduced the notion of the "smartness mandate" to describe the imperative which comes alongside any AI narrative, that is to "become smart or else go extinct as a species."[11] Smartness—as in smart phones, smart cities, etc.—is an epistemology, "that is,

7   Clive Hamilton, François Gemenne, and Christophe Bonneuil, eds., *The Anthropocene and the Global Environmental Crisis: Rethinking Modernity in a New Epoch* (Routledge, 2015).

8   Paul J. Crutzen and Eugene F. Stoermer, "The 'Anthropocene,'" *IBP Newsletter*, no. 41 (2000): 17–18.

9   Jason W. Moore "The Capitalocene, Part I: on the nature and origins of our ecological crisis," *The Journal of Peasant Studies* 44, no. 3 (2017): 594–630.

10   Werner Oechslin, "Ungewissheit, die einzige Hoffnung," Scholion: Bulletin 16 (2004): 5.

11   Orit Halpern and Robert Mitchell, *The smartness mandate* (MIT Press, 2022), 220.

a way of knowing and representing the world so that one can act in and upon that world."[12]

Beyond the usual critical voices, AI and its potential to change science and society are greeted with enthusiasm. This condition is the more surprising if we consider the vast history of the critique of technology and of future optimism, not least following the horrific consequences of the atomic bomb. One has only to think of Husserl's *The Crisis of European sciences and Transcendental Philosophy* (1936) or Adorno and Horkheimer's *Dialectic of Enlightenment* (1947), the former deploring the growing estrangement of human beings from the world and the latter describing how the promises of the Enlightenment have opened the way to political totalitarianism. And this is all the more relevant, as AI nowadays is becoming almost a cult, posing a fascinating paradox, as highlighted by Eduard Kaeser: while the Enlightenment and modern science fought against any form of devotion and superstition, AI and its algorithms are gaining an almost mystical aura.[13] More than ever, we need a critical stance that acknowledges the potential but also the pitfalls of the new technology and new world paradigm. This book is a step in that direction.

Architectural intelligence

Beyond the *depth* of AI, there is the *superficiality* surrounding the notion of intelligence. In the context of AI, the term "intelligence"—as is generally known, initiated by the Dartmouth Conference in 1956—is rather misleading. Human intelligence still goes beyond the comprehension of the science studying it[14] and the brain-computer metaphor, though still fashionable, has lost much of its appeal because it is rather shortsighted. However, AI indeed plays an "imitation game," mimicking human mental processes while expanding them to sometimes unexpected results. For this reason, and for the sake simplicity, in this book we still want to keep the notion of "intelligence" at the forefront of our

---

12   Halpern and Mitchell, *The smartness mandate*, xi.

13   Kaeser, *Trojanische Pferde unserer Zeit. Kritische Essays zur Digitalisierung*, 39.

14   "Few constructs are as mysterious and controversial as human intelligence. One mystery is why, even though the concept has existed for centuries, there is still little consensus on exactly what it means for someone to be intelligent or for one person to be more intelligent than another." Janet E. Davidson and Iris A. Kemp, "Contemporary Models of Intelligence," in *The Cambridge Handbook of intelligence*, ed. Robert J. Sternberg and Scott Barry Kaufmann (Cambridge University Press, 2011), 58.

discussion. We believe that the cross-mapping of "artificial," "intelligence," and "architecture" is fruitful for a theory of architecture and AI. Architecture has seldom been discussed in terms of intelligence, but as many of the essays in this book reveal, this appears to be a useful strategy to understand the implications of AI for architecture. Considering Howard Gardner's "theory of multiple intelligence" (1983), it is eminently possible to assume a specific intelligence for architects at the intersection of different types. This is in spite of the ironic quotation by Flaubert at the start of this text, which suggests that from the outside, people might believe that we architects lack such intelligence altogether.

Depth and surface are spatial metaphors, and built and imagined spaces are clearly at the core of architecture. Probably the most irritating thing about Midjourney images is that although they simulate space, they are clearly "flat" and not architecture. It is here that the expertise of architects remains vital. Architects have a specific spatial thinking that helps them to design spaces and navigate into these. Without this spatial thinking, spaces remain empty containers without meaning. And it is through space that architects are part of the form-giving process of society, culture, and politics.

What architects must learn—as many essays in this book discuss—is how to deal with these new tools and the possibilities they open. As Lidia Gasperoni argues, they call for a new form of agency, and a new "experimental user" and performative practices.

Even though architects have always been quite critical of technological transformations, the discipline has nonetheless absorbed many revolutions, as for example Alberto Pérez-Gomez has recounted for the profound transformation of architecture during the Enlightenment.[15] Yet architects have always found a way to recast tools against their intended use. Even Gottfried Semper revealed a certain interest in science and computation in his *Entwurf eines Systemes der vergleichenden Stillehre* (1884), where he made a quite astonishing reference to mathematics, describing the possibility to define an artwork through a function of the type $Y = F (x, y, z, etc.)$, only then to discard the possibility that reflection and calculation could replace talent and natural taste. In his words, he made use of this comparison only as a "crutch."[16] What appears new in the context of AI is that many tools are not only biased by the type of data they digest, but resistant to any use beyond the intended one.

---

15   Alberto Pérez-Gomez, *Architecture and the crisis of modern science* (MIT Press, 1983).

16   Gottfried Semper, "Entwurf eines Systemes der vergleichenden Stillehre," in *Kleine Schriften* (W. Spemann, 1884), 267–68.

With AI tools, there is a tendency to quantify architecture through the black box of certain programs, to automatically resort to a solution that is "good." This happens, for example when architecture is judged under the conditions of ecology and thus made to quantifiable parameters such as CO_2 emissions or embodied energy.

Fig. 1: Werner Hofmann, cover of the magazine "Aktuelles Bauen,"
January 1979

Fig. 2: Gottfried Semper, Entwurf eines Systemes der vergleichenden Stillehre, 1884, 267

Der Ausbruck wird angewandt zur Bezeichnung einer ge=
wissen Vollendungsstufe der Kunstwerke, welche erreicht werden kann :
    1. durch künstlerisch richtige Ausnutzung der Mittel,
    2. durch Beobachtung jener Beschränkungen, welche teils in
der Aufgabe selbst enthalten und gegeben sind, teils auch durch
die begleitenden Nebenumstände bedingt werden, welche die
Lösung derselben in jedem einzelnen Falle mobifizieren.
    Jedes Kunstwerk ist ein Resultat, oder, um mich eines
mathematischen Ausbruckes zu bedienen, eine Funktion einer be=
liebigen Anzahl von Agentien oder Kräften, welche die variablen
Koefficienten ihrer Verkörperung sind.

$$Y = F \; (x, y, z \; \text{2c.})$$

    In dieser Formel steht Y für das Gesamtresultat und
x, y, z 2c. stellen ebensoviele verschiedene Agentien dar, welche
in irgend welcher Richtung zusammen oder aufeinander wirken,

The point where AI and architectural intelligence diverge the most is in the absence of a sentient body for the former. Architecture and architectural theory have traditionally included—or explicitly rejected—the body as datum from which space is experienced.[17] Science and philosophy have debated the relation of body and mind and the possibility of thought without body for centuries. Whatever AI will generate, it will not come from some social/physical body and its interactions with the world, which on the contrary is fundamental for architecture and the spatial interaction/experience.

In that sense one can conduct a riveting experiment with AI. When prompted "what is the body of artificial intelligence," Midjourney will symptomatically deliver the image of a head without a body, as if cognizant of its own shortcomings. Prompting the same in ChatGPT generates the following answer (with "body" in brackets in the original):

The 'body' of artificial intelligence (AI) can be understood metaphorically or in a technical sense, depending on the context.
Metaphorical Body:

---

17   Harry Francis Mallgrave, *Architecture and Embodiment: The Implications of the new sciences and humanities for design* (Routledge, 2013).

In this sense, the 'body' of AI could refer to the way AI interacts with the physical world or how it performs tasks. For example, in robotics, an AI system might have a physical 'body' in the form of a robot that can move, interact with its environment, and execute tasks based on the AI's processing. The body here represents the tangible or mechanical form in which the AI operates.[18]

Fig 3: Midjourney, prompt: "What is the body of artificial intelligence," 2024

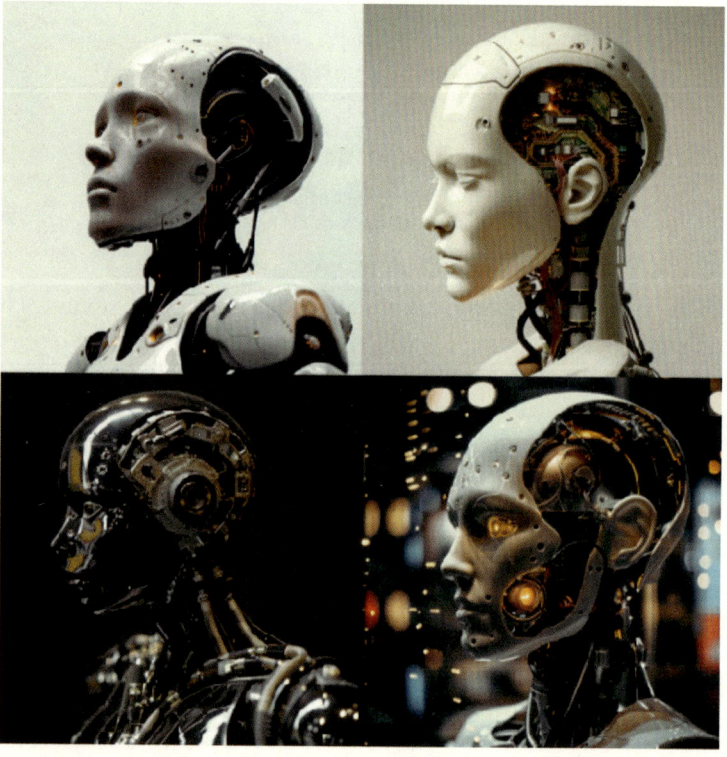

If one goes further and specifically asks how AI senses the world, the answer is equally interesting (again, "sense" in brackets in the original):

---

18   ChatGPT, March 15, 2025.

Artificial intelligence (AI) can 'sense' the world through various **sensors** and **data inputs**, which allow it to gather information from its environment, similar to how humans rely on their senses (sight, hearing, touch, etc.). The process of sensing in AI involves different technologies that enable AI systems to perceive, interpret, and respond to the data around them.[19]

AI thus suggests that it can overcome the absence of a physical body with a plethora of data and sensors that allow it to "experience" the world.

Desperately seeking theory

With this book we want to conceptualize AI in the context of architecture. That is, we want to establish theories—plural—that can help us to understand the multiple implications of architecture in this regard. To talk about theories in this specific context might appear outdated, at least in the classical Greek tradition of the word, where the *theoros* is just an observer. The literary critic Terry Eagleton famously declared in 2004 that "the golden age of cultural theory is long past," referring to theories from structuralism, poststructuralism, and postmodernism.[20] It is interesting that while few of the great thinkers of this "golden age" managed to remain relevant—we are thinking here in particular Foucault's concept of "biopolitics" or "governmentality"—authors such as Jean Baudrillard and Jacques Derrida are returning prominently to the stage and in contemporary discourse. Why not discuss, for example, the absence of authorship in AI tools with Roland Barthes' theory of the "death of the author," or the suppression of any disciplinary peculiarity with Derrida's theory of *différance*? Does Baudrillard's apodictic analysis and forecast about a world made only by "simulacres" not resonate with our present condition (a reference made by others in this book)?[21] The appeal these theories offer in this context resides not least in the fact that they are not classical theories, but hybrids. Falko Blask, for example, describes Baudrillard's theory as a "fictionalized theory."[22] Already, then, these authors experimented with new hybrid forms of theory to cope with the complex reality. We might need such hybrid theories to be able to grasp AI,

19   ChatGPT, March 15, 2025.
20   Terry Eagleton, *After Theory* (Penguin, 2004).
21   Jean Baudrillard, *L'échange symbolique et la mort* (Gallimard, 1976).
22   Falko Blask, *Jean Baudrillard zur Einführung* (Junius, 1995), 10.

which, as Elena Gavagnin describes in her essay, "can feel like trying to catch a slimy fish that keeps slipping when gripped, leaving you with only buzzwords in your hands."

But we might need go one step further, as theories nowadays seem not only to be outdated, but have been supplanted by simulations. As Eduard Kaeser ironically asks: why turn to the painful and "useless" path of theory when we have efficient means of prediction?[23] Martin Warnke and Anne Dippel have recently highlighted that our worldview, once based on evidence, laws, and principles, is now profoundly shaken. Flagging ideologies and weak theories have taken their place in a bottomless deconstruction of the world derived from algorithms.[24] One of the main problems with these simulations is that they are based on speculations and as such never fail, unlike theories.[25] AI indeed suggests a flawlessness which is disconcerting and false, as theories always fail and need to be reformulated, updated.

That said, we need a new form of theory that is operational and creates its own simulations. The *theoros* cannot longer be an observer but must become an actor interacting with AI and the world. We need to develop a "performative" use of the medium capable of destabilizing and transforming representational practices (see the essays of Lidia Gasperoni and Darío Negueruela del Castillo and Iacopo Neri in this volume). We need to develop specific and new forms of AI literacy, where we define ourselves on what knowledge this is based upon and how we can gain it. Doing so will probably keep us busy for several years.

Structure of the book

With all this in mind, we invited a series of authors—architects, historians, philosophers—to help to develop such theories and to better understand how AI could be used, and to what extent this will influence and change our practice.[26] The authors reveal different gradients of engagement, enthusiasm, and

---

23   Kaeser, *Trojanische Pferde unserer Zeit. Kritische Essays zur Digitalisierung*, 113.

24   Martin Warnke and Anne Dippel, *Tiefen der Täuschung. Computersimulationen und Wirklichkeitserzeugung* (Matthes & Seitz, 2022), 12.

25   Warnke and Dippel, *Tiefen der Täuschung*, 15.

26   The book has its origins in a conference we (Andri Gerber, Michael Mieskes and Atalay Franck) organized on May 3, 2024 at the ZHAW in Winterthur. Based on the findings and discussions of the conference, we invited the speakers, along with some additional experts, to contribute an essay to the volume.

criticism regarding AI as well as a more or less "conservative" view of architecture, and it was very important to us to represent this diversity in the book. The *depth* of their reflection also varies along their implication or critical distance. Ultimately, we are talking about something that is still in the making, but which, exactly because of this inchoate state, we might still be able to influence.

This introduction represents the first of four parts. In the second, titled "Fundamentals," we asked four non-architects to set the ground for the book. All four define boundaries and differences between AI and human intelligence/creativity.

Elena Gavagnin, a researcher and lecturer specializing in AI, data science, and computational astrophysics, introduces the concept of intelligence and how this is reflected in AI. She highlights shortcomings and differences, in particular how different learning modes blend in humans and not in AI, and how our physical presence is a fundamental aspect of human intelligence.

Further on, two philosophers, Dieter Mersch and Christian Georg Martin, contextualize AI in a broader history of intelligence, with particular focus on the role of creativity and thinking.

Against the backdrop of the history of computer art, Mersch makes the point that in the discussion of current AI-generated art, creativity and randomness are often confused. What we are missing in AI is an epistemic added value that makes the incompatible or the incommensurable significant. Creativity implies a "thinking of its own," which cannot be replicated by AI. AI will thus never be able to be "creative" in the terms defined by Mersch. Martin comes to a similar conclusion through another path and with a more general focus. The point of divergence he identifies between AI and human intelligence is in the role of concepts and conceptual activity which will never be comparable. Once we understand that AI is a tool, the main question is how to differentiate between use and abuse, and how to avoid the latter. The answer implies a use that allows us to improve and not to delegate our intelligent activities.

The last essay of this section is by artist and media theorist Michael Mieskes, who builds a bridge between philosophy and architecture by confronting—which might initially sound bizarre—baking and building. His point is indirectly also about use and abuse: AI should be there to expand our realm of experience, and not to lose contact with our environment. In his essay, he defines the terms by which we can discuss and approach AI in the context of architecture.

The third part is made up of two interviews. In the first, architectural historian Mario Carpo makes a plea for a return to the classical tradition, which was based on copying, much like AI today. That is, while we are all focused on looking forward into the future, we should instead look back at our history and learn from it.

In the second, visual artist Philippe Schaerer shows us, through the lens of his long expertise on reading and making digital images, how to better understand the images created by AI. AI tools in his understanding are useless without an author that comes with an idea or concept that AI would never be able to produce on its own initiative. Schaerer's own form of creativity will always be dependent on a human being. At the same time, reflecting on his own work after AI, he admits it has lost some of its artisanal practices and turned into a more curatorial stance.

Both Carpo and Schaerer stress the importance of teaching younger generations a critical approach to data and images, as they often lack a certain historical and cultural background.

The fourth part is the most substantial and divides the essays along four subjects: data, media and representation, practice, and teaching.

The first section tackles the fundamental question of what the data of architecture can be. If the answer is plans, elevations, sections, diagrams, and renderings, another question arises: How do we digitize this data, and how do we make the complexity of information contained in it accessible and translate it to CAAD? If the problematic bias[27] related to a certain type of data is well known and utterly problematic in replicating certain prejudices, what will be the bias of specific architectural data that can be found online?

Julia Krasselt, a linguist and professor for methods of language data analysis, discusses in her contribution one specific form of data—language—in the context of AI. Based on word embeddings, she presents the preliminary results of her research on the language of architecture, based on three Swiss architectural magazines published between 1977 and 2021.[28] Not only does she show the potential of such an analysis of a large corpus, but also the extent to which language and architecture are interrelated and the former can determine the latter. The "data" as such is not simply a representation of something, but itself

---

27   Joy Buolamwini, *Unmasking AI: My mission to protect what is human in a world of machines* (Penguin, 2023).

28   Julia Krasselt and Andri Gerber, "Sprache konstruiert auch etwas," interview by Tamino Kuny and Marcel Bächtiger, *Hochparterre* 3 (2025): 20–25.

influences architecture. Language cannot be thus considered neutral data for architecture. This reveals how complex and far from univocal the relationship between data and output is.

Based on examples from their teaching and research, Bige Tunçer and Cem Ataman discuss data-driven approaches in urban design and planning and the tension that results between the rich cultural, political, and historical tradition of urban environments on the one hand, and the uniformity that comes along with standardized data practices on the other. While acknowledging all the advantages that the integration of multi-modal data can bring for the practice, this calls for a paradigm shift, from data-driven design to design-driven data. The consequence would be a new "symbiotic relationship between intelligent workflows and human expertise"; that is, a new relationship between designers and AI tools. Urban design has to remain human-centric and data can help in this, by supporting "context-sensitive decision-making."

Darío Negueruela del Castillo and Iacopo Neri discuss how, in the context of the collective imaginary of urban environments, AI creates a digital shadow of these environments, which takes the place of the "real city" and of anything local and specific. This digital shadow is both the result of the "surplus data" and of "data colonialism." What appears to be an extension and an opening of reality is, rather, creating a closed system. Negueruela del Castillo and Neri make reference to three of their own projects based on AI-models, which allow them to engage with this reality and to render the contradictions of urban knowledge visible. Furthermore, the projects reveal the strongly political dimension of "urban AI." For them, this calls for an extension of the "right to the city" described by Henry Lefebvre to a "right to the algorithmic city," implying that we do not have to abandon computational tools, but work with them to create a more inclusive and open "reality."

The second section revolves around the mediality of AI and the relation of input, output, and representation. While AI is often described as a black box—a rather old metaphor—it displays a particular relationship between production and reproduction which appears to be quite new. AI tools are based on the reproduction of data and learning processes, but this reproduction seems to be at the same time a process of production, creating an interesting hybrid where the two are no longer clearly distinguishable. AI not only replicates data, but transforms it, creating a result which is strictly speaking the reproduction of these data. As a medium, it has a strong impact on the data and their transformation.

In the first essay, architect and researcher Roberto Bottazzi discusses the impact of "Deep Learning Models" (DL) on the practice of architecture and how these models transform the site of the user's agency from the process to the output, thus rendering the user a sort of curator. While designers in the past were acting upon the processes and could design/code them, with AI, they can only intervene upon input and/or output. With reference to his own teaching, Bottazzi pleads for a new strategic use of AI and a corresponding digital literacy which should allow boundaries to be broken and the limits of the influence of AI to be redrawn. Architects then can overthrow a passive posture and create an urgently needed "conceptual agenda for architecture."

The second essay, by philosopher and architectural theorist Lidia Gasperoni, starts from the question of how AI influences human interactions and the general experience of the world. To overcome the technological determinism of AI, Gasperoni postulates the need for new experimental practices and an experimental user, capable of introducing a performative use of the medium. These experimental practices have the potential to open AI as a medium and to introduce a counter-use of the technology.

The third section is the most "practical," as it approaches the question of how AI will impact the discipline and the practice of architecture. Here, four architects share their insights on how AI has impacted their work.

Architect and urbanist Stefan Kurath takes a mostly theoretical stance. He underscores how architecture is often oversimplified by excluding the complex production conditions which make every project something unique and hardly reproducible. As a consequence, he makes the case for a theory of architectural practice as a starting point for any discussion about AI's impact. He furthermore points out that data in architecture is always based on the known, and this known is what led us to all our contemporary crises. An AI-influenced architectural practice based on this data will thus only replicate them.

Adam Kiryk is Head of the AI Unit at Penzel Valier. In his essay he retraces the introduction of a newly created "AI-Unit" at Penzel Valier and describes the impact of the introduction of several AI tools in the office, in particular those based on LLMs. His experience in this sense is thoroughly positive, as these tools became "creative dialogue partners" for the employees of the office. The role of the architect then shifts from a *creator* to a *curator* of AI-generated ideas. Based on this experience, Kiryk argues that AI will be more of an evolution than a disruption.

Christoph Geiger and Clemens Lindner, both working at Zaha Hadid Architects (ZHA)—a practice at the forefront of digital architecture—underscore in their essay the huge potential of Generative AI, but at the same time warn about its present shortcomings, such as the absence of structured and labeled datasets and of a unified computational framework. To really progress in this domain, for Geiger and Lindner, there is the need for an independent architectural research ecosystem to ensure the advancement of the discipline.

The final section is dedicated to teaching architecture through and with AI. The approaches here could not be more different, while both remaining critical.

Giulio Bettini and Ron Edelaar describe in their essay a teaching experiment they introduced at ZHAW in 2023, which was accompanied both by the use of different AI tools and a theoretical framing of the phenomena through the inputs of a series of experts. The paper neatly sums up all the aforementioned differences between AI and human intelligence. Bettini and Edelaar underscore the human power of interpretation in the context of architecture, but also of experimentation, play, and even naivety. They describe a thought experiment comparing how AI and an architect would react to a specific task, and the result is quite revealing of the differences. As a conclusion to their teaching experiment, the reflection on what AI does and how it functions was more fruitful for the teachers and students than what it actually produced, as this also allowed them to reflect upon architecture and its conventions.

In the final essay of the book, Immanuel Koh describes his Codeless Studio in the context of the famous Paperless Studio, a didactic experiment by Bernard Tschumi in the mid-1990s at Columbia University. But as much as the Paperless Studio was not about getting rid of paper altogether, the term "codeless studio" is more of a conceptual provocation that describes the work with the new AI-native designers where coding will not completely disappear. Koh describes several experiments brought forward with students in the Spatial Design Studio and the theory of "neural tectonics" that emerged from these experiments. AI then becomes a tool that shapes "creatively desirable AI weirdness" and can be used also against its initial intentions. Once more, this calls for a critical embracing of AI, not least in order to understand its limits and potentials.

Engage with new forms of performative praxis. Open the closed box of AI and remain critical. Acknowledge the political dimension of AI and develop counter-practices. These are probably the most important takeaways from this book. The future will tell us to what extent this was possible.[29]

---

29   The authors would like to thank Tim Kammasch for his constructive criticism of this essay.

Part 2: Fundamentals

AI for Architects

Elena Gavagnin

Trying to define what "AI" is can feel like trying to catch a slimy fish that keeps slipping when gripped, leaving you with only buzzwords in your hands. The term in itself is much older than the current hype, which started in the second decade of the twenty-first century after the "data science" hype. The quest for machines to perform "intelligent" tasks, or tasks linked to the expression of some sort of intelligence, was formally recognized and named "AI" in the mid-1950s by researchers including John McCarthy, Herbert Simon, and Arthur Samuel. However, the conceptual groundwork can be traced back to Alan Turing, and even further if we consider the foundational algorithmic principles at the basis of much modern AI.

Clearly, in order to define and explain what AI is and how it works, a natural starting point is the definition of "intelligence." This, however, seems to be the critical yet crucial part in the "sliminess" of AI. One of the best definitions available is given by the very same John McCarthy and reflects the broader context in which it was formulated: "intelligence is the computational part of the ability to achieve goals in the world."[1] Intelligence is directly linked to the ability to compute something and the concept of intention. "To achieve goals" appears to be the distinguishing prerogative of an intelligent entity, even though this is an inherently relative concept, since the notion of a goal depends on the context and, in particular, on the perspective of an observer. Richard Sutton expands on this relativity, stating that "a goal-achieving system is one that is more usefully understood in terms of outcomes than in terms of mechanisms."[2] This suggests that an observer perceives such a system primarily through its outcomes rather than through the underlying mechanisms driving it.

---

1   John McCarthy, "What is artificial intelligence?" (Stanford University, 2007), 2, http://w
     ww-formal.stanford.edu/jmc/whatisai.pdf.
2   Rich Sutton, "The definition of intelligence," *Incomplete Ideas* (blog), July 9, 2016, http://
     incompleteideas.net/IncIdeas/DefinitionOfIntelligence.html.

The quest for intelligent systems is often, in a first approximation, reduced to the problem of "how to construct computer programs that automatically improve with experience."[3] This reflects the emergence of machine learning as a key branch of AI—one that approaches intelligence by enabling machines to learn from data and refine their performance over time, rather than relying solely on manually programmed rules. A formal and well-posed definition of learning is given by Tom Mitchell: "A computer program is said to learn from experience E with respect to some task T and some performance measure P, if its performance on T, as measured by P, improves with experience E."[4]

This definition broadly defines learning as any automatic improvement connected with experience. Historically, however, three distinct paradigms of learning have emerged: supervised, unsupervised, and reinforcement learning. Apart from involving different tasks and performance metrics, their main underlying distinction lies in the amount of human supervision required, which implicitly affects how and what kind of experience the system acquires.

Supervised learning assumes that a model's predictions can be verified against a human-defined ground truth, similar to checking answers at the back of a math textbook after solving a problem. The system compares its predictions with the correct answers, which must be explicitly provided.[5] In this case, experience consists of a collection of labelled examples—that is, data accompanied by their correct outputs. In contrast, unsupervised learning involves discovering patterns and structures in data without labels by analyzing distributions and relationships within the dataset.[6] Here, experience is represented by the amount of unlabeled data, which enables the detection of hidden structures and meaningful groupings. The third classic learning paradigm is reinforcement learning, in which an agent learns through trial and error, updating its behavior based on feedback from the environment.[7] In this case, experience is represented by the agent's interactions with the environment, where it takes actions, observes new states, and

---

3   Tom Mitchell, *Machine Learning* (McGraw-Hill, 1997), xv.

4   Mitchell, *Machine Learning*, 2.

5   Mitchell, *Machine Learning*, 2; Trevor Hastie, Robert Tibshirani, and Jerome Friedman, *The Elements of Statistical Learning: Data Mining, Inference, and Prediction*, 2nd ed. (Springer, 2009).

6   Christopher Bishop, *Pattern Recognition and Machine Learning* (Springer, 2006).

7   Richard S. Sutton and Andrew Barto, *Reinforcement Learning: An Introduction* (MIT Press, 1998).

receives rewards or penalties. The more it interacts, the more it learns and improves. These three classic learning modalities closely resemble how humans learn. We can intuitively recognize parallels with instruction-based learning,[8] discovery/statistical learning,[9] and operant conditioning.[10] However, in humans, these learning modes are not strictly separate—they often blend, overlap, and influence each other in complex ways.

In all cases, we have seen that the experience is represented by the data available, whether in the form of examples or interactions with an environment. The need for data to enable learning naturally leads to the necessity of collecting and representing these data. Recording as much data as possible becomes central for AI, hence the well-known hype around Big Data & Co. The fact that learning requires data is not surprising—after all, the same applies to humans—but AI models require a strictly numerical representation of information to perform computations. By having to define a way to "encode"—to represent—information numerically, it becomes clear that the choice of representation also influences the effectiveness of learning.

One major shift in AI research has been the recognition that the way data are represented internally by a system significantly affects its ability to generalize and transfer knowledge. Representational learning then emerged as a paradigm for automatically deriving abstract features.[11] Rather than manually engineering which edges, shapes, or keywords are important, the system learns a latent space that captures the intrinsic salient patterns. A latent space is a compressed, abstract representation of data in a lower-dimensional space. One form of representational learning is self-supervision, in which models learn general features from raw data without human-provided labels. This is made possible by designing so-called pretext tasks, where the "labels"

8   Robert M. Gagné, *The Conditions of Learning and Theory of Instruction* (Holt, Rinehart & Winston, 1965).

9   Jerome S. Bruner, "The act of discovery," *Harvard Educational Review* 31, no. 1 (1961): 21–32; Jenny R. Saffran, Richard N. Aslin, and Elissa L. Newport, "Statistical learning by 8-month-old infants," *Science* 274 (1996): 1926–28.

10   B. F. Skinner, *The Behavior of Organisms: An Experimental Analysis* (Appleton-Century-Crofts, 1938).

11   Yann LeCun, Yoshua Bengio, and Geoffrey Hinton, "Deep learning," *Nature* 521 (2015): 436–44, https://doi.org/10.1038/nature14539.

come automatically from the structure of the data itself. Autoencoders[12] can be considered an early approach in this direction: A network tries to reconstruct its own input, effectively creating "labels" from the input itself. In modern deep learning, language modeling (predicting the next word) also serves as a self-supervised objective, since the data themselves provide the target (the "next word"). Other examples of pretext tasks include predicting the context of an image patch,[13] colorizing a grayscale image,[14] or reassembling jigsaw puzzles.[15] Representational learning represents a further step in that not only are the model's parameters learned, but also the input features themselves.

Interestingly, the concept of representational learning finds an evocative, if more artistic, parallel in the Dear Data project.[16]

In this collaborative experiment, two designers collected personal data on aspects of their daily lives—ranging from coffee consumption to emotional states—and transformed those raw measurements into hand-drawn visualizations. Although not algorithmic, Dear Data demonstrates how the process of deciding what to collect and how to depict it can provide emergent insights. In AI-based representational learning, a similar but automated process unfolds at scale: data of various forms (images, text, sensor readings) are mapped onto multi-dimensional latent spaces that encode higher-level semantics within the data.

One of the advantages of having an abstract, multi-dimensional latent representation of a data point (e.g., an image) is that it transforms the original form (an array of pixels) into a more general encoding that captures distinguishing features and contextual meaning. Such a general representation be-

---

12   David E. Rumelhart, Geoffrey E. Hinton, and Ronald J. Williams, "Learning representations by back-propagating errors," *Nature* 323 (1986): 533–36, https://doi.org/10.1038/3 23533a0.

13   Carl Doersch, Abhinav Gupta, and Alexei A. Efros, "Unsupervised visual representation learning by context prediction," in *Proceedings of the IEEE International Conference on Computer Vision (ICCV)* (2015), 1422–30, https://link.springer.com/chapter/10.1007/978-3-31 9-46466-4_5.

14   Richard Zhang, Phillip Isola, and Alexei A. Efros, "Colorful image colorization," in *European Conference on Computer Vision (ECCV)* (2016), 649–66, https://link.springer.com/chapter/10.1007/978-3-319-46487-9_40.

15   Mehdi Noroozi and Paolo Favaro, "Unsupervised learning of visual representations by solving jigsaw puzzles," in *European Conference on Computer Vision (ECCV)* (2016), 69–84, https://link.springer.com/chapter/10.1007/978-3-319-46466-4_5.

16   Giorgia Lupi and Stefanie Posavec, *Dear Data* (Princeton Architectural Press, 2016).

comes universal and transcends data-domain boundaries—such as text versus visual data—since these representations can be put in mutual relation and jointly trained. Contrastive multimodal learning models (e.g., CLIP[17]) operate on multiple data modalities within this shared latent space, enabling them to learn representations that capture semantic parallels across different formats. As a result, they can generate captions for images or produce images from text. Another peculiar aspect is that in latent spaces learned by neural networks (especially in large-scale models), semantically-related items tend to be close together. Sampling near a known point produces outputs that share semantic meaning or structural appearance qualities, which is the idea at the basis of generative AI.

Fig. 4: Giorgia Lupi & Stefanie Posavec, Dear Data, 2016

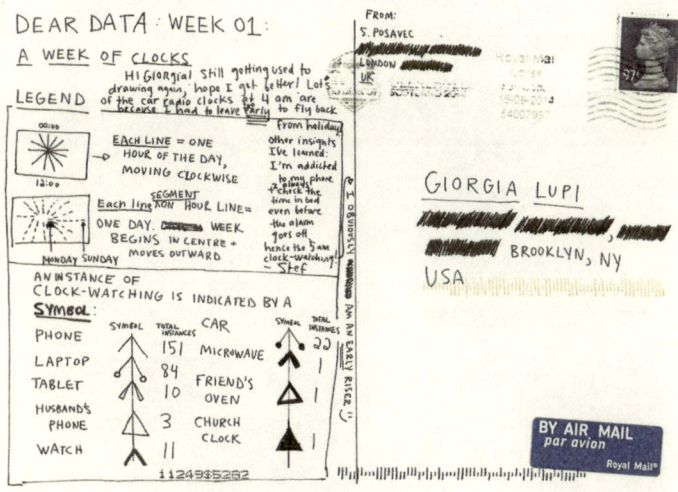

The euphoric advancements and remarkable successes of the described approaches—originally driven by the quest for intelligence and the ambition to build learning machines—can give the impression that modern AI is capable of almost anything. However, this is not (yet) the case. Asked, for example, to

---

17   Alec Radford et al., "Learning transferable visual models from natural language supervision," in *Proceedings of the International Conference on Machine Learning (ICML)* (2021), https://arxiv.org/abs/2103.00020.

distinguish which hand rests on Psyche's head in Canova's *Psyche Revived by Cupid's Kiss*, most visual-language models fail to provide the correct answer—a situation that, until recently, also applied to Leonardo's *Mona Lisa*.

Fig. 5: Antonio Canova, Psyche Revived by Cupid's Kiss, 1787

When faced with the same question, humans naturally answer from the perspective of the person whose hand it is, not from that of the observer. In other words, the right hand of a person is never referred to as the left one just because it appears on the left side from an observer's point of view. This, however, is not always the case for AI models. The surprising shortcomings in tasks that come naturally to humans—such as social and spatial cognition, especially perspective-taking—highlight an important gap. This ability, deeply connected to our innate sense of physical presence, our embodied experience of space, and our awareness that others have bodies both different from and similar to our own, invites deeper reflection on AI within an architectural context.

What does it truly mean to feel the space and immerse ourselves in it as well as in the people around us? And is this a prerequisite to achieve truly intelligent machines?

AI Creativity and Chance Operations

Dieter Mersch

The following considerations are devoted to determining the extent to which artificial systems can be creative in terms of artistic practices. Only those aesthetic productions that have been generated solely by means of AI programs are discussed. The central question concerns the nature of their "creative *momentum*," i.e., whether the attribution of genuine creativity to formal machine processing is adequate or stems from a category error. The thesis is that in all AI projects—whether historical ones or recent models such as Convolutional Neural Networks (CNN), Generative Adversial Networks (GAN), or Large Language Models (LLM) —random parameters are used at a central point in order to produce creative moments, confusing creativity and randomness.

Neural networks and machine learning

"Computer art" is not a precisely defined phenomenon; many forms can be distinguished, including collaborative projects between artists on the one hand and AI, robotics, and network systems on the other. In addition, there are all kinds of interactive projects in which control is achieved through dialogical interaction between humans and machines. In contrast to this, only *genuine AI projects*—those that claim to have already solved the creativity-problem by getting the machines themselves to act creatively—are considered below.

If one attempts to gain a heuristic overview of the various solutions that circulate today, three main forms can be distinguished so far:

a) *AI projects* that originate from identification programs such as image and facial recognition and use them against the grain. Images are generated depending on previously entered data sets that are taken from existing databases and whose character remains recognizable in the output of the programs. One example is the so-called "Inceptionalism" project founded by Alexander Mordvintsev and Mike Tyka, both Google employees.

b) *Compilative projects* that recombine a large amount of historically given input like works of art, either by imitating a certain style of painting or by mutating motifs over time on the basis of statistical averaging and thus creating new "works." Examples include *The Next Rembrandt* (2016), a project initiated by Microsoft in collaboration with Delft University of Technology, the Mauritshuis in The Hague, and Amsterdam's Museum Het Rembrandthuis on behalf of the advertising agency J. Walter Thompson, as well as the widely-discussed portrait *Edmond de Belamy* by the French artist group Obvious (2018), which was auctioned for USD\$432,500. They are mainly based on GAN.

c) *Prompt-based design projects* based on text-to-image generators such as DALL-E, Midjourney, or Stable Diffusion, to name just the best known. They are continuations of LLMs such as ChatGPT, which in turn has now gained a number of competitors including Grok and Lama. They react to certain textual descriptions, whereby the results vary greatly depending on the accuracy or vagueness of the input, but all in all they are nothing more than *illustrations of voice commands*.

This in turn must be distinguished from art productions in which artists misappropriate various AI systems and draw on specific "aesthetics" to create immersive or critical works of art based on (1), (2), and/or (3)—Mario Klingemann, Refik Anadol, Christa Sommerer, Travor Paeglen, and Hito Steyerl come to mind. Their discussion is omitted in the following because their works are based on artistic principles that conceal rather than exhibit the genuine share of AI-generated creativity. Instead, the focus is on programs that pretend to be creative in a human way in their own right. Prompt-based design projects based on text-to-image generators are also omitted because their creative potential is too meagre; not only because they depend on human-set prompts, but also because repetition and thus cliché reign supreme in them.

In contrast, the focus is on the first two image generators mentioned above in order to investigate their inner mathematical structure. Upon closer observation, they add something new to what the computer experiments of the 1960s launched, namely artificial productions by means of random parameters: statistical optimizations that proceed economically and thereby stage systematic mutation leaps alongside a much richer source material. They work through massive networking, above all by strengthening and weakening connections and their weights using matrix calculations into which filter functions are woven. The decisive factor here is the use of an "aesthetic" Turing test to verify the originality of their artistic and creative status by testing the quality of the results, comparing their artificial productions with works by existing artists *cora publico*.[1] The assertion is that, if no difference can be recognized for the time being, i.e., if we are dealing with an *undecidability*, we must credit computer art—as Turing postulated for machine intelligence—with an equally original and creative rank as artistic creations. However, the comparative situation fails to take into consideration, first, the difference between undecidability and indistinguishability, because it is not possible to infer the latter from the former, and second that, as Arthur Danto has demonstrated on the basis of Andy Warhol's *Brillo Boxes* (1964), the distinction between art and non-art is not a matter of the *aisthēsis* alone. The artistry of an object is by no means determined only by visual appearance; rather, art is first and foremost a way of thinking whose expression does not submit to the appearance of visibility.

The criticism presented below is thus based on the fact that the technical procedure of artificial art and creativity and, as a result, the recognition of a work or an action as "creative" or "artistic," differ seriously (i) from a proper understanding of creativity and art itself; and (ii) because AI is based on a short-circuited concept of art and creativity, since the actual momentum of artistic *creation* in all computer models in question comes from a *probabilistic caesura as a marker of difference* that promises the simulation of autonomous acts. In this way, (iii) the aesthetic Turing test—like the original one—turns out to be a paralogism that says nothing.

Aesthetic AI projects based on image and facial recognition programs

This refers us back to the actual, seemingly "creative" image generators, whereby for reasons of space we will focus paradigmatically to CNNs and GANs alone. In order to understand them and their potentials, one must

---

1   On the problem of an aesthetic Turing test, see Catrin Misselhorn, "Wie ein handelsübliches Urinal," *Süddeutsche Zeitung*, February 21, 2025, https://www.suedde utsche.de/kultur/ki-kunst-christie-s-auktion-li.3203930?reduced=true (last accessed 22.2.2025).

penetrate to the heart of their mathematical functions. In fact, the first models that triggered a certain hype about the intrinsic creativity of computer programs were, in addition to game programs—in particular chess computers such as Deep Blue or the AlphaGo from Deep Mind—and neural networks, preferably used for image classification or object recognition. The most powerful of these are CNNs, based on massive parallel connections of different *layers*.[2] Their mathematical structure is grounded in multidimensional, linear systems of equations, but in such a way that it is not their solution itself that is of interest, but the distribution and calculation of their "weights" or coefficients, whose order can in turn be written down as matrices. Decisive for their transformation, which provides the actual recognition, are again the so-called "convolutions," i.e., specific functions, which generate third functions by composition, which induce the strengthening or weakening of the network connections. A certain *black box character* is ascribed to their mode of operation, insofar as it is unclear even to their designers according to which criteria the machines make their decisions—which are of course not *theirs*, but effects of their calculations. Above a certain level of complexity, *emergences* necessarily arise which—even in equation systems—no longer appear logical, but rather approximately so. Where darkness prevails, people tend to attribute independent or magical properties, as if machines resemble living creatures.

In addition, the functional structures used, by focusing on frequency distributions, deviation rates, or Gaussian curves, i.e., on statistical measurements, make the results appear as if they exceed the simple determinative random processes of earlier eras. In truth, they do nothing more than shift them.[3] Correspondingly, their systematic application—according to Margaret Boden's theory of creativity,[4] which underlies most descriptions of AI art projects as authoritative—produces "interesting," sometimes "surprising" or "unanticipated," results, superficially appearing to be "new." The attributes that Boden herself classified as insufficient, however, seem to be enough for

---

2   Cf. Yann LeCun, *Generalization and Network Design Strategies*, Technical Report CRG-TR-89-4 (University of Toronto, 1989), https://yann.lecun.com/exdb/publis/pdf/lecun-89.pdf. For the history see: K. Kavukcouglu and C. Farabet, "Convolutional Networks and Application in Vision," in *Circuits and Systems (ISCAS): Proceedings of 2010 IEEE International Symposium* (2010), 253–56.

3   For an overview, see Philip Galanter, "Computational Aesthetic Evaluation: Past and Future," in *Computers and Creativity*, ed. Jon McCormack and Mark d'Inverno (Springer, 2012), 255–93.

4   Margaret Boden, *The Creative Mind: Myths and Mechanisms* (Routledge, 2003).

many *artificial artists* to promote their productions as "creative," even if they are selective and lack a sense of global narratives, let alone whether they meet human-relevance criteria. In contrast, there is a *persistent precedent for reception-aesthetics* in computer-art theories, that, where confronted with opacity, sense the potential for authentic creative leaps, because it looks as if the programs generate original material. However, it is not aesthetics of reception that are decisive for art and creativity, but aesthetics of production: It is not *what appears* a surprising twist that is essential, *but the underlying artistic thinking, its experimental arrangement and its epistemic content*, that is decisive, and in contrast to that, *what happens in the machines mathematically when they generate their artifacts*. To speak of "art" or authentic creativity therefore indeed seems hypertrophic.

Fig. 6: Alexander Mordvintsev, image from the Deep Dream series.

Look for instance at Alexander Mordvintsev's Deep Dream series (Fig. 1). What is happening here? The image shown is based on an application of CNN, but oblique to its actual function.[5] A large number of hidden "computer layers" are interconnected and provided with a large number of equally standardized inputs, usually simple animals or objects, which in turn are converted into discrete sets of numbers in order to be computable: in this case dogs and other animals. A primitive semiotic approach is at the basis here in order to teach machines recognition. It is important to pay attention to the theoretical foundations in order to understand their reductionism. This is because the method imposes specific conditions on the input, *namely clearly labelable data sets* that originate from plain representation (the primitive semiotic approach)—i.e., clearly specified objects that can be assigned the name "dog," "cat," and the like. The recognition process is thus basically rooted on an *indexical orbis pictus system* that, after a period of avant-garde abstraction, literally makes pictorial representationalism absolute again. It is not necessary to know what "cats" and "dogs" are; rather, their recognition requires quantifications which, as with facial identifications, are based on measurements—e.g., of *landmarks*, a procedure from cartography—which, as we know, can occasionally lead to confusion in the case of cats and dogs.

According to his narrative, Mordvintsev, from Google Zurich, had the idea one sleepless night, supposedly in order to understand how the machines work internally, to stop their processes in the middle, as it were, and feed the intermediate result back into the recognition machine as a new input, and to do this repeatedly, contrary to the original intention. Then, in the middle of the recognition process, discrete sets of numbers emerge, which, retranslated into images, reveal strange entities—chimera-like hallucinations that still prove their dog-like nature, but distorted. We are thus dealing with a mixture of indices, i.e., the production of hybrids or bastards that seem to resemble unusual, uncanny nocturnal creatures, but whose random generation is by no means compatible with what we understand by creativity or art. Although, according to Margaret Boden's minimal criteria, they certainly represent "the surprising," "the unpredictable" or "the unusual," and "newness," this is not enough to see

---

5   For more details on how it works, see Alexander Mordvintsev, Christopher Olah, and Mike Tyka, "DeepDream: A Code Example for Visualizing Neural Networks," *Google Research* (blog), July 1, 2015, https://research.google/blog/deepdream-a-code-example-for-visualizing-neural-networks/. See also Alexander Mordvintsev, Christopher Olah, and Mike Tyka, "Inceptionism: Going Deeper into Neural Networks," *Google Research* (blog), June 18, 2015, https://research.google/blog/inceptionism-going-deeper-into-neural-networks/; Arthur I. Miller, The Artist in the Machine: The World of AI-Powered Creativity (MIT Press, 2019): 58ff.

the pictures as a creative work of art worthy of being exhibited. "Mordvintsev's adventure ... was to completely transform our conception of what computers were capable of. His great idea was to let them off the leash, see what happened when they were given a little freedom,"[6] comments Arthur I. Miller in *The Artist in the Machine*, one of the seminal monographs on machine creativity. Their "little freedom" gives rise to phantoms like those from schizophrenic drawings, whose stylistic presence Mordvintsev dubbed, together with Google employee Mike Tyka, who enthusiastically embraced the idea, "Inceptionalism."[7]

An exhibition at Google Art Space in San Francisco in 2015 displayed the collection to the public, with such success that both Mordvintsev and Tyka have since described themselves as computer scientists and computer artists at the same time. However, it is no coincidence that the name "Inceptionalism" is reminiscent of avant-garde styles. So here we have the first "works" of a new generation of AI-supported computer "art" which, however, does not present a new movement in art, but at best some *psychedelic kitsch*.[8]

Compilative AI art projects

The next stage of so-called "creative" AI programs is far more sophisticated, in particular the GANs designed by Google employee Ian Goodfellow in 2014, as well as the subsequent CANs by Ahmed Elgammal. Goodfellow's GANs, which are the paradigmatic focus here, were originally used to generate "realistic" looking images from certain templates. In other words, it is the exact reverse of image recognition: images of objects or faces are generated synthetically from large amounts of data, for example by changing resolutions, filling gaps, applying styles or composing new images from a series of historically predetermined ones.[9] GANs are the basis of most of today's "creative" image generators, but we owe their misappropriation for art production to such spectacular examples

---

6   Miller, The Artist in the Machine, 59.
7   Miller, The Artist in the Machine, 66.
8   Cf. Dieter Mersch, "Creativity and Artificial Intelligence. Some remarks on a critique of algorithmic rationality," *Zeitschrift für Medienwissenschaft*, no. 21 (2019): 65–74; Mersch, "Ideen zu einer Kritik 'algorithmischer' Rationalität," *Deutsche Zeitschrift für Philosophie* 67, no. 5 (2019): 851–73.
9   See Ian Goodfellow et al., "Generative Adversarial Nets," in Advances in Neural Information Processing Systems 27 NIPS 2014) (2014), https://papers.nips.cc/paper_files/p aper/2014/hash/5ca3e9b122f61f8f06494c97b1afccf3-Abstract.html.

as the aforementioned portrait *Edmond de Belamy* by the French arts collective Obvious, which first triggered the hype surrounding "AI art."

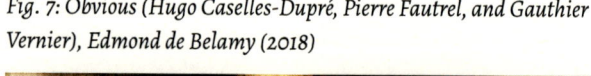

Fig. 7: Obvious (Hugo Caselles-Dupré, Pierre Fautrel, and Gauthier Vernier), Edmond de Belamy (2018)

GANs operate dialogically on the basis of two CNNs that compete with each other. The aim is to create structurally random but creative, i.e., autonomous, images. The first program acts as a *generator* (G), the other as a *discriminator* (D), which evaluates the output of the former according to certain criteria, which in turn are derived from an underlying input set. So, what "dogs" and "non-dogs" are for the classical image recognition of *convolutional networks*, real or non-real or artistic or non-artistic-looking images are for the GANs, whereby "creation" and "criticism" alternate—however, the anthropomorphizing way of speaking should not obscure the fact that we are still dealing exclusively with the *operativity of pattern recognition*, which works statistically and does not "judge" at all.

As the actual aim of the GANs—in contrast to predecessor models—is to *simulate image models by using mathematical patterns*, only the *generator* is initially relevant, while the *discriminator* has restrictive functions. Like Bense's concrete poetry of the early 1960s, the generator starts with random numbers, while the discriminator comes up with the image material trained from the databases and corrects it by simply deciding if p ε G also belongs to D or not. Hence, we are dealing, right from the start, with a twofold concept of chance: First, the random selection of an initial image p in G, and second, the randomly selected set of images as a benchmark for D, which serves as a criterion for the entire process of competition. What then happens is the successive generation of order from random chaos, which converges approximately to a certain point by using optimization processes. As with all recognition and generation programs, the discriminated evaluations are thus based on probability values, so that a third random measure comes into play, because none of the programs work exactly; we are always confronted with statistically-smoothed threshold values that break off where no further substantial improvement can be achieved. Both pre-trained *convolutional networks* in this way compete against each other, whereby, in accordance with the competitive situation of the two networks, we are confronted with a game manual that emphasizes the ludic character of the overall production. The generator G, hence, delivers improved outputs step by step along the outputs of the discriminator D, thanks to so-called *loss functions* known from economics, until D no longer considers them as errors or deviations.

Mathematically, the process is based on formal game-theoretical premises, as introduced by Oskar Morgenstern and John von Neumann, in particular the so-called mini-max-method and the so called "Nash equilibrium for zero-sum games," which can be used to solve optimization processes with the help of gradient methods according to the formula

$$\min \max E_X [LOG(D(X))] + E_z \log(1 - D(G(z)))]$$

The formula is also known from the signature of the portrait of *Edmond de Belamy*, whereby the name "Belamy" as a French translation of "Goodfellow" not only pays homage to the architect of the GANs, but the signature also serves as a reproduction of the central algorithm—standard to machine learning programs—on which Goodfellow grounded the entire two-sided generation process. However, this process should not be regarded as straightforward, inevitably leading to a hypothetical convergence point, for a number of "accidents" can happen along the way—such as the frequent "mode collapse," which consists of concentrating on a certain type of image so that the various outputs are too similar, and the process is ineffective. Sometimes the game also ends in circulation or empty noise, especially if the networks are dysfunctionally coupled. Moreover, the parameters can be set too tightly and the gradients too small, so that the process expands endlessly. The mathematics of systems is therefore by no means devoid of experimentation; rather, it is the product of a pragmatics based on various tests and trial-and-error procedures.

At the same time, one can see what this kind of "creative" image generation aims at, especially when it is used to generate art. We are consistently dealing with (i) *probabilistic functions* and (ii) *optimization procedures*; while (iii) the generation of images owes itself to a *ludic procedure* that Roger Caillois, in his classification of the ludic, would have assigned without hesitation to the category "agon," i.e., to a very specific, binary-structured form of play, typical of economical conflicts.[10] All three elements enter into the process of *creatio* and, together with the actual parameters of chance, define the specific *momentum* of machine creativity, which is only indirectly able to depict the necessary difference, the acausal "leap." The ludic reason (iv), on the other hand, also has its origins in the economic with its game strategies trained on a competitive situation, so that the underlying type of reason forms an *economic rationality* alongside the *functional-mathematical* one.

The production of creativity and art is therefore not based on *aesthetic principles*, but exclusively on *mathematical and economic decisions*. If we move specifically from pure image generation—which can encompass any type of imaging, including fictitious photographs such as those on the website *This Person Does Not Exist*[11]—to the question of artworks that make an *explicitly creative claim*, a fifth element should be added, because (v) the "art machines" incorporate *material extracts from all possible art-historical epochs* in the first place. They therefore obtain their basic data from museum repositories or public databases such as Rhizome Artbase and the like in order to elicit the characteristic features that are used to generate "new" products as genuine AI creations; for example, in the case of *Edmond de Belamy*, 15,000 head portraits from the period between the fifteenth and twentieth centuries.[12] Using mini-max-functions, the AI averages these historically canonized works of art and emulates from them what

---

10   Cf. Roger Caillois, *Man, play, and games* (University of Illinois Press, 2001).

11   https://thispersondoesnotexist.com/.

12   Miller, *The Artist in the Machine*, 119ff.; Hanno Rauterberg, *Die Kunst der Zukunft. Über den Traum von der kreativen Maschine* (Suhrkamp, 2021), 48ff. See also Ahmed Elgammal, "What the Art World Is Failing to Grasp about Christie's AI Portrait Coup," Artsy, October 29, 2018, https://www.artsy.net/article/artsy-editorial-art-failing-grasp-christies-ai-portrait-coup.

appears to be "new." The crucial point then is that *the source of machine creativity* is *the art of mankind*, so that the machines *"learn"* and continue into the future what has already been done in the past. There is no artificial newness in a machine-like sense, but only human creative work and its variation or permutation. The writer Daniel Kehlmann therefore aptly referred to AI as a "secondary user" in his Stuttgart speech on the future, *Mein Algorithmus und ich*,[13] just as Noam Chomsky has flatly accused it of ongoing plagiarism.[14]

However, because machines *project into the future what was already there in the past*, they lack any actual innovativeness. Instead, the possibility of their *inventio* remains tied to the past, true to Nelson-Goodman's dictum that "to create" means "to re-create."[15] Indeed, the quantity of existing works is multiplied many times over in an arbitrary way, so that the creative shrinks to a certain manner of mutation or varying repetition. Caesuras—such as the historical caesura around 1800, the transition to subjective-romantic art, or around 1900, the change to the disruptive avant-gardes—do not occur in this way. The radicality of a break is not in the disposition of machines; it takes humans to break and—as Hannah Arendt characterized the creative act—to begin anew. It is therefore no wonder that, projected into the future, machine creativity and its capacity will gradually become weaker and poorer because it is based solely on *repetition, chance, and variation*. In other words: *AI creativity and AI art necessarily tend to degenerate* successively *with increasing use*.

Evaluation and analysis

This brings us to the end of a brief evaluation, which again can only be sketched for reasons of space. The deception and misdirection of the entire debate about "genuine art and creativity from computers" obviously lie in the fact that the concept of creativity remains essentially misunderstood or naïve, because in its kernel human creation originates from a *reflexive mode*. It cannot be substituted by random processes, just as it is not sufficient to rely just on evolutionary mutation or on repetition and variation. Reflexivity is to be understood in

---

13   Daniel Kehlmann, *Mein Algorithmus und Ich. Stuttgarter Zukunftsrede* (Klett-Cotta, 2021).

14   Cf. Noam Chomsky, Gary Marcus, and Jeremy Kahn, "Debunking the great AI lie," Web Summit, November 14, 2022, YouTube video, 32:23, https://www.youtube.com/watch?v=PBdZi_JtV4c.

15   Nelson Goodman, *Ways of Worldmaking* (Hackett Publishing Company, 1978).

the literal sense: as *reflectere* in terms of referring back or turning around. We therefore understand creativity not as *a positive capacity of producing something new*, nor as *invention*, but as a primarily *negative force*, as expressed in turning back the gaze, or turning around thought. We do not deny that the concepts such as intuition, inspiration, imagination, or even association and figuration, can be useful; however, at best they refer to the *condition of the creative*, not to its *source or leap and thus to what creativity does or causes in particular, and what makes it happen in the first place.*[16]

Every *creatio*, to begin with this Latin term, reveals itself through its situatedness, i.e., its temporally boundedness, and its relation to the intrinsic constellation of a cultural epoch. It thus *responds* to its inner contradictions and unsolved problems, its obstacles or fundamental impossibilities as they show themselves in the limits of what can be said, imagined, and thought. Their structure and conditions, their excluded and included, enter into the creative act which, as a negative practice, literally seeks to leap over and resolve them (and not "solve" them in a solutionist sense). Creativity thus requires a "leap out," as it were, as the Polish aphorist Stanislaw Jerzy Lec said about the "Open Sesame": "I want to get out."[17] Therefore the actual *creatio* does not seek the entrance, but the exit. The primary experience that ignites the creative *momentum* is thus an act of liberation in the face of closed orders, being trapped in obstructive structures and the apparent hopelessness of opening or unlocking them. *For this reason, the paradox is the prime place where creativity arises*; the creative does not follow any derivation or deviation from rules, no sudden occurrence or coincidence, and certainly not the deterministic mathematical operations. Nor is its source the "nocturnal shaft" of Hegel's images[18] or Sigmund Freud's unconscious or the *écriture automatique* of surrealism. Rather, the creative act derives from the undecidability of paradoxical constellations, their "impossible possibility," and the attempt to destroy their confinement and limitations. It is precisely this impossible possibility that the concept of creativity shares with that of art, which is why there is an intimate connection between them.

---

16   On the connection between creativity and reflexivity, see Dieter Mersch, "Sprung in eine neue Reflexionsebene," in "Ressource Kreativität," special issue, *Kunstforum International* 250 (2017): 136–49.

17   Stanislaw Jerzy Lec, *More Unkempt Thoughts*, trans. Jacek Galazka (Funk & Wagnalls, 1964).

18   Georg Wilhelm Friedrich Hegel, *Werke*, vol. 10, *Enzyklopädie der philosophischen Wissenschaften* [1817] (Suhrkamp, 1979), 258ff.

The fact, however, that creativity has its reason in something other than a combination of chance and variation, that it is fulfilled in "the different" rather than the revelation of the new, and that art has its meaning in liberating thought and perception from the narrowness of the common-sense-cage rather than in some spectacular aesthetic appearance that at best serves decorative purposes, should be outlined in more detail with respect to a few basic principles of its significance. They anchor their practices, as a social institution, together with science in the open space of what can be addressed as "cultural *episteme*." In contrast, AI art localizes the artistic solely in the ludic as well as in design practices; therefore, it devotes its value exclusively to the visible or audible and relates it to the externality of its bare appearance and the experience it induces. It thus restitutes an understanding of art that consecrates it again to *aisthesis*. This is why values such as beauty, intensity, and immersiveness return as preferred aesthetic feelings and criteria of its evaluation. This in turn is opposed to concepts of art developed in the entire history of aesthetics, i.e., those from Antiquity, handed down through medieval and modern art, and peaking in recent avant-gardism and post-avant-gardism. It also contrasts any understanding of art from the perspective of the aesthetic and its epistemic impact. Correspondingly, what art is and what leads us to label certain objects, representations, images, musical compositions or installations, performances, novels, and the like as "artistic" lies deeper than what is simply accessible to the senses.

This requires a consistent shift from a preference for reception aesthetics to a perspective of *production*. Consequently, an aesthetic is advocated that understands art and creativity from *practices of composition* in the literal sense of *com-positio*, the *interconnection of the disparate*. Here, disparity aims at the heterogeneous, i.e., recalcitrant material, visual, or acoustic breaks, incomparable things or incommensurabilities that react alien to one another and whose gaps or cracks allow the happening of another appearance and thus make the invisible visible or the inaudible audible. A *specific form of thinking* is embodied in this exposition of the invisible or the inaudible. It can be apostrophized as an independent cognitive practice. Our crucial point is: it is incongruous with any act AI is capable of. This is because this exceeding concept of aesthetic thinking cannot be traced back to the formal *logos* or to structures of logical rationality, as embodied in mathematics, or to statistical or numerical pattern recognition, as used in machine learning. *Logos* refers to the mind, to order; likewise, logical rationality must be separated from reason. Instead, AI, whether algorithmically terminated or grounded in probability theory, remains anchored in pure logic and "formal syntaxes." They not only lack meaning—at best, the modeling of the semantic in AI models follows a second-order syntax—but above all the uniqueness of a *sense of meaning*. It also follows from this that the concept of thinking in general and of aesthetic thinking in particular cannot be predetermined "logocentrically"; rather, any logical or logocentric concept of thinking is misleading. This is why, in our *Epistemologies of Aesthetics*,[19] we spoke of "art" being a *different kind of thinking* and at the same time *something other than thinking*, i.e., thinking outside the logocentric mode.

How is this otherness to be understood? More fundamental than rational structure in thinking is, as Kant rightly emphasized, *synthesis*. *Synthēsis* literally means "bringing together"; that is, in thinking, linking different or disparate elements together, placed in a series or related to one another. The standard form of this sequence or connection is "predication," which admittedly privileges a certain form of *synthēsis*, namely the propositional statement "A is p," which assigns a property to a subject and identifies its determination with this feature. Propositional thinking is rooted in the identification of the non-identical, as Theodor W. Adorno put it,[20] which in turn obeys the logic of inclusion: substances are broken down into a number of attributes and conversely "de-identified" by this number.

In contrast to the discursive, the aesthetic is about a *different kind* of connection. It can best be understood in terms of "montage": different things are "tied together" in their very differentiality (*com-positio*) and thus left in their difference as well as their disparity. They resonate with each other in such a way that an epistemic added value emerges from them. Therefore, if logical thinking is founded in the logic of identity, aesthetic thinking obeys an "alogic" of differences. This means that art proves to be a different way of thinking in the sense of an other-than-logocentric way of thinking, namely a specifically *aesthetic–practical way of "heterogeneous interconnection."* The expression "heterogeneous interconnection" deliberately makes use of a *contradictio in adiecto*, because the preferred form of such connections is disruption, contradiction, or the paradoxical. Adorno therefore defines their structural mode in particular—as the core concept of his philosophy of art—as a "synthesis without judgment."[21] It is non-judgmental because it gets by without concepts

---

19   Cf. Dieter Mersch, *Epistemologies of Aesthetics* (Diaphanes, 2015).

20   Cf. Theodor W. Adorno, *Negative Dialectics*, trans. E. B. Ashton (Routledge, 1990).

21   Cf. Theodor W. Adorno, *Ästhetik (1958/59)*, ed. Eberhard Ortland (Suhrkamp, 2017); see, especially, the 19th lecture, 294ff. See also Dieter Mersch, "Die ästhetische Synthesis.

for the time being, because it does not proceed in a determinative manner, but rather brings non-identical things together in a "constellation" or "configuration," whereby the prefix "con" again reminds us of the "together with" of the compositional. The decisive factor in this *nondeterminative syntheses of the aesthetic* is thus the "compositional" in its literal meaning of linking or interweaving disparate elements in its singularity, whereby everything possible can be linked or put together: blocks of different sounds, narrative strands, individual words or colors, things that are foreign to each other such as felt and grease or the like. You could argue that AI does this too. But its image processes systematically synthesize pixel by pixel and step by step *from bottom up*. The nature of the compositional proves to be *atomistic* in the same sense *as analytic and syntactic*. Moreover, as we have seen, AI compiles; it assembles different patterns that it has taken from human arts and the "art of the world" and combines them together into new meaningless sensations without any sense of their compositional "drama" and thus without any epistemic surplus.

Conclusion

Combing entities and putting different objects together is therefore not enough to turn them into something that we perceive as "creative" or "artistically significant" or to produce something that we are inclined to call "art." Any kind of combination can lead to an artistic *momentum*, but not every kind induces an *artistic* momentum. So, what must be added? In our opinion, the decisive moment that brings an artistic and creative *surplus* lies in the fact that we are dealing with bulky, contrary, or contradictory constellations, with the interconnection of the incompatible or incommensurable, which can become significant because it creates a tension in itself and uses contradictions to "make the constellated elements dance," as Karl Marx said of social relations. The thesis is then that an epistemic added value, a reflexive gain, can emerge from the combination of disparities, and it is only this epistemic added value and its immanent reflexivity that trigger a creative leap and turn an *aesthetic* artifact into an *artistic* one.

Zur Form künstlerischen Denkens," in *Praktiken ästhetischen Denkens*, ed. Silvia Henke, Dieter Mersch, et al. (transcript, 2021), 53–82.

Creative thinking "thinks" in this mode of its own. AI cannot work in this way.[22] At best, it generates something that allows such events to occur by chance. But this emergence is not a matter of the programs, but a happening in the eye of the beholder. This is why the randomness and chance that come into play here again are not in themselves creative but, rather, like those famous monkeys randomly hitting keys on typewriters for an infinite amount of time who must "almost surely" eventually produce the complete works of Shakespeare.[23]

22   For more details, see Dieter Mersch, *Kann KI Kunst?* (Halem Verlag, forthcoming 2025).

23   The infinite monkey theorem was first published in Émile Borel, "Mécanique Statis-
tique et Irréversibilité," *Journal Phys.*, 5th series, 3 (1913): 189–96. It exemplifies a statistical lemma concerning the relationship between probability and infinity.

The Simulation of Intelligence and Creativity: On the Foundations of Machine Learning

Christian Georg Martin

Introduction

Ever since its inception in the 1950s the research program of AI has been marked by a profound ambiguity which is still with us today. The proposal for the 1956 "Dartmouth Summer Research Project on Artificial Intelligence," to which that program owes its name, was based on the "conjecture that every aspect of learning or any other feature of intelligence can be in principle so precisely described that a machine can be made to *simulate* it."[1] In 1957, Frank Rosenblatt, the forefather of the deep learning approach to AI which has regained prominence in recent decades and is currently the field's leading AI paradigm,[2] characterized the perceptron, the first artificial pattern recognition system imitating the human brain, as "*a model* of a system which is primarily concerned with the recognition of the forms, sounds, and other stimuli which make up the ordinary physical world, as we know it through our senses."[3] While on the one hand conceiving of AI as a *simulation* or *model* of human intelligence, the forefathers of AI, on the other hand, viewed the creation of *"fully intelligent* machines" as imminent.[4] The same ambiguity can

---

1   John McCarthy, Marvin L. Minsky, Nathaniel Rochester, and Claude E. Shannon, "A Proposal for the Dartmouth Summer Research Project on Artificial Intelligence: August 31, 1955 [1955]," *AI Magazine* 27, no. 4 (2006): 12, https://doi.org/10.1609/aimag.v27i4.1904.

2   See Melanie Mitchell, *Artificial Intelligence: A Guide for Thinking Humans* (Random House, 2020), 7–9.

3   Frank Rosenblatt, *Two Theorems of Statistical Separability in the Perceptron* (Cornell Aeronautical Laboratory, 1956), 2.

4   Rosenblatt, *Two Theorems*, 5.

be observed at present, for instance, insofar as large language *models* such as ChatGPT are often credited with thought, meaningful speech, and creativity.

It only makes sense to speak of a "model" or a "simulation" if there is a difference in kind between the model or simulation and what it models or simulates: a model or simulation is not "the real thing." Accordingly, if a machine could indeed be granted thought, understanding, or creativity, it would not just be a model or simulation thereof. In many cases, it is easy to tell a model or simulation and its object apart. There is no temptation, for instance, to confuse a climate model run by a computer with climate itself, i.e., the actual weather conditions on earth over a period of time. In other cases, however, a simulation might resemble its object in ways that give rise to confusion. Such confusion can also be deliberately created so as to illicitly substitute an established practice with one that merely simulates it. The simulation of democratic procedures in a nascent authoritarian state, for instance, is designed to conceal the fact that the state in question isn't a democracy any more. If a human practice is being replaced by a simulation of it, what ultimately results is deskilling: an impoverishment of the capacity to engage in the original activity.

As I shall argue, the deep neural networks underlying contemporary AI can only provide us with more or less impressive simulations of intelligent activity. That something is a mere simulation does not mean it couldn't be useful. However, if the output of AI amounts to a simulation of intelligent and creative activity, this raises the question of what kinds of *subservient* use we can or should put it to within our own intelligent and creative activities. The question of how to distinguish between potential use and abuse of AI within human practice is vastly complex and deeply variegated, depending on the particular activity in question and its place within our forms of life. To dispel some of the fog that currently surrounds the deep learning approach to AI, it seems helpful to compare an elementary and pervasive example of intelligent activity of ours with its machine learning counterpart so as to precisely explain why the latter amounts to a mere simulation of the activity in question. Accordingly, rather than aiming to compare human and artificial intelligence, broadly speaking, the present contribution contents itself with confronting them with regard to an elementary example, the use of ordinary concepts such as *red* or *inside*.

When reflecting on what humans or machines *can do* we compare *capacities* rather than particular *occurrences*. Many of *our* capacities are self-constituting, i.e., we learn them by doing and deepen them by way of ongoing exercise. Deep neural networks, in turn, acquire their capacities in a process of training. A capacity is a potential to engage in a certain kind of activity that can be exercised on an indefinite number of occasions. The capacity is defined by what it is the capacity for, i.e., by examples of its successful exercise. All kinds of things might in fact go wrong when a capacity is exercised, and its exercise will then be flawed. Nonetheless, what the capacity is for can only be grasped by recourse to what is achieved if things go well. It is therefore misguided to compare human and artificial intelligence, as is usual in the machine learning community, by comparing *average* scores on a certain kind of task. Instead, one needs to ask with an eye on the particularly felicitous exercise of a human capacity whether a machine could in principle do *that*.

The following comparison between intelligent activity on our part and the output of deep neural networks is conceptual rather than observational. We dispose of a certain understanding of our own intelligent activities by virtue of engaging in them rather than based on observing ourselves doing certain things. It cannot happen, for instance, that I'm baking a cake or getting married without me knowing that I am. Such knowledge is not based on observation of an independent object, but is internal to the activity known. It is philosophy which clarifies and deepens the self-knowledge that is inherent to our intelligent activities such as thinking, speaking, or artistic creation. Such clarification is required since the inchoate self-knowledge inherent to our intelligent activities tends to be confused.

It might require observation to find out whether a machine can in fact do what we designed it to do. It does not require observation to find out whether a machine that has only apparently been designed to engage in full-blown intelligent activity might in fact exhibit such activity. For intelligent activity does not just happen to occur. If a machine had been designed to randomly print letters on sheets of paper, we could know *by way of reflection* that this machine does not produce meaningful texts. We would not have to compare its actual output with meaningful texts. Analogously, we might recognize by way of reflection that deep neural networks do not use concepts, but rather simulate their use. Thinking otherwise would then amount to a confusion, which this essay seeks to highlight. It is structured into three parts. Part one sheds light on human thought by clarifying what concepts are and what using them amounts to. In part two it is argued that deep neural networks can only simulate conceptual activity. The third and final part exhibits the challenge that AI poses to us, namely to distinguish between use and abuse of machine generated simulations of intelligence within our human form(s) of life.

Human Thought: The Use of Concepts as Involving Reason and Creativity

Traditionally, the idea that we are intelligent beings has been spelled out by conceiving of ourselves as rational animals or finite thinkers.[5] An animal is a creature whose cognitive access to its environment depends on that environment appearing to it by way of the senses. As animals, we are finite insofar as we do not know everything all at once. That we are *rational* animals means that we aren't lost in ever-changing environments but have the ability to expand our acquired understanding to unforeseen situations that we thereby integrate into a unified horizon in which *anything* that might occur to us can be placed. As such, we are creatures who live in a *world*. To integrate unforeseen circumstances into our world-view we can neither treat them as entirely novel and incomparable, nor can we simply assimilate them to situations that are already familiar. We steer through the unknown by way of using concepts. Concepts are representations which allow us to recognize a unity between otherwise different situations. The rose and the sunset, for all their difference, can both instantiate the concept *red*. Using concepts is thinking. Concepts allow us to anticipate future situations such as the next red sunset. However, they do not make us infinite thinkers: grasp of a concept does not allow us to partition "all possible" situations into those that fall under the concept at hand and those that don't. Our grasp of a concept is always partial in that it doesn't rule out unforeseeable situations that defy the concept as we understand it: situations in which we no longer know how to apply the concept as it was hitherto understood and in which we thus run the risk of losing it, not knowing what to say. It is part and parcel of the capacity to use concepts to come to terms with such situations by *expanding* a concept in a way that allows it nonetheless to be applied to a situation which defies its usage as hitherto understood. The successful *modification* of a concept in light of an unforeseen situation that at first defies its application is an act that is both creative and rational. It is *creative* in that it involves doing something novel and original that does not simply result from the application of conceptual resources already available. For it is precisely these resources which have proven insufficient when faced with the given situation. The novelty is *rational* insofar as the successful modification

---

5   Matthew Boyle, "Essentially Rational Animals," in *Rethinking Epistemology: Volume 2*, ed. Günter Abel and James Conant (de Gruyter, 2012), 395–428.

of a concept in light of that situation isn't arbitrary but can be justified *in retrospect*, insofar as it allows us to overcome the conceptual predicament and to thus find a way out of the dead end which our previous understanding of the concept had led us into.

Concepts thus have a more complex texture than one might imagine: they involve an inner articulation insofar as they record critical junctures of their application which motivated their expansion. Not all of those who grasp a certain concept have an equally refined understanding of the junctures it incorporates. However, even those whose understanding of a concept is relatively limited have the general ability to move from one stage to another, i.e., to expand their understanding in a way that is both creative and rational. What the capacity for conceptual expansion amounts to can best be seen by looking at examples. As our example we can take the run-of-the-mill concept *red*. If we looked at *water* or *number* instead, we would arrive at essentially the same results. Reflecting on how we apply the concept *red* and how we have learned to expand it in the face of situations that at first seemed to defy its application will reveal that we tend to imagine concepts and conceptual activity in ways too simple to do justice to the intricacies of actual usage.

At first sight, it might seem that there must be some sort of shared ingredient that corresponds to the concept *red* on the part of the things that fall under it. However, things can be red in different ways, to which different shades of red correspond. No shared ingredient, then! Accordingly, it might seem more appropriate to view the concept *red* as delineating a certain *region* within a "space" whose dimensions are given by three axes of possible variation: hue, saturation, and brightness. Any point falling within a certain somewhat blurry region of this color space would count as red. Applying the concept *red* to a thing encountered in real life would accordingly amount to placing that thing, or a monochrome part of its surface, inside or outside the respective region in the same immediate and effortless way as we can imaginatively insert a red circle in its proper region within a color space.

Following Wittgenstein, we can call an imaginary scene that is supposed to illustrate our use of a concept, a picture of that concept. The philosophical picture of color concepts as delineating a certain region of a color space and of the application of such concepts as an immediate placing of a sample inside or outside such a region cannot do justice to the intricacy of our color concepts and their actual application. This can be seen by paying close attention to the application of such concepts in real life situations.

Fig. 8: Inserting a red circle in its proper region within a color space

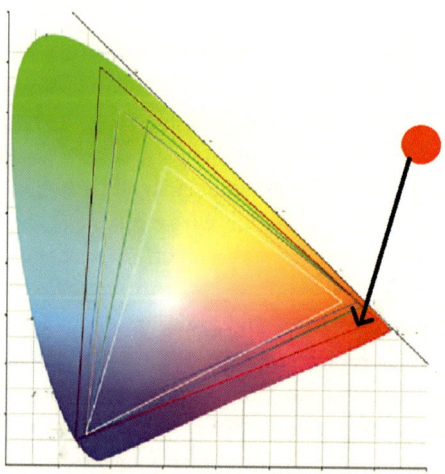

First, the picture of placing a thing inside or outside a region of a color space is static insofar as it does not take into account the temporal extension of things. One way of running into trouble when applying the concept *red* is occasioned by a thing changing its chromatic appearance when moved to a different place, due to diverging lighting conditions. Let us assume that our original concept of *red* had been formed ostensively by recourse to samples of red in plain daylight. It is part of our rudimentary color concepts that things do not simply change their colors upon being moved. Accordingly, when faced with a thing that reliably changes its chromatic appearance from red to brown while being moved to-and-fro between two places, we have run into trouble, risking losing our concepts of *red* and *brown* in the face of a situation that makes them inapplicable as they are. The trouble we have run into has the form of a dilemma: Neither saying of a thing which, in plain daylight, we took to be red and which now, indoors, appears to be brown, that it is *just* red or *just* brown, nor saying that it is *both* red *and* brown will do, for both involve a contradiction, either with what we see or within what we say. On the one hand, the thing viewed inside and viewed outdoors looks too different to be attributed one and the same color, while stating that the object simply changes its color from red to brown contradicts the principle that things do not just change their colors when moved. The predicament is resolved by expanding our concepts of *red* and further colors so as to allow for a distinction between standard lighting conditions in which things exhibit the color they have and deviant lighting conditions in which their color looks different from what it is. The *expanded* color concept thus comes with an inbuilt distinction between *is red* and *looks red*, which can be applied in the kind of situation that beforehand defied its application. It follows from this that the expanded concept of *red* cannot appropriately be visualized as a continuous region in color space. For it essentially involves discontinuous junctures: it is part and parcel of the expanded concept of *red* that its instances are subject to abrupt shifts of chromatic appearance depending on lighting conditions.

Second, even given constant lighting conditions, e.g., plain daylight, the subsumption of a thing under a color concept does not consist in *immediately* placing it, *without further ado*, inside or outside a certain continuous region of the color space as the philosophical picture that holds us captive makes it appear. The principle that things do not abruptly change their color can not only be challenged by a change of lighting conditions, but also by unexpected behavior of things under given lighting conditions. A glistening object such as a bronze pot might *momentarily* have the same appearance as a yellow object, while its manipulation, e.g., rotation, will bring out that its color isn't in fact yellow, but golden. Accordingly, we cannot properly attribute a color to an object viewed *in an instant*, but subsuming a thing under a certain color concept amounts to placing it in the same class with other objects that change chromatic appearance in a similar way when subject to certain kinds of manipulation.[6] Techniques of manipulation which we are used to applying, unreflectively, and which serve to ascertain the real color of a thing are part and parcel of our ordinary application of color concepts and can be viewed as the result of an expansion of rudimentary color concepts in light of the trouble we run into when taking the momentary chromatic appearance of things at face value.

What has been exemplified by color concepts applies to any concept whatsoever. In our ongoing use of any concept we can meet with situations which defy its application and occasion a sort of modification of the concept which is both creative and rational, i.e., retroactively justifiable insofar as it allows us to apply the expanded concept to the situations which rendered its unexpanded

---

6   Mark Wilson, *Wandering Significance: An Essay on Conceptual Behavior* (Clarendon Press, 2006), 104–06 and 454–67.

version inapplicable. Each mature concept thus involves a series of inbuilt logical junctures which result from the resolution of a certain kind of dilemma to which its previous application gave rise.

The Simulation of Conceptual Activity by Deep Neural Networks

Having shed light on what concepts are and what conceptual activity amounts to in our own—human—case, we now turn to the attempt to build machines that can be trained to exhibit conceptual behavior. We will focus on deep learning, the now-dominant branch of AI research. In contrast to the symbolic approach to AI that had been prevalent for decades, the deep learning approach is subsymbolic: It does not conceive of intelligence first and foremost on the model of rule-governed manipulation of symbols, but on the model of neural activity in the brain. Accordingly, it does not seek to make machines exhibit conceptual behavior by feeding them with detailed instructions about how to manipulate symbols in the face of certain external inputs, but seeks to construct a mechanism that allows them to learn concepts on their own in the course of responding to input in a way that is based on trial and error. This approach might seem promising insofar as it is analogous to how we humans acquire our first concepts, given that infants cannot acquire concepts by following explicit rules or instructions given to them, for in order to understand such rules or instructions they would already have to grasp the concepts involved in their formulation. It should be noted, though, that both the symbolic and the subsymbolic approach to AI involve algorithms, i.e., recipes for step-by-step procedures that yield well-determined results. For in order to learn by trial and error in the course of humanly-supervised training, it needs to be uniquely determined how the machine is supposed to change its own parameters if its response to a certain input doesn't comply with the response human trainers have labelled correct.

It is characteristic of the deep learning approach to view conceptual activity in terms of input–output behavior that is evaluated statistically. The question of what a concept even is and whether it exhibits a certain kind of inner articulation is largely absent. It is assumed from the outset that a device can be granted mastery of a certain concept if its outputs partition inputs that do or do not instantiate the given concept into two classes in a way that is statistically reliable. In that case the machine is said to be able to recognize a pattern. It is thus fair to say that the deep learning approach assumes without further ado that a concept can be represented by a set of isolated instances, the so-called training set, and that grasp of a concept consists in a reliable responsive disposition that allows to sort sample items into two classes—the class of those which instantiate the concept and the class of those which don't. However, as we have seen, conceptual capacities do not simply consist in the ability to uniquely partition a set of samples into two disjoint subsets, but essentially involve the capacity to *creatively and rationally* extend a concept in light of unforeseen situations which defy placing a sample in one class or the other. One might therefore venture that the machine learning approach to conceptual activity is a non-starter: It can at best result in a model or simulation of conceptual activity, because it bypasses what concepts are right from the start.

We need to take a closer look, though, to substantiate this conjecture. As indicated, the paradigm on which the deep learning approach models intelligent behavior is the brain and its characteristic cells: neurons. A neuron allows electro-chemical signals sent out by other neurons to be received and processed. These signals can have a different importance or weight. The neuron works by summing up its weighed inputs, and if the resulting value exceeds a certain threshold, the neuron "fires," i.e., it has a non-zero output. Otherwise, it does not fire, i.e., its output is zero. The guiding idea of automated pattern recognition as viewed from the perspective of deep learning is to construct networks of artificial neurons which learn to specifically and reliably respond to inputs caused by instances of a certain concept with the output 1, while yielding 0 in all other cases.

Fig. 9: The neuron and the perceptron

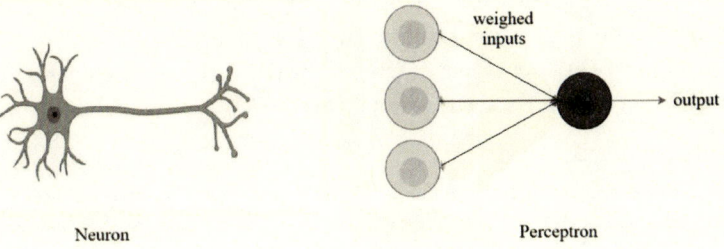

Neuron   Perceptron

Neural networks are supposed to learn to recognize certain patterns in their environment by trial and error, i.e., by a process of adaptation where inappropriate responses to environmental stimuli result in a certain change of weights within the network, while appropriate responses leave it as it is. Even while the initial responses of the network and the changes of weights occasioned by inappropriate responses might be random, the whole setup is such that the network gradually organizes itself so as to make appropriate responses more likely. Frank Rosenblatt's original idea about how to achieve this was to construct an artificial neuron, a so-called perceptron.

The perceptron gradually acquires the appropriate responsive dispositions by way of trial and error, guided by mathematical approximation techniques implemented in a digital computer endowed with a sensor for environmental stimuli. The sensor might be a camera yielding images that comprise a number of pixels to which a number of inputs or entryways on the part of the perceptron corresponds. Initially, the weights of these inputs and, hence, the output of the perceptron are random. However, this is supposed to be changed through training. The so-called training set might consist of images that have been labelled by humans according to whether the image instantiates a certain concept or not. Whether a neural network can actually be trained to learn to recognize a certain pattern depends not only on its architecture but on the algorithm or recipe that determines how its weights are supposed to be changed if its response to a test sample deviates from the expected result. By repeating the training process time and again the weights are supposed to be gradually changed until the network reliably responds to samples with the appropriate response. While still following what is essentially the same kind of procedure, modern day neural networks have a much more complex architecture than Rosenblatt's perceptron, consisting of multiple layers of artificial neurons. For this reason, they are called *deep* neural networks.[7]

By now, such networks are astonishingly good at certain pattern-recognition tasks. Does this mean that they can be granted conceptual capacities? In order to answer this question, AI researchers have designed benchmarks that are supposed to test the ability to form concepts. A benchmark that is thought

---

7   On the invention of the perceptron and its relation to deep neural networks, see chapter 9 of Matteo Pasquinelli, *The Eye of the Master: A Social History of Artificial Intelligence* (Verso, 2023). Pasquinelli's book provides a critical history of the AI paradigm as driven by the capitalist attempt to automate labor from the vantage point of historical epistemology.

to be particularly precise and challenging is the so-called "abstraction and reasoning corpus" (ARC) designed by François Chollet.[8] The benchmark consists of tasks that are supposed to test the capacity to form a concept by learning from examples. These examples consist of simple shapes within a grid that illustrate elementary concepts such as *inside*, *square*, or *even*. Abstraction, i.e., the acquisition of a concept, is supposed to be tested by the task of completing further grids involving similar shapes.[9]

Fig. 10: Example of an ARC task. The challenge is to demonstrate grasp of the abstract rule governing the demonstration transformations by completing the test input.

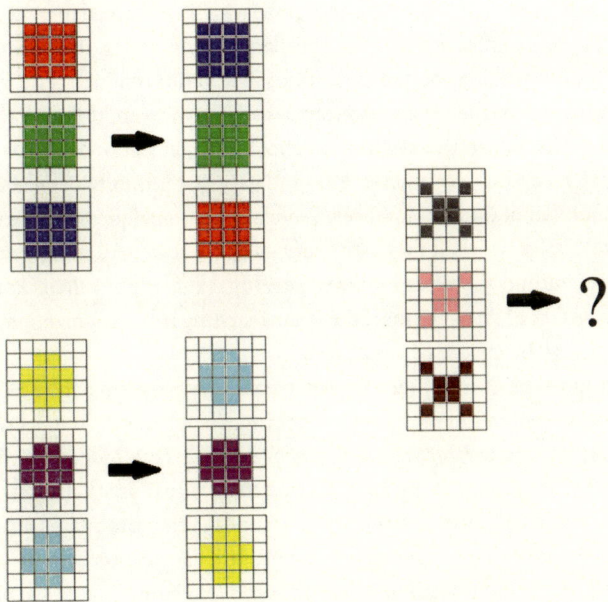

8   See François Chollet, "On the Measure of Intelligence" (2019), https://arxiv.org/abs/191
     1.01547.
9   See Arseny Moskovichev, Odouard Victor, and Melanie Mitchell, "The ConceptARC
     Benchmark: Evaluating Understanding and Generalization in the ARC Domain" (2023),
     https://arxiv.org/abs/2305.07141.

In December 2024 it was found that certain AI tools score higher at ARC tasks than humans.[10] Chollet and others have suggested that this shows such tools can be credited with the ability to abstract, i.e., to form concepts.[11] Other members of the AI community have been more critical, pointing out that immense human effort had gone into tailoring AI tools that fit the purpose which makes it somewhat difficult to say to what extent the machines should be credited with success and to what extent the credit goes to their human designers.[12]

From a philosophical vantage point, the assumption that deep neural networks can acquire conceptual capacities can be criticized in a more fundamental manner. The misguided assumption underlying attempts at teaching deep neural networks to form concepts is to assume that a concept could somehow be contained in a set of its instances. Teaching a machine to form a concept would accordingly mean making it recognize what is contained in such a training set. The sets comprise a number of isolated items, and training consists in making the network respond to these items in isolation, one at a time, without explicit recourse to the others. Concepts, as we have seen, do not have their place in things, but in the eye of the beholder: a concept is the content of a capacity to recognize a characteristic similarity or continuity between an indefinite number of things. Moreover, a concept is rationally extendable in light of circumstances which at first sight defy its application. Teaching a machine to acquire concepts therefore requires teaching it something *intangible* that *we can do* in the face of sets of items rather than teaching it to recognize something that is supposedly *contained* in such sets.

If training sets don't contain concepts, trying to make a machine recognize what is contained in a training set cannot in principle result in it acquiring a concept. How to then interpret the fact that machines can indeed successfully be trained to respond to samples by sorting them into those that instantiate a certain concept and those that don't, sometimes even more successfully than humans? The first thing to stress in response to this question is that *we* select the training samples in a clear-cut way so as to avoid borderline cases that defy

---

10   See François Chollet, "OpenAI Breakthrough High Score on ARC-AGI-PUB," *Arc Prize* (blog), December 20, 2024, https://arcprize.org/blog/oai-o3-pub-breakthrough.

11   See Chollet, "OpenAI Breakthrough," and François Chollet, Mike Knoop, Gregory Kamradt, and Bryan Landers, "ARC Prize 2024: Technical Report" (2025), https://arxiv.org/abs/2412.04604.

12   See Melanie Mitchell, "Did OpenAI Just Solve Abstract Reasoning?," *AI: A Guide for Thinking Humans* (blog), December 23, 2024, https://aiguide.substack.com/p/did-openai-just-solve-abstract-reasoning.

being put in either of two boxes. When trying to teach a machine the concept *inside*, for instance, it is exposed to figures either fully enclosed by or fully outside of a bounded area, rather than situated at the margin of a half-open form. This seems justified since acquisition of the rudimentary concept *inside* that is applicable to a continuous range of unproblematic cases has to precede its *extension* in light of borderline cases. However, as we shall now see, a neural network that reliably responds to a continuous range of unproblematic cases can neither be credited with mastery of a rudimentary concept nor is it in principle capable of rationally extending a rudimentary concept when faced with deviant situations.

The reason why a neural network that has successfully been trained to reliably respond to a range of unproblematic instances of a concept which are continuous with one another cannot even be credited with mastery of a rudimentary version of that concept is that it isn't able to recognize similarity or resemblance *as such*. Similarity and resemblance are *relations between* samples. A neural network, on the other hand, responds to samples *in isolation*, possibly adapting its weights, while being unable to explicitly compare a new sample to a previous one. The successfully trained network exhibits the same reaction—producing the output 1—on different occasions to different samples that instantiate the same concept, but it does not recognize sameness as such. Mastering a rudimentary concept instead means relating an indefinite range of multiple items to one another as partaking in one and the same trait and thus *viewing them as characteristically similar*. That there is a difference between reacting in the same way to isolated items and recognizing their similarity as such can be illustrated by the shift in appearance of a figure that we recognize as similar to others. The well-known duck-rabbit, for instance, changes it appearance when first seen as a duck and then recognized as a rabbit.

However, the difference matters nonetheless. For it is on account of not being able to compare items to one another and to recognize relevant continuities and discontinuities as such that a neural network is in principle unable to *rationally* extend rudimentary concepts in the face of circumstances which require such extension. The extension of a concept requires two things: Recognizing a novel circumstance as one that makes the concept as hitherto understood inapplicable by threatening its application with contradiction, and modifying the conditions of application of that concept in a way that allows to apply it to such circumstances without running into contradiction. Artificial neural networks are built in a way that prevents them from achieving either of these.

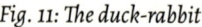

Fig. 11: The duck-rabbit

Such a shift of appearance can only occur to one who can *compare* items to one another, e.g., drawings to certain animals one has seen. There can clearly be a device that responds to two items in the same way without ever comparing them. This difference, however, might appear too subtle to matter when it comes to assessing the ability of humans and machines to recognize recurrent patterns. If performance is all that matters, it might indeed be safe to say that the machine simulation of a rudimentary concept can indeed outperform the human original.

In order to recognize a novel situation as one that requires the concept that is being applied to be extended (or its whole network of weights to be changed, for that matter) the machine would have to be able to compare its response to the new situation with earlier responses and to recognize that the two systematically contradict each other. Remember how the dilemma that gives rise to the extension of our rudimentary color concepts arose from comparing the color of the same object in situations that differ with regard to lighting. An artificial neural network that is being trained cannot compare samples and situations, because it can only respond to one sample at a time, adapting its weights accordingly, while not storing its own reactions to previous samples *as such*. Even if it did store these reactions, it could not detect a contradiction between them, because its only possible outputs are 0 or 1, i.e., yes *or* no, rather than 0 *and* 1.

A neural network might very well be trained to affirmatively respond to red items in standard lighting conditions *as well as* to samples that appear to be brown in green light. This, however, would not show that it now masters an extended concept of *red*. For in order to do that it would have to be able to distinguish between *one coherent* concept that exhibits a certain internal articulation by virtue of having been extended in response to a dilemma to which its application to a novel kind of circumstance gave rise, and *a mere combination* of *two incoherent* concepts such as *red and blue*. However, the network is built in a way that prevents it from noticing the *logical* difference *in kind* between *red and blue*, on the one hand, and *red in normal light while brown in green light*, on the other.

Why should it not be possible, though, to connect two parts of a neural network in such a way that a contradiction is indeed registered, if the response of one partial network to a thing is 0, while the other's response to the same thing is 1? If the machine is supposed to recognize these two responses as contradicting each other, it would have to recognize them as responses to *the same* thing, rather than just responding twice to what in fact is the same thing without noticing it to be so. Why should a machine not notice sameness and difference, though? Sameness and difference are neither contained in things, nor are they real relations between them such as spatial distance. Envisaging sameness and difference requires *comparing* things, and things do not compare themselves with one another, *we* do. A neural network accordingly cannot learn the concepts of sameness and difference by being exposed to things which *we* recognize to be the same or different. The network also cannot come up with these concepts on its own initiative, because the only thing it can change are the weights between its nodes. Each weight is an isolated numerical value that simply is what it is and thus cannot represent a distinction between itself and something else. If neural networks are constitutively unable to recognize dilemmas to which the application of a concept in a novel kind of situation gives rise, they cannot recognize a situation as one which requires the rational modification of the concept at issue.

That deep neural networks cannot engage in conceptual activity neither means that they couldn't do astonishing things, nor that they couldn't successfully do things we are unable to do or do less successfully. When asking what it is that successfully trained neural networks actually do, we shouldn't forget that their behavior matters to us, because we view it in light of intelligent activities *we* engage in and care for, rather than independently of them. Insofar as their behavior strikes us as meaningful and perhaps astonishing, it is because we assess this behavior, perhaps unwittingly, in a way that is parasitic on ours. In view of our understanding of a concept and a certain range of unproblematic applications that don't give rise to dilemmas, we might marvel at how much better the machine is at putting samples into that range. It is only better than us, though, at a kind of activity *we* know of, while it doesn't, in the same way litmus paper is better than we are at reliably responding to slightly acidic liquids. It being better than us obviously doesn't mean that litmus paper could be credited with understanding the concept of an acid or that we care for what it does independently of viewing its behavior in light of the concept of acid *we* dispose of.

A Challenge for Our Times: To Distinguish between Use and Abuse of Simulated Thought

It has been argued that deep neural networks as conceived in machine learning can at best simulate the use of concepts rather than actually apply them. It remains to be asked what kinds of use *we* human beings who actually engage in conceptual activity might have for machines that simulate conceptual activity. While automated pattern recognition might turn out to have all kinds of meaningful uses that cannot yet be fully anticipated, it is important to point out that the simulation of our own intelligent activities by way of machines allows both for meaningful uses on our part as well as for abuse. Abuse is inevitable if we attribute to machines intelligent capacities which in fact only we humans possess, and which the machines themselves can only simulate. A simulation per definition deviates from the reality it simulates. However, within a certain limited range of application, we might be struck with how compelling, life-like, and maybe even statistically superior the simulation is with regard to its output. This fascination might make us overlook how poorly the system performs outside of that range of application. Even while deep neural networks might ultimately be more reliable than we are at sorting items within a continuous range of unproblematic cases, they are constitutively unable to recognize and rationally respond to situations which defy being assessed according to a given pattern. For that very reason, deep neural networks cannot be credited with conceptual capacities. Assigning machines tasks that indeed require conceptual capacities that put one in a position to both creatively and rationally respond to tricky cases can only result in failure, and possibly disaster.

A device for the automated recognition of a pattern, X, will not be able to recognize borderline cases which defy being classified as either X or non-X and to rationally respond to such cases by diversifying the pattern that is being sought. Instead, the device will inflexibly stick with putting samples in one of the two boxes it has been trained to recognize. We do not need to elaborate here on the possible consequences of entrusting devices for automated pattern recognition instead of human administrators with the classification of social affairs.

It might be objected, though, that nothing speaks against training devices for automated pattern recognition to distinguish between clear cases for which automated classification is sufficient and borderline cases which require special—human—attention. This solution, however, is spurious. For it is written on the sleeves of our concepts that we are finite thinkers: our concepts cannot rule out the emergence of unpredictable situations which defy their application and require us to both creatively and rationally modify them in a way that allows us to continue using them. The machines which we might build to simulate conceptual activity inherit the finitude of our concepts and, hence, the partial unpredictability and elusiveness of reality in the face of our attempts to put it into boxes. In consequence, we might very well construct a device for automated pattern recognition that can recognize *a certain determinate kind* of situation as a borderline case that requires special—human—attention. However, no machine simulating the use of concepts can be trained to recognize *all relevant kinds* of borderline cases for what they are. For in order to do that we would have to be able to *conceptually anticipate* all possible situations that *defy* the application of a certain concept, which is a contradiction in terms.

There is no general reason why learning machines that we have trained to simulate conceptual activity by reliably responding to input within a certain standard range of application should not prove to be better than us at putting samples into their proper box. This doesn't make them, rather than us, authorities on the general distinction between unproblematic and borderline cases which require *thoughtful* responses, namely comparisons between cases, recognition of contradictions, and rational modification of our concepts. Ultimately, in the same way as microscopes or telescopes are tools that can help us to see things that we otherwise couldn't see, learning machines are *tools* that might help us to improve our own intelligent activities rather than delegating them to seemingly autonomous non-human agents.

I have argued in this essay that pattern recognition as conceived in deep learning only amounts to the simulation of concepts rather than proper conceptual activity. It is not immediately clear what this implies for the realm of Generative AI, which is not just about machines reliably responding to certain kinds of stimuli but about generating meaningful text, images, videos, etc. when prompted in a certain way. If it could be shown that concepts are involved, in some way or other, in meaningful speech as well as in the creation of images and the like, it would follow that Generative AI can generally only simulate these activities rather than ever properly and autonomously engage in them.

Baking and Building: Reflections on Architecture and Artificial Intelligence

Michael Mieskes

> Just as technology is always revealing
> nature from a new perspective, so also,
> as it impinges on human beings, it
> constantly makes for variations in their
> most primordial passions, fears, and
> images of longing.[1]
> Walter Benjamin

The following article addresses students and practitioners in the field of architecture who, in the future, will be dealing with particular technological questions in their profession. For this purpose, short "everyday scenarios" are designed to illustrate different relationships with *objects, things*, and *"automated" processes*. Examples labelled *Scenario B* illustrate these relationships with a simple object of comparison: baking bread. Those labelled *Scenario A* meanwhile translate these observations into the more complex field of architecture. The similarities in content between *B* and *A* can be conceptually related to each other. The aim of this contribution is, first, to describe our relationship to *objects* that appear to us as clear and comprehensible (i.e., *bread* and *architecture*), second, to distinguish conceptually that we name objects that we cannot grasp clearly and comprehensibly as *things*, and third, that the comprehensibility of objects is determined by our deep engagement in producing them which is affected by *"automated" processes*—understood as the division of labor through both human or machine work. The essay tries to show how our historically

---

1   Walter Benjamin, *The Arcades Project*, trans. Howard Eiland and Kevin McLaughlin (Harvard University Press, 2002), 392.

determined *concepts* and current *experiences* of objects, such as architecture or technology, are crucial for recognizing both the design of our environment and the technological possibilities and limitations—here, the automated processes of so-called "Artificial Inteligence" ("AI").[2]

This short essay will not pursue a stringent differentiation of the individual philosophical concepts or an emphasis of their "adequate" scientific contextualization. Rather, it aims to set a few emphases that are as comprehensible as possible, using the designed scenarios to provide points of reference for a practice that can be used to develop independent thinking.

Currently, there are still no fully-applicable methods of AI for generating constructions for buildings. As interesting as the results of the various AI methods are, given the current debates and effects of AI, it seems more urgent to assume a critical perspective that counteracts its mythologization driven by tech companies and the adapted everyday language.[3] However, a quote by the philosopher and sociologist Theodor W. Adorno should be prefaced to guide our endeavor. Although he probably never dealt with AI, he made a remarkably current statement about the computer in 1968:

> It is likely with computers, as with numerous other phenomena, precisely because the disenchantment of the world is progressing as it is, institutions and things that are themselves part of the mechanism of demystification are then magicalized by the general consciousness, made into a fetish. [A]nd I would think that the less people seriously understand about this, and above all the less they are aware that these are highly enhanced calculating machines, the more they are prepared to trust these machines to be able to replace living, productive thinking.[4]

---

2   The term "Artificial Intelligence" was coined in the course of a conference in Dartmouth in 1955: John McCarthy, Marvin L. Minsky, Nathaniel Rochester, and Claude E. Shannon, "A Proposal for the Dartmouth Summer Research Project on Artificial Intelligence: August 31, 1955 [1955]," *AI Magazine* 27, no. 4 (2006): 12–14, https://doi.org/10.1609/aimag .v27i4.1904. In the following, the prefixes are omitted.

3   For a socio-critical perspective on AI, see, for example, Matteo Pasquinelli, *The Eye of the Master: A Social History of Artificial Intelligence* (Verso, 2023). For a critical localization of AI in the context of architecture see, for example, Sandra Meireis, "Sinnliche und maschinelle Intelligenz. Zehn Thesen zu 'KI' in der Architektur," in *Ästhetik und Architektur, Schriftenreihe des Weißenhof-Instituts zur Architektur- und Designtheorie*, ed. Daniel Martin Feige and Sandra Meireis (transcript, 2023), 269–89.

4   This quote comes from an unpublished interview held in German that can be found in the Theodor W. Adorno Archive and will be published at the end of 2025 in my disserta-

Let's keep that in mind and focus on the scenarios now.

Scenario B_1 —We want to have some bread for dinner. We go to the bakery and name the bread we have in mind: "The wholegrain bread, please!" If the baker then gives us a pretzel, we will say, perhaps even pointing with our finger for a clearer understanding: "That was a misunderstanding, we would like that bread—there!" Our formal familiarity with the objects *bread* and *pretzel* helps us to get what we have in mind.

Scenario B_2 —Same scenario: We go to the bakery, order the wholegrain bread, pay for it, receive it, and enjoy it. In this scenario, we enjoy the "privilege" of the *division of labor*. The production of the bread appears to us as an "automatic" process, as the object is accessible to us without having to produce it ourselves.

Scenario B_3 —We have a problem: The bakery is closed, and so we want to bake bread for the first time in our lives. Suddenly, from this perspective, bread no longer seems as self-evident as before. The production of bread now seems distant or unclear.

To approach the matter, we will gather *information*. We never start from scratch; we can rely on historical accounts that describe this process to us: the recipe lists the ingredients as well as the procedure. The recipe contains the idea of production. This process is thus reproducible; with the same ingredients and the same process, we get "the same" bread every time. The production process is no longer a "thing" to us, but a tangible "object" that we have been able to differentiate through our engagement. The object *bread* is now even more familiar, even "closer" to us than it appeared before our own attempts.

Scenario B_4 —Through our experience, we have noticed qualitative differences between the purchased and homemade bread. As we delve deeper into the matter, we will distinguish which ingredients or steps need to be changed to make

---

tion, which gives more theoretical context to Adorno's theory. Michael Mieskes, "Technologische Bildlichkeiten. Digitalität und Mimesis nach Adorno" (PhD diss., Goethe University Frankfurt/M., forthcoming end-2025). See Theodor W. Adorno und [Peter?] Beike, "Zeitalter des Computers", Theodor W. Adorno Archiv, Frankfurt am Main, SK 63/2, https://archiv.adk.de/objekt/3285076. All subsequent translations are by the author, except where otherwise stated.

the bread tastier. We will begin to adjust the recipe—the reproducible process—based on our experience. If we succeed, we will have developed not only a more differentiated relationship with our object, *bread*, but also with our object of *production*. We possess an experience that has brought us closer to these objects.

Scenario B₅ —We didn't have time for baking and after a long time, we go back to our old bakery. We try our favorite "wholegrain bread" and notice: it doesn't taste as good anymore! This is because our understanding of bread has become more differentiated through our closer engagement. We draw on our experience and realize: Not all bread tastes the same, not all bread has the same qualities. The object, *bread*, is familiar to us in a special way, so we can see that we will not get this object—in the way we understand it—if we continue to go to that bakery.
—How should we now locate our relationship to the "wholegrain bread" in *Scenario B₃*? Did we have a "blind spot"—a "thing-side"—on our supposedly concrete object?

Scenario B₆ —We visit different bakeries and notice qualitative differences. We can identify that this is due to the production process, which we understand better through our new experiences. We can locate the "automated" processes because we have experience with our object, *bread*. We can differentiate: "This may formally look like a rustic loaf of bread, but its substance is like that of spongy toast. Its production process is reduced to cost optimization, profit, and the design of a desirable appearance." Or: "That small loaf over there looks modest, but it is tasty, and two small slices are filling." Even if the homemade bread still tastes better, we can better navigate within the various "automations."

A brief interlude —What can we take from this everyday relationship between thing, object, and automation for our consideration of architecture and AI? Obviously, we need to have a certain nearness to be able to understand an object as such. Of course, with architecture and AI, we are dealing with more complex objects, and we would hardly claim that we could do without the division of labor to explore and implement everything ourselves. However, we can proceed methodically, similar to baking bread, by dealing with historical circumstances on the one hand and collecting our own experiences with the production process on the other. We turn to the given circumstances, engage with the experiences of others, but we are also ready not to rely solely on their information, instead mobilizing and adapting our own approach through our own experience. Such an engagement could lead to the ability to differentiate the object *architecture* even though we have not performed every task ourselves or determined and shaped every material. Such an engagement would bring us closer to the object *architecture* in a way that allows us to differentiate the qualities it possesses and how it could be realized.

Scenario A₁ —We stroll through an unfamiliar city and see a particularly striking silhouette in the distance, a structure that stands out from its surroundings due to its shape. Advancing a few steps closer, we identify it as a magnificent building, and say: "Look at that architecture!"

Scenario A₂ —During our walk through the streets, we don't encounter a baker, but an architect, who responds to our statement as follows: "Architecture is a *gesture*. Not every purposive movement of the human body is a gesture. Just as not every purposive building is architecture."[5] We need to think about that for a moment, but we have already learned: not every object that looks like a delicious, substantial loaf of bread is actually such.

Scenario A₃ —Let's take this architect's statement seriously and ask ourselves: what is a "purposive movement"? And accordingly, what could a "purposive building" be?

(We scratch our heads.) It must be related to the everyday movements of our body. We need to ask ourselves what needs we can satisfy with it, what technical–functional actions can be performed in it, and what goals can be achieved with it. We need to start dealing with how we can create such a building. Let's use existing reports of experiences for this!

We follow some philosophical wisdom from a book published in 1570 called *The Four Books on Architecture*. In the first chapter, it states that certain things "must be considered and prepared before building can start." Besides "usefulness or convenience," "durability" also plays a central role in the construction of "every building."[6]

---

5   Ludwig Wittgenstein, *Vermischte Bemerkungen*, ed. Georg Henrik von Wright (Suhrkamp, 1977), 86.

6   Andrea Palladio, *The Four Books on Architecture*, trans. Robert Taverno and Richard Schofield (MIT Press, 1997), 6.

First, we set a purpose. "Convenience will be provided for when each member [*membro*] is given its appropriate position"[7]—for our purpose, an exemplary fragment: an apartment. We must therefore consider that objects and actions required for cooking, baking, eating, washing up, sleeping, etc., must be contained or take place in it. Through these conditions and individual elements, the *volume* required for the purpose of an "apartment" can be determined. How can we now construct the building that defines this volume and is characterized by a certain "durability"?

> Durability will be guaranteed when all the walls are plumb vertical, thicker below than above, and have sound and strong foundations; and further, when the columns above stand vertically over those below and all the openings, such as doors and windows, are one above the other: so that solid is above solid and void above void.[8]

A building constructed in this way would be a purposeful one!

Scenario A_4 —It seems, therefore, that purposefulness can be determined by clear rules. For "durable construction," we can also rely on "recipes" based on existing experiences. For example, material properties such as hardness, density, flexibility, tensile strength, load-bearing capacity, etc., are based on *measurements*. Through these measurements, we can *quantify* the materials and derive the necessary construction dimensions based on them: we can determine through formulas how material information relates to formal dimensions. This numerical, formalizing activity gives us certainty that our planning approach and the subsequent implementation are physically sound. In a way, we create a formalizing principle based on data that provides us with stable components.

Put very simply: By stacking and lining up these components, we achieve an order that ensures the structure holds together. This order can be derived through formalizing activity because it must also take physical numerical values into account. If we can rely on this order, it is a process that enables the reproduction of our object. The process could be described as an "algorithm": because this process can be broken down into small, numerical basic operations ("Elementarity"), because it is determined by compliance with their clearly defined sequence ("Determinacy"), because it is available in a general

---

7   Palladio, *The Four Books on Architecture*, 7.
8   Palladio, *The Four Books on Architecture*, 7.

form and can be executed as such ("Generality"), and finally, because there is a completed result that can be achieved again by the same procedure ("Finiteness").[9] With algorithmic operations, we can thus determine our purposeful, technical–functional structure for a building.

Scenario A_5 —Algorithmic operations, as is well known, can be solved not only by human activity but also by computing machines.[10] For *Scenario A_4*, however, a parametric system would suffice;[11] there is no need for an AI system. AI systems are characterized by their ability to determine their computational paths in a self-learning manner. Through various clever programming methods, they can respond flexibly to tasks and represent complex issues accordingly.[12] However, all AI methods are fundamentally based on algorithms, meaning they rely on familiar, rule-based mathematical forms:

> Formal thinking ... is based on the possibility of replacing the operation with thoughts by the operation with patterns of signs, so that the rules according to which the construction and alteration of the patterns of signs take place no longer refer to the content of the thoughts, but only to the structures of the patterns themselves.[13]

A rule-based following of signs, which delivers a correct result without human thought (and therefore without thinking!), as generative systems adopt and even adapt, suggests reliability—but we know from our experience with bread that we must relate these general "patterns" back to our physical world.

---

9   See also the "intuitive" (since not mathematically provable) concept of algorithm by the philosopher Sybille Krämer, *Symbolische Maschinen, Die Idee der Formalisierung in geschichtlichem Abriß* (Wissenschaftliche Buchgemeinschaft, 1988), 159.

10   Krämer, *Symbolische Maschinen*, 3.

11   For example, Autodesk's software, Fusion 360. See Bryce Heventhal, "Generative Design in Autodesk Fusion: Revolutionizing Design with AI," Autodesk, September 30, 2024, https://www.autodesk.com/products/fusion-360/blog/generative-design-in-autodesk-fusion-revolutionizing-design-with-ai/.

12   There are various AI methods, each with its own strengths and weaknesses. For example, one distinguishes between Machine Learning, Neural Networks, and Deep Learning. For a general technical overview, see Clemens Heitzinger and Stefan Woltran, "A Short Introduction to Artificial Intelligence: Methods, Success Stories, and Current Limitations," in *Introduction to Digital Humanism: A Textbook*, ed. Hannes Werthner (Springer, 2024), 135–49, https://link.springer.com/book/10.1007/978-3-031-45304-5.

13   Krämer, *Symbolische Maschinen*, 102.

Nevertheless, we maintain, it is very likely that certain AI methods can adapt and support the constructive, planning approach (A_4) of humans, as they can determine formalizing processes based on data that represent material properties or a physical environment, and thus ultimately generate technical–functional forms.[14] Furthermore, they could carry out formalizing procedures that exceed the computational capacity of humans in their complexity and information density, and potentially offer technical–functional optimizations that also consider the scope of ecological aspects, for example. In summary, we can say: Machines seem able to serve our required technical–functional purposes, which we achieve through formalization, even if we have to pursue them critically!

Scenario A_6 —We now know that machines can support us in the realization of our desired, purpose-built objects. We know that we need to understand this object—the technical–functional building construction—so that the manufacturing process also turns out as desired. For all problems that can be solved by a rule-based procedure, there are ways to develop corresponding formalizing procedures. We can also call this a "program." Programs can be created and followed by both humans and machines. But what happens outside of this problem-solving area, outside of formalization? "The limits of formalizability are the limits of a mechanical, unimaginative mind."[15]

Scenario A_7 —Let's look beyond these limits. The building fulfills a purpose, but not every building is architecture, it was said. Architecture is a "gesture." We are familiar with this word from our everyday lives: the friendly wave of a person greeting us expresses the gesture of welcoming. It is a physical movement that follows the purpose of the greeting, but adds a certain "warmth" to it—one could say that the movement is filled with a vivid expression that not only greets the newcomer in a matter-of-fact way, but welcomes them warmly. We recognize the purposefulness of the greeting movement, but *it shows* that it is *more* than a purposeful movement, more than a transmission of information. How could this be transferred to architecture?

---

14   One possible approach here could be Reinforcement Learning, a category of Machine Learning in which a so-called Agent learns based on a Rich Environment. See, for example, Richard S. Sutton and Andrew G. Barto, *Reinforcement Learning: An Introduction* (MIT Press, 2018).

15   Krämer, *Symbolische Maschinen*, 181.

An architectural gesture could be characterized by possessing a similarly "vivid expression" that is familiar to us through that physical gesture of our body. This would be the case if architecture succeeded in enriching the *volumes* of purpose with "more" in developing a vivid *space*. Since it has neither an organic body nor a language of words, it is faced with the challenging task of realizing this "more" through form and material[16]—for example, a gesture of welcoming as a reception. We would have to use our experience to find out which gesture—measured against its purpose—would be considered a more exuberant or appropriate expression in architecture; we would have to find a contemporary measure of form and material to do so. This measure is not found through formalization or quantification, but through our physical experience that takes part in our environment.

We conclude: the gestural entrance fulfills its purpose with expression. The entrance of a building therefore differs from that of architecture in that it has no gesture, but we can still walk into the building. We can now grasp our object, *architecture*, a little more clearly than before.

Scenario A_8 —A great friend of *architecture*—as his expression, the "art of master builders" (*"baumeisterliche Kunst"*[17]), reveals—was the composer and philosopher Theodor W. Adorno, who recorded his experiences with such art forms in a number of notes. Among other things, he was concerned with constructive procedures that were limited to technical–formal correctness and deducible order. He also verified such procedures based on existing objects—in one of his notebooks, it says that "in the architecture of the eighteenth century" one encounters "similar circumstances [of a supposedly systematic necessity of compositional logic], where 'compelling' symmetrical relationships prevail *without* constructive necessity in the strictest sense. My suspicion: that contingency increases the more rigid the regularity becomes, i.e., the more it dispenses the subject from experience."[18] If we depend on formal regularity, the quality of our object can suffer under certain circumstances, which we only notice when we have come closer to it through experience (i.e., B_5). But the first

---

16   Here I allude to Theodor W. Adorno, "Funktionalismus heute", in *Gesammelte Schriften, Band 10.1, Kulturkritik und Gesellschaft I / II*, ed. Rolf Tiedemann (Suhrkamp, 1977), 388.

17   Arnim Regenbogen and Uwe Meyer, eds., *Wörterbuch der philosophischen Begriffe* (Meiner, 1998), 63.

18   Theodor W. Adorno, "Graeculus (I), Musikalische Notizen," in *Frankfurter Adorno Blätter VII*, ed. Rolf Tiedemann (edition text + kritik, 1992), 21. Emphasis by Adorno.

sentence of this quote initially sounds paradoxical: "'compelling' symmetrical relationships ... without constructive necessity in the strictest sense?" So, construction here must be understood as something different from what we have worked out in scenario A_4. Adorno seems to be referring to a form of experience through which we can make constructive decisions that cannot be derived in a technical–functional sense. It is an experience that does not provide retrievable knowledge, let alone allow one to enrich formal rules. So, we need to be more precise here: The gesture that we experience through our body is a form shaped by our senses, it is determined by our aesthetic perception. The task of such an architectural construction would therefore be to translate these gestural experiences into the ("wordless") language of architecture—through form and material.[19] As in our everyday gestures, organic, asymmetrical moments would creep into the technical–functional construction or systematic order. These—in an aesthetic sense—constructive "irregularities" could be experienced as gestures.

Let us specify this experience, which is *essential for the construction of architecture*: aesthetic experience needs a body. It enriches our small, purposeful everyday situations with vividness. It opens up a realm that we cannot summon in a controlled manner, but which happens to us involuntarily and immediately: we are momentarily distracted and disrupted from our everyday, purposeful courses of action because we are somewhere in between fascinated and shocked. In this, we experience a participation in our environment. The term we use to outline such "small" or "large" phenomena of an object is "beautiful."[20]

We conclude: "Construction" in architecture does not only mean serving purposes, but also mobilizing its purpose-bound order according to the experience of the living body. Construction is therefore not a purely rule-based, dominant activity, but rather also needs non-intended impulses to flow into itself through aesthetic experience. We can thus distinguish that there is both technically-functional and vividly-gestural construction, which do not stand in opposition to each other but go hand in hand. Such a construction would be called "supra-functional" by Adorno.[21] Supra-functional constructions need a

---

19   Adorno, "Funktionalismus heute," 377.

20   On the concept of the "beautiful" in Adorno, see Theodor W. Adorno, "Ästhetik (1958/59)," in *Nachgelassene Schriften, Abteilung IV: Vorlesungen, Band 3*, ed. Eberhard Ortland (Suhrkamp, 2009), 157; Theodor W. Adorno, *Aesthetic Theory*, ed. and trans. Robert Hullot-Kentor (continuum, 2002), 44 and 61.

21   Adorno, *Aesthetic Theory*, 44.

body. With a nod towards AI, a technical formulation: the body as an aesthetic measuring tool.

Scenario A₉ —What does this mean in conclusion for a current architectural practice that will deal with the future developments of AI?

We can localize the answer. The potential of such technologies lies not only in making our lives easier by taking over or accelerating work but also in expanding the realms of experience. In the worst case, automated processes can lead to us losing sight of our objects without realizing it. This turns objects into things in a bad sense. The simple abundance of our shaped environment also suffers as a result: Our functional forms without the quality of gesture would be sober and dead, "gesture" without purposeful orientation would become an empty play with material and form. An alternative scenario would be if we were to embark on an "excessive," friction-generating exploration between thinking and perceiving, between conceptual apperception and liberating, aesthetic experience. This could give us a refreshing perspective on architecture and technology, if we were to allow ourselves to be driven to our limits, to free ourselves from "classical" design processes in order to open our perception to the qualities of architectural space, however this may be technically produced. This would place the architectural object at the center: It would differentiate the purposes up to ecological questions, would interlock it with "nature," and pleasantly remove the so-called "creative subject" from its center, without forgetting that it corresponds with man in its language-like form.[22] If we could gather unexpected, unintended experiences in the new technologies, and if these could help us to realize a living habitat that is characterized by numerous constellations that create an equivalent, gestural vessel for our everyday life in any modes and ways of existence—that would be an urban, architectural habitat for man and nature.

Outlook —With this openness to experience, equipped with a rich concept of our object—architecture—we could re-engage with its obscured, distant "thing-side": "to produce what is blind, expression, by way of reflection, that

---

22   Adorno, "Funktionalismus heute," 376.

is, through form; not to rationalize the blind but to produce it aesthetically, 'To make things of which we do not know what they are.'"[23]

---

23   Adorno, "Funktionalismus heute," 114. Here Adorno quotes himself: Theodor W. Adorno, "Vers une musique informelle," in *Quasi una Fantasia, Essays on Modern Music,* trans. Rodney Livingstone (Verso, 2002), 322.

Part 3: Interviews

The Classical Tradition of Artificial Intelligence

Andri Gerber in Conversation with Mario Carpo, February 11, 2025 (online)

Andri Gerber: AI has been a hot topic in architecture for some time. What concerns us all, is to what extent it is transforming or might transform our profession.

Mario Carpo: In order to discuss this, we have to start by acknowledging that, in the context of architecture, there is not much you can do with the available AI tools at the present. There are offices training their models on past work, so that they can replicate their style. Coop Himmelb(l)au is one example. They published an article about their AI model, which can reproduce the office's house style. They call it "Deep Himmelblau."[1] But in this case it is rather easy, because the office has a distinctive style. But many offices don't have a specific style, so they can't do this kind of exercise. Even for Coop Himmelb(l)au this is mainly a marketing tool and, I understand, they use it primarily as a first step when discussing initial ideas with clients. If the client is convinced, then the real work starts.

AI has already replaced quite a number of jobs. Think of all those working on images. Generative AI can do better image editing than humans. But it's not a design tool. My argument would be that generative AI is not changing the way we work, but rather the way we look at architecture. We are talking about a cultural and conceptual impact, and this leads us to look at architecture in ways which are not new, but revived and brought back to us. We have to go back and consider how architecture was seen in the European classical tradition since Antiquity. This way of thinking was cancelled by twentieth-century modernism for many reasons. Indeed, I was a modernist myself, at least in

---

1   Wolf Prix, Karolin Schmidbaur, Daniel Bolojan and Efilena Baseta, "The legacy sketch machine: From artificial to architectural intelligence," *Architectural Design* 92, no. 3 (2022): 14–21.

spirit, so I know something about it. If you believe that form follows function, any idea of creative and stylistic imitation becomes obsolete.

AG: Do you yourself use any AI tools in your teaching?

MC: Many students use a category of software called "Style Transfer." The idea is that there is something from which you can draw inspiration. Even though design students often don't know art history, they are nonetheless constantly talking about "style." So the idea of style comes—literally—from the program they are using. But the term was very important in art history. Think, for example, of German architectural theory in nineteenth century, about Heinrich Hübsch and his book, *In What Style Should We Build?*, from 1828.[2] Or think about Vasari and his idea that some paintings have something in common, what he calls *maniera*.[3] One could even go as far back as Cicero to find a reference to the concept of style.

In the classical tradition, imitation meant inspiration, transposition, and transformation. Imitation was part of creation. There is no creation without some component of imitation, and there should be no imitation without some component of creation. That's the classical tradition. With German art theory in the nineteenth century, in particular, style became an inevitable term in architecture.

We thus have two terms—imitation and style—which are embedded in the classical tradition. They rose then fell together under the guillotine of modernism. We should not forget that the first modernists were still trained in the academies and in this tradition, which they then rejected, but, regardless, they wanted to create a new style. When modernism went to America it became "the international style," named after Philip Johnson's MoMA exhibition.[4] Tradition, style, and imitation became forbidden words only with later modernism.

For these architects, imitation meant copy, and hence plagiarism, and hence a crime, something to be reprimanded and repressed. They even came up with a totally new vocabulary to avoid these words.

When I was a student, you could not mention the word "imitation" without being considered an idiot. At the same time, we were all looking at references for our projects. [laughs]

---

2   Heinrich Hübsch, *In welchem Style sollen wir bauen?* (Müller, 1828).

3   Giorgio Vasari, *Le vite de' più eccellenti pittori, scultori, e architettori* (Giunti, 1568).

4   Philip Johnson and Henry Russell Hitchcock, *The International Style* (Norton, 1932).

So, we did imitate, but we were forbidden to conceptualize imitation. You could do it, but you shouldn't talk about it.

AG: Absolutely, that was the same for my generation during our studies!

MC: Imitation and precedent returned with postmodernism, but the situation remained complicated, and the terms "imitation" and "style" were never really rehabilitated. Think about one of the bestsellers of the 1970s: Harold Bloom's *The Anxiety of Influence*, published in 1973.[5] Interestingly, you have here a book which is all about tradition and imitation, but these two terms are never mentioned!

In my understanding, thinking in terms of style and imitation is an inevitable component of the human mind. You may repress it as modernists did, but now it is coming back with generative AI, which is rather ironic.

AG: Imitation forces us to talk about copyright.

MC: Well, in the classical tradition, the notion of copyright could not exist, because it was a right, even a necessity, to be inspired by precedent. With mechanical reproduction—for example, the copy of a photograph—copying became an identical reproduction. Hence the idea of plagiarism. There is a right of copy, but there is no right of inspiration.

There are no royalties to be paid for influence, for the intellectual property of influence. You go to a museum, see a painting, and that might inspire you. With modernism, to copy became to cite. The idea that you need quotation marks. Collage is a typical modernist technique where you take fragments and put them together.

The classical tradition was different; there you look at something, you absorb it, you digest it, you transpose it, and then you create something new. You are inspired by something, and make something out of it, but you won't be able to reveal the ingredients you were using. Gottfried Semper, following Bötticher, would define this process as *Stoffwechsel*,[6] which we can translate as "metabolism." We can explain it by a metaphor: it's about the difference between French *potage de legumes* and Italian minestrone. In the first soup, you

---

5   Harald Bloom, *The Anxiety of Influence: A theory of poetry* (Oxford University Press, 1973).

6   Gottfried Semper, *Der Stil in den technischen und tektonischen Künsten* (Frankfurt 1860/3).

can't identify the ingredients, except from the color; in the second you can recognize all the vegetables. The French soup is the classical tradition; minestrone the modernist.

There is a nice story about the Greek painter Zeuxis. He was invited to the south of Italy and asked to make a painting of Juno. He asked for the most beautiful girl in the region, in order to use her as model, but could not find anyone quite to his taste. Instead, he chose five models, not one, and composed a painting out of the most beautiful features of all five.

And this is exactly what AI is doing. It's merging, transforming, transmogrifying. But the data set today is not made of five models but a gazillion. And with generative AI, anybody can do that! And this is what we used to do in the past, with the exception of the last seventy to eighty years of modernist dogma.

AG: The story of Zeuxis resonates with how Alberti developed his own proportional system. Rejecting Vitruvius' assumption of a fixed system, in which the head is always 1/7 of the body, and knowing that this system does not apply to many people, he made a new system out of the proportions of several individuals.[7]

MC: And that is where his machine to transpose proportions he describes in *De Statua* comes from.[8]

AG: Let's go back to teaching. Before you said that the first modernist architects were taught in the classical tradition and rejected it. Their students then grew up with the new tradition, but without any knowledge of what their masters rejected, and this led to a great ignorance and finally also to the dogma you described. My question then would be, how do we teach our students for them to really understand what these tools mean in the context of our rich history?

---

7   Andri Gerber, Tibor Joanelly, and Oya Atalay Franck, *Proportions and Cognition in Architecture and Urban Design* (Reimer, 2019).

8   Leon Battista Alberti, *Della Pittura* (1435).

Fig. 12: Leon Battista Alberti, Finitorium, 1435

MC: As I said before, our students use these programs, which were invented around ten years ago, but they don't know what the notion of "style" implies. But what is even more problematic is that we are missing a culture of creative imitation. We are not capable of dealing with imitation in critical and creative terms, because we are not teaching imitation anymore.

And this is not the consequence of a new technology. It is a consequence of modernism, which decided that all forms of imitation were a crime. Imitation was eliminated from our discourse for a very long time. We were trained to imitate without having a concept or a theory for it. We lacked the terms to describe it; we did it in an idiotic way in the technical sense of the term, without having a language to describe what we were doing.

We have lost the classical tradition, which was based on imitation. Don't forget that tradition means transmission. For centuries we had a huge body of consensual thinking to theorize what imitation is and to make a distinction between bad imitation and good imitation.

We have to ask again: what is the pedagogy of imitation? Think about learning languages. You learn them at school through rules, declensions, etc. But before school, we speak the languages without any rules, without any grammar, by simply imitating the sounds coming from the mouths of the people living next to us.

Imitation as a practice without a theory is embedded in the technical history of computer science. From its beginnings in 1956, AI had two styles, so to speak: the rule-based, or symbolic, and the connectionist, which was based on trial and error. Now you have large language models (LLM) and Chatbots. This led to large behavioral models which are used to train robots, so that they can repeat gestures. These kinds of experiments were first conducted by Google a couple of years ago. They positioned a robot to observe a person through computer vision. The person was sorting cubes of three colors—red, blue, and yellow—into a pile under the watchful eye of a computer with AI. This was next linked to a robot, which did the same by imitating what it saw. There is no scripted rule to explain what the robot should be doing. It is not scripted in the sense that the robot will lay a brick in position x, y, z because of some code. Rather, it is being trained and driven by AI. It looked at something and repeated what it had seen. It learned. This can be also explained by the notion of "tacit knowledge"; something that you learned and know, but cannot verbalize. You cannot explain it. The only way to teach an artist in that way is to have an apprentice learn next to the master. In the medieval craft tradition, for example, you would live in the same house as your master and just observe him working for twenty years until you knew what to do—by replicating what he did.

Machines today are automating tacit knowledge, which for a modernist, as I was by training, is somewhat perplexing, because I always thought that tacit knowledge is a shortcut we have invented to hide our incompetence [laughs]

The idea that AI is vindicating the stupidity which was always embedded in a non-rational way of doing things by imitation learning, or model teaching, which is the way we still tend to teach many arts and crafts, is fascinating.

That's what AI is now doing, which is fascinating, perplexing, and worrying at the same time.

So, to return to your question, what is the consequence for teaching? The question then is who is learning from whom.

AG: So, there is this historical background, but now concretely on this aspect of imitation, what is our role as teachers, and what is the role of the students?

MC: I don't have a direct answer. There is one thing we could do, but I hesitate to advocate it: restart teaching in the classical tradition. Not all of it, not what it did, but how it worked. Because there is a body of theory we now need. In order to have a dialogue with post-industrial machines, we should learn from the tradition of a pre-industrial age.

AG: That's a fantastic and quite radical idea!

MC: One problem is that although classical theory has recently been revived in architecture, the revival was not for good reasons. It is all about *looking* like the classics, not *thinking* like them. Advocating for the classical tradition today could be misunderstood, because of these references.

AG: Let's change subject for a moment. You have often used metaphors in this interview to explain your thoughts and I am also a big advocate of them, as they were the subject of my PhD. If we consider AI as a way to organize knowledge, it seems to do so without reference to architecture. In the past architecture was one of the preferred metaphors for knowledge systems. Think of the two-partite tower used to describe the relationship of the quadrivium to the trivium, the theater of memory by Giulio Camillo Delminio, or the music temple by Robert Fludd. Is the fact that architecture has lost its capacity to be a metaphorical vehicle for AI symptomatic?

MC: The art of memory goes as far back as Quintilian and Cicero, to name but two examples. It used the physical configuration of spaces to store and order memory. If Cicero had to deliver a speech in the Senate, where he would speak for hours, he first had to memorize it. To do so, he would subdivide his speech in units of arguments and place them in physical spaces, in order to pick them up at the right moment.

Now, AI doesn't work that way. Google has already replaced sorting, as you would do with a traditional library, where every book has its place, with coding and searching, where things have a code and not a physical position.

AG: The generic warehouse could then be the architectural metaphor of AI.

MC: You could say so. And if you look at the classical model of the library, the organization is based on several theories, such as the arborescent subdivision of topics, which was invented by Pierre de la Ramée (Petrus Ramus) in the sixteenth century or the Dewey Decimal Classification—named after Melvil Dewey—where every book has a place based on its subject. And when it comes to sorting images, we could refer to art historian Aby Warburg and his iconology and the arrangement of images in his *Mnemosyne Atlas*.

If you take a book and don't place it back in the right slot on shelf, it is lost forever. Nowadays the warehouses, which are organized by AI, don't have any sorting principle, because each item has a code which can be read by a robot moving from a distance. The logic behind this organization is that of minimizing the distance a robot has to run in order to pick a piece. Items which are most frequently sold are put next to each other, etc.

Ideally, the library of the future would make a huge pile of real books. Books would just be piled up without any order upon arrival. Each book would have a QR code or a code legible at a distance. When you looked for that book, you would put on a pair of Google glasses and say: "hey Google, where is that book?" And in the Google glasses, that book would become luminescent. So, you would go and pick it up. Automated searching has replaced human sorting.

We humans need to sort things. We put things in a certain place, so we know where they are when we need them. AI does not need sorting, because it can search without any order. Unfortunately, the profession of the librarian is one which will probably become obsolete because you won't need to put books on shelves anymore, assuming that books will continue to exist, which I think they will.

AG: We all hope so! But at the moment, we don't need sorting, we don't need a spatial order, and thus architecture as a way of organizing space.

MC: Searching is for computers. That's what they do. The question, then, is how this affects us and the way we think. This happened already before the rise of generative AI with the Google search, which has become a cultural technology. This has definitively produced some kind of mental adaptation already. And speaking for myself, I remember fewer things, because I know I can find them anytime I need them. Thus, my memory is declining because the artificial memory I can use is now so effective.

AG: This makes me think of the famous study of taxi drivers in London who developed larger hippocampi due to their navigational skills, which demonstrates the plasticity of our brains.[9]

MC: Neuroscientists are no doubt currently studying the plasticity of a human brain adapting to these new ways of organizing knowledge.

AG: You have talked about the classical tradition. There is another tradition which is embedded in the etymology of certain word. Think about the word "artificial." If you look at its etymology, it goes back to Latin *artificialis*, which is derived from *artificium*, meaning realized skillfully or artfully. In German there is a nice mirror effect between *künstlich* (artificial) and *künstlerisch* (artful) which does not work in English. Something is artificial because it is artfully done. In architecture, the term *artificiale* was mainly used to describe visual effects and illusions. When we talk about AI, the connection to the origin of the word seems completely lost, as we don't think about something which has been done by humans but is somehow generated by algorithms.

MC: Well, "artificial" is not the only word to lose its original meaning in this context. Another word which has lost its original meaning in the context of AI is "generative." We do not talk about *creative* AI, but about *generative* AI. Here we have to go back to the history of Christianity. Generation and creation are important terms there. All this goes back to the Nicene Creed and one line in it, which says (in Italian): *generato non creato* (Latin *genitum, non factum*). Generated and not created. God creates, the son is generated; he is not made from nothing, he is made from something that is already there. Now think of what that means for generative AI. Nothing is created out of nothing. Everything is generated after something which is already out there. What do we call that in

---

9   Eleanor A. Maguire, David G. Gavian, Ingrid S. Johnsrude, and Christopher D. Frith, "Navigation-related structural change in the hippocampi of taxi drivers" *Proc. Natl. Acad. Sci. U.S.A.* 97, no. 8 (March 2000): 4398–4403, https://doi.org/10.1073/pnas.07003 9597.

architecture? Precedent, tradition, or history? There is no innovation without tradition. There is no license without rule. There is no invention without convention, and we always knew that. And now, AI is proving it.

AG: Absolutely. Again, we are back at tradition.

MC: Except that it's not intelligent: it can imitate, but it cannot creatively imitate. There is innovation, but based on tradition. Think of the famous metaphor of dwarfs standing on the shoulders of giants.

AG: I was rereading your introduction to the English edition of *Architecture in the age of printing* where you end the preface with the following words: "This book, which recounts how architecture came into the age of printing, implicitly suggests that architecture will also manage to get out of it—and survive. After all, we did well without printing for quite a while."[10] I was wondering what your outlook is nowadays, with all the experience that you have gained. Are we and architecture going to survive?

MC: That was thirty years ago! [laughs] Times have changed and we all have mixed feelings about technology. The problem in the first place is political. In 1996, 1997, a lot of architectural students were going into computers and the Internet, and wanted to be the next Bill Gates. But nowadays, I don't know anybody who wants to be the next Elon Musk ... It is not a civilizational problem; it has become a political problem in the sense that we must ask who owns the technology. Don't blame the technology, blame the person who owns it.

AG: I think that is an excellent conclusion. Thank you very much for your time!

---

10   Mario Carpo, *Architecture in the Age of Printing: Orality, Writing, Typography, and Printed Images in the History of Architectural Theory*, trans. Sarah Benson (MIT Press, 2001), viii.

Learning from Images

Andri Gerber in Conversation with Philipp Schaerer, Zurich, February 5, 2025

Andri Gerber: We had the pleasure of inviting you to give a talk at ZHAW two years ago, and I was honestly a little surprised when you spoke so positively about AI and its possibilities. It was a time when there was a very negative attitude towards AI, especially in the architectural context, and when I think of your work, I associate it with a very elaborate "digital craft" that is now being greatly shortened by AI.

Philipp Schaerer: Perhaps I should first clarify: when I talk about AI today, I am primarily referring to AI image generation—just as I did back then in my presentation.

Automated image description through captions has already been around for some time and is still widely used today for image tagging. This almost inevitably led to the question of whether this process could be reversed—i.e., whether images could be generated automatically from text fragments. A first significant step in this direction was taken in the mid-2010s by Elman Mansimov and his team. They developed an AI image-generation prototype that showed that this was possible in principle. This opened the door, so to speak, for the further development of more powerful models, which were refined further and further in the following years and finally made available to the public.

From 2020 onwards, AI-generated images spread rapidly—especially via social media. I think we were all fascinated by these images: their unusual softness, their precise attention to detail, and their deceptively real, almost photographic aesthetic. The countless curtains were particularly striking in these architectural fantasies [laughs].

This realistic aesthetic was simply astounding. Suddenly, anyone could translate their architectural fantasies into photorealistic images—without much effort, using text instructions alone, without any in-depth understanding of images, and without any knowledge of the optical laws of photography.

I found this fascinating, but at the same time it raises fundamental questions about authenticity. The fragile boundary between appearance and reality, between truth and staging, has preoccupied me since my first series of images, "BILDBAUTEN" (2007)—and has become all the more relevant with these new technologies.

Fig. 13: Philipp Schaerer, Bildbau No 1, 2007

AG: How do you deal with this new condition in your work?

PS: The effort required to generate such images is relatively low, and the resulting image often only approximates the idea you originally had in your head.

That's why it's out of the question for me to consider an AI-generated image as the end product.

In my works, AI-generated images serve mainly as building blocks—be it in the form of textures that I have specifically generated or as representational fragments that I then integrate into a pictorial ensemble using a conventional image montage. One example of this is my latest work, "Crossbreeds—Imaginary Still Lifes," in which individual fragments come from AI-generated images or were rendered directly into the image by me.

For me, making pictures is still a manual process, a continuous development and creation in which I always want to consciously decide in which direction the picture should develop.

Fig. 14: Philipp Schaerer, from the series "Crossbreeds – Imaginary Still Lifes", 2024

AG: You mentioned the subject of "authenticity." If you look at your earlier works—I'm thinking in particular of your "BILDBAUTEN"—the observer always asked himself whether these architectures were real or not. The pictures were very ambivalent, which was also their great quality.

PS: Technically speaking, the "BILDBAUTEN" series are image montages, i.e., composites of various photographic fragments—image constructions that have been created "by hand." Despite minor image inconsistencies or irritations, they deliberately play with photography's claim to credibility.

In the context of AI image generation, it is important to emphasize that such image montages previously required in-depth prior knowledge and technical expertise. The seamless and deceptively realistic weaving of image fragments into an image surface required experience in image processing—just as the use of 3D-rendering programs to simulate photographic representations demanded a certain amount of specialist knowledge.

However, this has changed fundamentally with the advent of AI image generators. Today, simple text-based descriptions (prompts) can be used to generate images at the touch of a button that simulate the photographic representation in a deceptively realistic way. This process takes seconds and requires no technical knowledge on the part of the user. Anyone is now able to create realistic images of fictional content—a development that also brings the problem of deepfakes into focus.

This development requires a critical examination. We need to address not only the possibilities but also the risks of this technology and ask ourselves how we want to deal with the increasing manipulability of images.

AG: Let's take a concrete example: you did an exercise with your students at EPFL called "Original & Replica." You set them the task of reproducing a photograph as accurately as possible using prompts in an AI image generator. I find this exercise extremely valuable from an educational point of view because, on the one hand, through this process you understand the mechanisms of these image generators and, on the other, you realize the value of the "original" and the difficulty of reproducing it

PS: In the first module, "My Choice," each student selected four images that either had a special meaning for them or that they felt were outstanding due to their aesthetic quality. The aim was to develop the ability to talk about the qualities of an image and formulate a convincing case for it. Through this endeavor, the students engaged intensively and analytically with their chosen image. Either personal memories played a role or aesthetic aspects such as composition, coloring, or lighting determined their selection.

In the second module, "AI Reconstruction," the task was to recreate the previously selected original images as accurately as possible using AI image generators. The aim was to use targeted text prompts to create an image that was visually as close as possible to the original.

However, this proved to be challenging. The students had to constantly adapt their prompts in order to achieve a closer approximation to the original and at the same time understand the effects of different formulations (prompt engineering) on the generated image.

It quickly became clear that an exact 1:1 reproduction of the original image using AI image generators with text prompts alone is simply impossible. In addition, there were striking differences in image quality and visual style between the various AI generators. Regardless of the model used, the students also discovered numerous inconsistencies and image errors in their AI-generated images: inconsistent perspectives, faulty depth gradation, problems with fine textures, distorted object shapes, inconsistent light and shadow casts, and faulty reflections on reflective surfaces.

A central aim of the module was therefore to sensitize students to the importance of looking closely at images. They should learn to devote more time and attention to images and consciously pay attention to possible inconsistencies—especially at a time when images are omnipresent, mass-produced, and consumed at high speed on social media.

Fig. 15: / imagine: A tall construction building in a foreboding landscape, in the style of dark, thin steel forms, photo -ar 127:128 (Reference Image: "Brasilia", c. 1958, Marcel Gautherot). Text prompt (above) and AI generated image (Midjourney), 18.10.2023. AR-329: Constructing the View: Built Images, Autumn Semester 2023, EPFL. Student: Darmezin Sidney

Fig. 16: / imagine: A realistic photograph of a thin rectangular black rear-view mirror of an old scooter, a beige sand dune in the background in the distance in front of the observer, the clear blue sky which takes up three quarters of the image, the trail of a plane in the sky, the rearview mirror reflecting another lighter, sunnier beige sand dune, the real dune and the dune reflected in the rearview mirror aligning perfectly as if it were a single dune, no vegetation and no people in the image, the rearview mirror at the bottom right of the image (Reference Image: "Coincidence Project", 2012, Denis Cherim). Text prompt (above) and AI generated image (Adobe Firefly), 20.10.2023. AR-329: Constructing the View: Built Images, Autumn Semester 2023, EPFL. Student: Alix Eggli

Fig. 17: / imagine: Café interior scene viewed from the front. The overall tone is warm. The bottom of the image is in a shadow and the top of the image is illuminated with a warm sunset light. The floor has square white tiles, the wall is composed of a medium dark green panel in its base and mustard yellow paint on the rest of the wall. On the right side of the wall, a landscape painting illustrating a view from a shore with trees on a sea with boats floating is hung. The furniture is 3 sets of rectangle-shaped tables with rounded edges with an off-white color, around each table are 4 dark jean blue plastic chairs with a tall curved back support. Three red bottles of sauces are on top and two spice holders are on each table (Reference Image: "Summerstown", 2019, Niall Mc-Diarmid). Text prompt (above) and AI generated image (Adobe Firefly), 20.10.2023. AR-329: Constructing the View: Built Images, Autumn Semester 2023, EPFL. Student: Sahar El-Zein

AG: This inevitably leads to the question of what an original is. In his famous essay, "The Work of Art in the Age of its Technical Reproducibility," from 1936, Walter Benjamin draws a history of art from the perspective of its reproducibility, from the manual to the technical, lamenting the loss of the aura. Benjamin writes above all against the backdrop of the development of film, to which he attributes a new form of participation, but one that takes place in a state of distraction. This resonates with many phenomena that have intensified through social media. If we now apply this to AI image generation, we are dealing with something new: on the one hand, it is about reproduction—the data that is recorded—and the algorithms that learn from the tasks and produce new images/texts. We are therefore dealing with a peculiar overlapping of production and reproduction, in which the question of an original takes on a whole new meaning, as there are probably many originals that are combined to create something new.

PS: Walter Benjamin was primarily concerned with the fact that the aura of a work of art is inextricably linked to its uniqueness and non-reproducibility—and thus directly integrated into its embedded context. A classic example of this would be a fresco or a wall painting that is tied to a very specific location. However, the situation is different with lithography or photography, which make it possible to produce numerous identical copies or prints of a work of art. These multiplied images can take on very different meanings depending on their context and intended use.

However, AI image generation is difficult to categorize clearly in this context. It is not a pure reproduction tool, as can be seen from the fact that it never generates exactly the same image despite identical prompts. Instead, a new image is created each time, which is difficult to embed in a clearly defined context—as it is not derived from a physical reality, but is based on a complex, data-based construct.

AG: Let's talk about prompts and language. It is exciting that today, images are gaining a new significance, but so, too, are texts. Writing, and especially describing, is taking on a new relevance

PS: In the 1990s, the terms "pictorial turn" and "iconic turn" described the increasing pictorial nature of social communication. To exaggerate and simplify it: the image replaces the word. Today, we are experiencing an interesting kind of reversal of this principle with AI image generation. In order to generate images, we first have to formulate text input (prompts)—the word once again becomes the central element of image production. This is an exciting development: whereas images used to be seen as a substitute for language, we now use language as a tool to generate images.

Furthermore, images are an extremely democratic medium, as they can be grasped intuitively and understood largely independently of prior linguistic or technical knowledge. AI image generators open up a new dimension of accessibility here: they make it possible to sketch and articulate visual ideas and visions of the future without the need for traditional artistic training.

I see this development as highly positive, as it significantly simplifies the production process and makes it more inclusive. The use of AI image generators requires little prior technical knowledge, which underlines their democratic character. Everyone can develop their own images, concepts, and visions of the future—regardless of their creative skills—and thus actively participate in the creative discourse.

AG: Pictures are an important form of communication, especially when it comes to selling a house.

PS: Yes, it is impossible to imagine architecture today without images. In recent years, however, there has been a strong trend towards increasingly photorealistic project visualization—often at the request of clients or project developers.

However, this type of representation can be problematic, especially in the early design phase. Highly realistic renderings give the impression of an already finished result, leaving little room for open design processes. This can not only restrict creative development, but also mean that alternative approaches are no longer even considered.

I therefore encourage my students to try out different aesthetic approaches in order to expand their digital visual vocabulary and develop a more conscious approach to images. Instead of being guided by a single, supposedly "correct" way of representation, they should learn to use images as tools for thinking and designing—and not just as a final form of presentation.

AG: In this context, there is a lot of talk about creativity, and we also have two texts on this topic in the book. Creativity is seen as the only human ability that · cannot be taken over by AI, because the technology can only reproduce.

PS: From my point of view, it is quite clear: AI does not replace creativity but remains dependent on humans as authors. It needs an idea, an intention, a creative decision, which is then further developed with the help of an image generator. Without conscious control, a concept, or an artistic question, the generated image remains just a random arrangement of pixels.

AG: One topic that comes up again and again in this context is the speed of processes. We are dealing with an acceleration that is overwhelming many people. How do you see this development? I imagine that your work on the picture is a very lengthy process; is this now accelerated with AI?

PS: Yes, many things have indeed become faster—that's true. But this acceleration also has positive sides. Today I have a much greater variety of image material and variations at my disposal than was previously available. This opens new possibilities and considerably expands the creative scope.

However, this unlimited variety can also seem overwhelming. I would see it less as overwhelming and more as a constant surprise at how many possibilities arise in a very short space of time. The challenge lies in making the right decisions and not getting stuck in the flood of options.

Ultimately, for me, it's about using the technology sensibly—as a tool that supports my creative process, but doesn't determine it. I use AI where it helps me to explore things faster without losing focus on the content.

AG: So you have adapted a new tool to your old working method.

PS: Yes, I think we can say so. In the past, my work may have taken more time in terms of craftsmanship than it does today. In this sense, the work actually loses some of its artisanal character, as I can now generate fragments in a more targeted and efficient way. The creative process shifts more to the curatorial and conceptual level, which is about making the right decisions from the multitude of possibilities.

AG: But that also means, when we come back to teaching, that students have to understand this decision-making process.

PS: Yes, exactly. Students must learn to consciously cultivate the decision-making process and develop cultural depth—a skill that is always linked to their own biography, perception and experience. It is also about gaining confidence in this role. The ability to make a choice and to make well-founded decisions is not self-evident—and is otherwise rarely taught systematically. It is therefore crucial that they learn to reflect on the medium and the image in order to sharpen their own visual language and deal more consciously with the flood of possibilities.

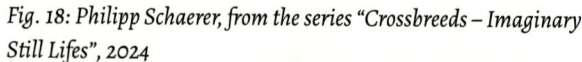

Fig. 18: Philipp Schaerer, from the series "Crossbreeds – Imaginary Still Lifes", 2024

AG: Where do you see the potential of AI in architecture?

PS: AI image generation is ideal for initial image approximations, concept images, tests, and variant studies. But architecture is precise: tied to a specific location, and usually thought through down to the smallest detail. It is simply impossible to precisely describe and fully control all the image-specific elements of architecture with text prompts alone.

It is true that it is now possible to upload images in addition to text instructions and link these to the prompts, which improves the result to a certain extent. However, even this method cannot meet the requirements of an architect's planning precision.

The further development of AI models in a direction in which 3D data of the architecture and the context with material assignments are uploaded instead of text prompts to describe the architecture seems more promising to me. Text-based input would then only be used to define stylistic image features. I am convinced that this is only a matter of time—initial approaches to such models already exist, even if they are not yet fully developed.

I have always been interested in hybrid image constructions—in other words, images with breaks and varying degrees of abstraction. These include, for example, photographic fragments that at first glance appear to be "illogically" integrated into an ensemble or interwoven with more abstract pictorial elements.

In general, I believe that we should take a step back in architectural representation—especially when it comes to communicating ideas and designs. We need to move away from the exclusively photographic visual language that increasingly serves as the standard for communicating concepts and possibilities.

This is precisely where I see great potential in AI image-generation programs: they could help us to explore and test new image approaches and more abstract aesthetics.

AG: Last but not least, I would like to address the question of authorship. What about the authorship of an AI-generated image when, in principle, potentially thousands of other people's images are recorded there in the form of data?

PS: The issue of authorship and copyright is important and real. A current example is the lawsuit filed by the *New York Times* against Microsoft and OpenAI because they believe that their copyrighted content was used on a large scale without permission. However, only large media companies can afford such lawsuits—many artists and creatives do not have the resources to legally defend themselves in this way.

It is therefore all the more important that we talk to students about the ethical aspects of AI in image production. Transparency plays a crucial role here—both in terms of the tools used and the creation processes. Today, it is more important than ever to declare the techniques and methods used to create images. This not only reflects the respective authorship but also reveals how and by what means an image was created. At a time when digital image production and AI generation continue to advance, it is becoming increasingly difficult to distinguish between handmade, photographed, or synthetically generated images. The open labeling of the tools used creates transparency and enables a critical examination of the image source and production.

Part 4: Essays

A: Data

What can a Multidimensional Language Model Tell Us about Architecture?

Julia Krasselt

Why look at language in architecture?

Language and architecture have much in common. Both function as semiotic systems—they convey meaning beyond their immediate form.[1] Just as a building can be "read" as a text that structures and organizes space,[2] language serves as a fundamental medium for communication. Both language and architecture are inherently social practices: They shape and are shaped by human interaction, structuring communication, behavior, and collective meaning within cultural and societal contexts. Moreover, language and architecture interact with each other. Research in linguistics has shown that the way we conceptualize and communicate about space is shaped by language, with different languages providing different spatial reference frameworks.[3] When people interact with architectural spaces, their perceptions are shaped by linguistic categories and culturally-specific spatial lexicons. Conversely, space and architecture shape the way we speak and communicate. Even in everyday interac-

---

1   Umberto Eco, *A Theory of Semiotics* (Indiana University Press, 1976); Gabriele Aroni, "Semiotics in Architecture and Spatial Design," in *Bloomsbury Semiotics Volume 2: Semiotics in the Natural and Technical Sciences*, ed. Jamin Pelkey and Stéphanie Walsh Matthews (Bloomsbury, 2023), 277–96, https://doi.org/10.5040/9781350139350.

2   Bryan Lawson, *Language of Space* (Taylor and Francis, 2007), 6.

3   Barbara Landau and Ray Jackendoff, "What and Where in Spatial Language and Spatial Cognition," *Behavioral and Brain Sciences* 16, no. 2 (June 1993): 255–65, https://doi.org/10.1017/S0140525X00029927; Peggy Li and Lila Gleitman, "Turning the Tables: Language and Spatial Reasoning," *Cognition* 83, no. 3 (April 2002): 265–94, https://doi.org/10.1016/S0010-0277(02)00009-4.

tions, space becomes a communicative element: "When we talk to each other, the space between us is part of our communication."[4]

But the relationship between language and architecture is also a complex one. As a physical object, architecture poses a challenge to language because it is primarily experienced through sight, touch, hearing, and smell. The material properties of a building, surface textures, spatial acoustics, and atmospheric qualities all contribute to architectural perception. These elements influence human interaction with the built environment but are not easily translated into verbal descriptions. In addition, architecture involves movement and embodied interaction, adding complexity to linguistic representation.

Yet, language plays a crucial role in conceptualizing, communicating, and theorizing about architecture and architectural practice. Without language, it would be difficult to communicate design intent or analyze the social and cultural roles of architecture. Architectural theorist Tom Markus emphasizes this by stating that "language is at the core of building, using and understanding buildings."[5] Language also structures architectural discourse, allowing professionals to communicate ideas systematically. As the architectural theorist Branko Mitrovic notes, certain aspects of architecture, such as function, social history, or cultural role, are primarily verbal and cannot be visualized.[6]

This article explores the relationship between language and architecture by using word embeddings, a computational method for representing word meanings based on their contextual relationships.[7] Word Embeddings are a fundamental component of Large Language Models (LLMs), serving as the representational backbone that allows these models to efficiently process, understand, and generate human language. Through an exploratory analysis, this study demonstrates how word embeddings can be used to investigate the meaning of key architectural concepts at a given point in time.

The research presented here follows a discourse-analytic perspective. Building on constructivist theories, this study considers language not as

---

4   Lawson, *Language of Space*, 8.

5   Thomas A. Markus, *Buildings and Power: Freedom and Control in the Origin of Modern Building Types* (Routledge, 1993), 4.

6   Branko Mitrovic, "Architectural Formalism and the Demise of the Linguistic Turn," *Log* 17 (2009): 20.

7   Tomas Mikolov et al., "Distributed Representations of Words and Phrases and Their Compositionality," *Advances in Neural Information Processing Systems 26* (2013): 3111–19; Alessandro Lenci, "Distributional Models of Word Meaning," *Annual Review of Linguistics* 4, no. 1 (2018): 151–71, https://doi.org/10.1146/annurev-linguistics-030514-125254.

a neutral medium reflecting an objective reality but as an instrument that actively constructs it.[8] The way society discusses architecture shapes collective knowledge and influences architectural perception. From a linguistic perspective, discourse analysis involves examining the meaning of words—semantics—to understand how concepts are constructed. By exploiting the power of word embeddings to map semantic relationships, this study offers a novel approach to analyzing architectural discourse.

Word Embeddings

Word embeddings operationalize the distributional hypothesis, a linguistic theory which proposes that the meaning of a word is derived from the contexts in which it occurs.[9] This approach to semantics was established long before the advent of LLMs and Generative AI, both of which rely heavily on it. Instead, distributional approaches to semantics were already being expressed in the 1950s, as the following quotes from Wittgenstein, Firth, and Harris show:

> [T]he meaning of a word is its use in the language.[10]
> You shall know a word by the company it keeps.[11]
> ... difference of meaning correlates with difference in distribution.[12]

The distributional hypothesis allows researchers to model the semantic similarity of words, phrases, and even larger syntactic structures based on real-world language usage, rather than relying solely on (native) speakers' intuition. According to the distributional hypothesis, meaning emerges from patterns of

---

8   Jürgen Spitzmüller and Ingo H. Warnke, "Discourse as a 'Linguistic Object': Methodical and Methodological Delimitations," *Critical Discourse Studies* 8, no. 2 (May 2011): 75–94, https://doi.org/10.1080/17405904.2011.558680; James Paul Gee, An Introduction to Discourse Analysis: Theory and Method, 4th ed. (Routledge, 2014).

9   Magnus Sahlgren, "The Distributional Hypothesis," Italian Journal of Linguistics 20 (2008): 33–53.

10   Ludwig Wittgenstein, *Philosophical Investigations*, trans. G.E.M. Anscombe (Basil Blackwell, 1958), PU §43.

11   John Rupert Firth, *Papers in Linguistics 1934–1951* (Oxford University Press, 1957).

12   Zellig S. Harris, "Distributional Structure," WORD 10, no. 2–3 (August 1954): 156, https://doi.org/10.1080/00437956.1954.11659520.

word co-occurrence. Thus, words that frequently occur in similar linguistic environments tend to have related meanings. Rather than considering contextual features such as time or place, this approach focuses on co-text—the words that commonly surround a given term.

Contextual patterns can be systematically identified in large collections of text. While early theories conceptualized meaning through linguistic context, modern AI techniques have operationalized this principle computationally.[13] Word embeddings model semantic similarity by mapping words into high-dimensional vector spaces: each word from a given corpus is represented as a vector in such a space. The position of each word in this space is determined by the surrounding words with which it appears. The following sentence from a corpus of Swiss architectural magazines (see the following section) shows the word *Beton* ("concrete") in its immediate context:

left context (10 words)	node	right context (10 words)	source text id
Stahlbeton eingebaut und die hangseitige Wand mit einem Vorbau aus	*Beton*	*versehen. Der neue Betonkubus unterteilt den Keller in eine*	Schweizer Bauzeitung, 142/2016
"Reinforced concrete was installed and the wall on the slope side was covered with"	"concrete"	"The new concrete cube divides the basement into a"	

A word such as *Beton* is likely to be repeatedly embedded in similar contexts, meaning that one would find similar sentences like those shown above, giving rise to specific patterns of use. Large linguistic corpora are particularly effective in identifying these patterns. They not only allow the identification of patterns for individual words but also reveal patterns that emerge from clusters of words. Put differently, by applying such a distributional, context-based approach to all the words in a corpus, they can be clustered according to their similar contexts. This is achieved by constructing a co-occurrence matrix that captures word-context relationships, as shown in the following simplified example:

---

13   Lenci, "Distributional Models of Word Meaning."

	Gebäude ("building")	bauen ("to build")	malen ("to paint")	skulptural ("sculptural")	Wendel-treppe ("spiral stair-case")	...
Beton ("concrete")	6	5	1	1	1	...
Holz ("wood")	5	7	3	0	0	...
Gemälde ("painting")	2	1	7	0	0	...
Porträt ("portrait")	1	2	8	0	0	...

By representing words as numerical vectors, word embeddings allow semantic similarity to be measured mathematically. For example, words that occur in similar contexts (e.g., *Beton* and *Holz*) will have similar vectors and will be positioned closer together in the vector space (see fig. 20). In practical implementations, word embedding models go beyond simple co-occurrence matrices. Using neural network-based learning techniques, models such as Word2Vec, GloVe, and FastText generate vector representations that capture complex semantic relationships.[14] These models compute word embeddings with hundreds of dimensions, allowing them to reflect nuanced word meanings. While co-occurrence matrices provide valuable insights, they are limited by sparsity and dimensional constraints. Neural network-based models overcome these limitations by producing dense vector representations that capture more nuanced semantic relationships.

A simplified 3D representation can be used to visualize word embeddings. In such a representation, words with similar contexts will be closer together, while unrelated words will be further apart (typically measured by cosine similarity or Euclidean distance). Fig. 21 illustrates how words such as *Beton* ("concrete"), *Holz* ("wood"), *Gemälde* ("painting"), and *Porträt* ("portrait") are

---

14   Piotr Bojanowski et al., "Enriching Word Vectors with Subword Information," Transactions of the Association for Computational Linguistics 5 (June 1, 2017): 135–46, https://doi.org/10.1162/tacl_a_00051; Mikolov et al., "Distributed Representations of Words and Phrases and Their Compositionality"; Jeffrey Pennington, Richard Socher, and Christopher Manning, "GloVe: Global Vectors for Word Representation," in *Proceedings of the 2014 Conference on Empirical Methods in Natural Language Processing* (EMNLP), ed. Alessandro Moschitti, Bo Pang, and Walter Daelemans (Association for Computational Linguistics, 2014), 1532–43, https://doi.org/10.3115/v1/D14-1162.

positioned in a vector space based on their contextual similarity. For example, the vectors for *Beton* and *Holz* are closer together than *Holz* and *Gemälde*, indicating a stronger contextual similarity between building materials. This method allows for accurate modelling of word relationships, even in high-dimensional spaces.

Fig. 19: 3D vector space as visualization for word embeddings.

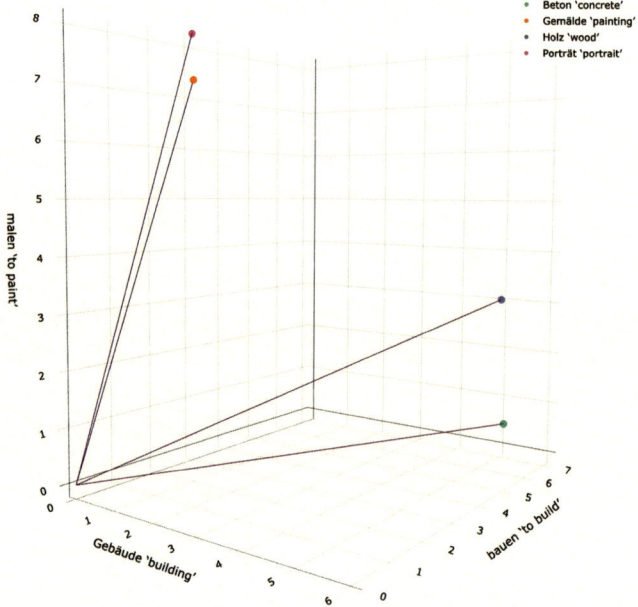

Nearest neighbor analysis in a word embedding model is a powerful tool for semantic analysis, revealing how meaning is structured within a corpus. It allows researchers to empirically identify dominant semantic fields without relying on manually-assigned categories, providing a data-driven linguistic perspective. In addition, nearest neighbor analysis helps uncover conceptual metaphors and highlight patterns in language use that reflect underlying discourse structures.[15] In the following analysis, this method is applied to examine how the architectural concept of spatiality is used within specific discursive contexts, namely within architectural magazines.

Data

For the study, a corpus of three Swiss architectural journals was compiled: *Werk, Bauen und Wohnen* (1977–2021), *Schweizerische Bauzeitung* (now *Tec 21*) (2001–2017), and *Hochparterre* (1988–2022). All issues of these journals were provided by the ETH Zurich Library in a digitized XML format. The corpus includes all textual elements from the three journals (e.g., articles and image captions) but excludes images (see Table 1).

Table 1: Corpus of Swiss architectural journals.

	words	documents	time span
Werk, Bauen und Wohnen	17.96 million	10,418	1977–2021
Schweizerische Bauzeitung/Tec21	6.76 million	4,231	2001–2017
Hochparterre	20.4 million	10,092	1988–2022
Total	45.12 million	24,741	

The corpus was processed using an automated linguistic processing pipeline[16] and contains various linguistic annotations (e.g., word and sentence boundaries, parts of speech) as well as text-based metadata (e.g., publication date and issue number). For the corpus, a word-embedding model was computed using word2vec (100 dimensions, context window size of 5).

---

15   Austin C. Kozlowski, Matt Taddy, and James A. Evans, "The Geometry of Culture: Analyzing the Meanings of Class through Word Embeddings," *American Sociological Review* 84, no. 5 (October 2019): 905–49, https://doi.org/10.1177/0003122419877135.

16   Described in Julia Krasselt et al., "Swiss-AL: A Multilingual Swiss Web Corpus for Applied Linguistics," in *Proceedings of the Twelfth Language Resources and Evaluation Conference* (European Language Resources Association, 2020), 4145–51.

The Concept of Spatiality in Architectural Magazines

Spatiality is a central concept in architectural discourse, making it an ideal focus for this exploratory analysis. To analyze how spatiality is represented linguistically, the nearest neighbors of the words *Raum* ("space") and *räumlich* ("spatial") were examined in the word embedding model (Fig. 21). By manually clustering the nearest neighbors, we identified different linguistic dimensions of spatiality in architectural discourse.

1) Functional Spaces

Nearest neighbors in this category refer to spaces with a specific use or purpose in architecture, emphasizing their designed function. Examples include *Wohnraum* ("living space"), *Stadtraum* ("urban space"), *Kirchenraum* ("church space"), *Arbeitsraum* ("workspace"), and *Bewegungsraum* ("movement space"). These terms highlight how space is structured and given meaning through its functional role in architectural contexts.

2) Social Spaces and Interaction

This category includes terms that emphasize space as a site of human interaction and social exchange. Examples include *Begegnungsort* ("meeting place"), *Kommunikationszone* ("communication zone"), *Gemeinschaftsbereich* ("community area"), and *Bewegungsraum* ("movement space"). The presence of these terms suggests that spatiality in architecture is not only physical but also relational, shaped by social dynamics and interaction.

3) Private and Intimate Spaces

Certain terms emphasize the personal or secluded aspects of space, emphasizing privacy and intimacy. Examples include *Privatraum* ("private space"), *Intimität* ("intimacy"), *Geborgenheit* ("sense of security"), and *Privatheit* ("privacy"). These words suggest that spatiality can also be framed in terms of emotional and psychological experiences, emphasizing the importance of enclosed, protective environments.

Fig. 20: Screenshot of word-embedding model calculated for the three Swiss architectural journals. The screenshot shows the 100 nearest neighbors for the word räumlich, "spatial."

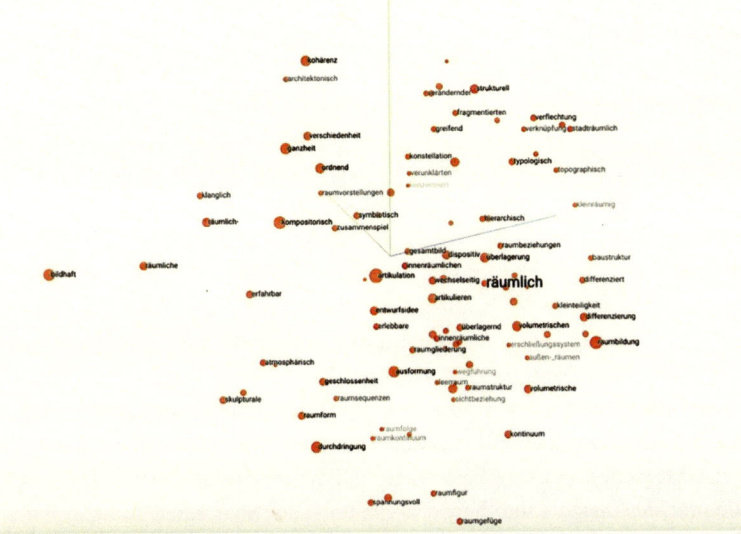

4)   Spatial Boundaries and Containment

Some words define space in terms of enclosure or extension, reflecting different ways of structuring space. Examples are *Innenraum* ("interior space"), *Aussenraum* ("exterior space"), and *Umraum* ("surrounding space"). Within this category, we also found the metaphors *space as a stage* (*Bühne* "stage," *Szenerie* "scenery", *dramaturgisch* "dramaturgical") and *space as a container* (*Gefäß* "vessel," *Leere* "emptiness"). These findings suggest that architectural discourse often conceptualizes space in terms of containment and permeability. Furthermore, the blurring of boundaries (*durchlässig* "permeable," *fliessender Übergang* "smooth transition," *verschränken* "entangle") reflects a linguistic tendency to describe space as fluid rather than rigidly bound.

5)   Spatial Relationships and Connectivity

Words in this category describe how spaces are linked, interwoven, or structured in relation to each other. Examples include *Verflechtung* ("interweaving"),

Verknüpfung ("connection"), *Überlagerung* ("superimposition"), *Raumgefüge* ("spatial structure"), *symbiotisch* ("symbiotic"), and *kompositorisch* ("compositional"). This cluster suggests that space in architecture is not static but dynamic, with an emphasis on relationships between spatial elements rather than isolated units.

6)   Sensory and Multimodal Aspects of Space

Beyond its geometric and functional properties, spatiality is also described in experiential and sensory terms. Examples include *Atmosphäre* ("atmosphere"), *Raumerlebnis* ("spatial experience"), *Raumgefühl* ("sense of space"), *erlebbar* ("perceivable"), *spannend* ("tense"), and *klanglich* ("acoustic"). These words indicate that spatiality in architectural discourse extends beyond the visual and geometric to include atmospheric and sensory dimensions, in line with phenomenological perspectives on space.

The identified semantic categories reveal that architectural discourse constructs spatiality as a multidimensional concept, encompassing functionality, social interaction, sensory experience, and dynamic relationships. This analysis provides insights into how space is linguistically framed and conceptualized, reflecting broader architectural thinking. A notable observation is the absence of regulatory and political aspects in the nearest neighbors of *Raum* ("space") and *räumlich* ("spatiality"). While spatial planning, zoning laws, and urban policies play a crucial role in shaping architecture, these aspects do not feature prominently in the linguistic model for architectural journals. This suggests that spatiality in the analyzed architectural journals primarily reflects descriptive and experiential meanings rather than regulatory language.

The exploratory analysis focuses on the linguistic representation of spatiality. The findings open up further research avenues in architectural, sociological, and philosophical contexts. For example, future work could explore how these linguistic structures align with architectural theories of space and whether similar patterns emerge in other domains of architectural discourse.

Outlook

The findings of this study demonstrate how a linguistic approach using word embeddings can reveal underlying semantic structures in architectural discourse. By analyzing the nearest neighbors of *Raum* ("space") and *räumlich* ("spatial") in a large corpus of Swiss architectural journals, we identified different linguistic dimensions of spatiality, including functional spaces, social interaction, private spaces, spatial boundaries, spatial relationships, and sensory experience. This analysis reveals how spatiality is constructed in discourse and provides new insights into the way language encodes architectural concepts.

For architectural research, this study provides a framework for understanding how linguistic patterns reflect and shape architectural thought. While architects are primarily concerned with visual and material forms, their discourse is inherently structured by language. The semantic categories identified in this study suggest that certain aspects of space—such as functionality and connectivity—are linguistically dominant, while regulatory and political dimensions are less prominent in the analyzed corpus. This raises questions about how different genres of architectural writing (e.g., policy documents, academic texts, practitioner discourse) construct space differently.

These findings suggest several avenues for future research, such as how architectural discourse changes over time. By applying diachronic word embedding models, researchers could trace shifts in spatial conceptualization over time, revealing how the meanings of spatial terms evolve in response to architectural trends and societal changes. Another way forward could be to integrate linguistic analysis with architectural theory. While this study focuses on linguistic structures, a next step could be to systematically link the identified semantic categories to architectural and spatial theories (e.g., phenomenological perspectives in architecture).

From Data-Driven to Design-Informed: A Socio-Technical Dialogue on AI, Context, and Design Futures

Bige Tunçer, Cem Ataman

Introduction

In contemporary architecture and urban practices, the interplay between standardized data protocols and the unique complexities of local contexts presents both a promise and a challenge. Standardized methodologies—emerging from the software industry's focus on uniform data structures—enhance efficiencies, interoperability, and AI analyses. However, built environments are shaped by cultural, social, historical, and environmental factors that defy uniformity. This chapter examines the tension between these imperatives, arguing that while standardized data practices can streamline large-scale projects and uncover spatial patterns, they may erode the characteristics that define distinctive urban and architectural settings. By integrating multi-modal data—from geospatial analytics and sensor readings to ethnographic insights and participatory contributions—this work comprehensively advocates a shift from data-driven design to design-driven data. In this approach, computational tools are employed not to dictate outcomes but to support creative exploration and critical reflection through collaboration among engineers, social scientists, and community stakeholders. Ultimately, this chapter contends that achieving a balance between technical optimization and contextual sensitivity is essential for fostering resilient, inclusive, and culturally responsive design.

Navigating Uniform Protocols Amid Local Complexities: Standardization or Context?

In contemporary architecture, urban design, and planning, a persistent tension arises between the drive for standardized data protocols and the imperative to account for the distinct complexities of local environments. The software industry has long prioritized uniform data structures and rigid frameworks, yielding efficiencies in collaboration and enabling advances in AI.[1] However, architecture and urbanism operate within a fundamentally different paradigm shaped by cultural, social, historical, and climatic specificities. The imposition of a singular standardized model risks homogenizing diverse urban and architectural settings, eroding the unique spatial, social, and material characteristics that define buildings, neighborhoods, and cities.

Despite these concerns, the rationale for standardization remains compelling. By systematizing data collection, classification, and processing, standardized methodologies enhance operational efficiency and facilitate interoperability across digital tools.[2] Large-scale urban projects, particularly those involving extensive datasets, increasingly depend on such efficiencies to optimize decision-making and coordination among stakeholders.[3] The growing reliance on big data further amplifies this trend, as the potential to uncover latent spatial patterns and generate predictive models exerts considerable influence on urban strategies. Yet the rigidity of standardized metrics poses a critical challenge: reducing architectural and urban complexity to quantifiable parameters risks constraining creative agency and diminishing sensitivity to local contingencies. When stakeholder perspectives, historical contexts, and site-specific constraints are abstracted into uniform indicators, the value of place-based interventions may be compromised.

This challenge is further complicated by the expanding array of data sources that inform design and planning decisions. From microclimate

---

1   Daochen Zha et al., "Data-Centric Artificial Intelligence: A Survey," *ACM Computing Surveys* 57, no. 5 (2025): 1–42.

2   Matthias Buchinger, Peter Kuhn, and Dian Balta, "Towards Interoperability of Data Platforms for Smart Cities," in *Handbook of Smart Cities*, ed. Juan Carlos Augusto (Springer International Publishing, 2021), 1–22.

3   Simon Elias Bibri, "Data-Driven Smart Sustainable Cities of the Future: Urban Computing and Intelligence for Strategic, Short-Term, and Joined-up Planning," *Computational Urban Science* 1 (2021): 8.

sensors and transportation analytics to participatory workshops and ethno-graphic fieldwork, the proliferation of data streams presents both oppor-tunities and obstacles.[4] On the one hand, these diverse inputs offer a more granular understanding of spatial dynamics, revealing overlooked interde-pendencies and challenging entrenched assumptions. On the other hand, the vast volume and heterogeneity of data risk overwhelming stakeholders, fostering selective engagement that may reinforce preexisting biases rather than fostering genuine insight. As a result, the question extends beyond the mechanics of standardization to a more fundamental inquiry: which data are most relevant, and how should they be contextualized to support context-sensitive decision-making?

Ultimately, architects and urban practitioners must navigate this inter-section of globalized technical infrastructures and locally-situated identities with caution. Striking a balance between efficiency and legitimacy requires a comprehensive approach that leverages the benefits of standardized protocols without compromising the specificity of context. The challenge lies not in rejecting standardization outright but in developing adaptable frameworks that accommodate both the demand of data-driven methodologies and the irreducible complexity of built environments.

Data as a Socio-Technical Lifeline: Keeping Designers in the Loop

The built environment is shaped by a complex interplay of social, economic, and technological factors, which collectively influence its design, function, and evolution over time.[5] While quantitative metrics—such as land-use ef-ficiency, resource consumption, and cost-benefit analyses—play a crucial role in informing design and planning decisions, an overreliance on techno-cratic methodologies risks neglecting the social and cultural dimensions that shape how built environments are experienced and interpreted.[6] Cultural

---

4   Constantine E. Kontokosta, "The Quantified Community and Neighborhood Labs: A Framework for Computational Urban Science and Civic Technology Innovation," *Journal of Urban Technology* 23, no. 4 (2016): 67–84.
5   Matthew Carmona, *Public Places Urban Spaces: The Dimensions of Urban Design*, 3rd ed. (Routledge, 2021).
6   Cem Ataman, Bige Tunçer, and Simon T Perrault, "Asynchronous Digital Participation in Urban Design Processes: Qualitative Data Exploration and Analysis With Natural Language Processing," in *POST-CARBON—Proceedings of the 27th CAADRIA Conference,*

norms, local power structures, and everyday practices often elude purely data-driven analyses, necessitating a more integrative approach. In this context, human-centered inquiry remains indispensable. By engaging with the lived experiences and cultural values of communities, such inquiry transcends the limitations of quantitative methodologies, capturing the subtle ways in which individuals perceive, navigate, and interact with their built environments.

Architects and urban practitioners, therefore, do not simply interpret pre-existing datasets but actively mediate between algorithmic insights and contextual realities. Their role extends beyond passive engagement with standardized metrics; instead, they formulate hypotheses about behavioral patterns—such as how pedestrians interact with a new shopping center or how perceptions of trust shift in response to digital tool interventions—and validate these assumptions through both quantitative datasets and qualitative observations. This interdisciplinary collaboration among engineers, software developers, and data scientists, as well as community stakeholders, social scientists, and environmental scientists, further ensures that design and planning decisions remain technically robust, culturally sensitive, and ethically responsible.

In this socio-technical paradigm, data is not a neutral or static entity but an active agent in collaborative exploration. Rather than dictating deterministic outcomes, data serves as a medium through which competing perspectives and complex urban systems can be reconciled. Architects and urban practitioners, in turn, assume the role of facilitators across disciplines for inclusive decision-making processes. By resisting the reductive impulse to optimize environments solely according to measurable metrics, data-driven approaches can instead cultivate built environments that skillfully balance operational performance with a profound sense of place, ensuring alignment with the lived experiences and cultural needs of communities. This shift is particularly critical in ensuring that communities marginalized by digital exclusion—those unable or unwilling to generate extensive data footprints—are not rendered invisible within design and planning frameworks. Ultimately, integrating both computational and human-centered perspectives enables the built environment to remain functional, responsive, and contextually meaningful.

---

ed. Jeroen van Ameijde et al. (2022), 383–92, https://doi.org/10.52842/conf.caadria.20 22.1.383.

Data Fusion and Intelligent Workflows:
Toward Complex Design Scenarios

Contemporary design and planning processes necessitate a robust method-ological framework, allowing stakeholders to synthesize diverse datasets—rang-ing from geospatial analytics to ethnographic observations—into holistic, context-sensitive strategies. By integrating varied, multi-modal datasets that are multi-source, multi-scale, and multi-temporal, architects and urban practitioners can construct a systemic understanding of built environments from otherwise isolated parameters, revealing the complex interdependen-cies among infrastructural demands, environmental conditions, and human behaviors. While this integrated perspective enhances descriptive analyses, it also informs predictive modeling and scenario-based simulations, where AI-driven decision-support tools enable the exploration of "what-if" scenarios for urban interventions—such as public space design, amenity distribution, or climate-adaptive strategies. Supported by well-curated and integrated datasets, these systems illuminate trade-offs that might otherwise remain obscured, ensuring that design and planning decisions balance technical feasibility with socio-environmental responsiveness.

Nevertheless, the increasing reliance on algorithmic processes introduces challenges related to transparency, interpretability, and trust. AI-driven mod-els, particularly those employing deep learning techniques, often function as "black boxes," generating outputs with limited traceability.[7] This opacity tends to weaken stakeholder trust and process reliability, especially in public sector contexts where accountability and democratic decision-making are paramount.[8] Consequently, ensuring the accountability and interpretability of such algorithmic processes is critical. Clear documentation of data sources, modeling assumptions, and computational outputs, along with consistent stakeholder communication, is essential for shifting from passive acceptance of opaque system outputs to critical engagement with data systems and de-sign workflows. The development of a shared interpretative framework—one

---

7   Mohammad Amir Khusru Akhtar, Mohit Kumar, and Anand Nayyar, "Socially Responsi-ble Applications of Explainable AI," in *Towards Ethical and Socially Responsible Explainable AI, Studies in Systems, Decision and Control* (Springer Nature Switzerland, 2024), 261–350.

8   Cem Ataman, Simon Perrault, and Bige Tunçer, "Fostering Inclusive Urban Design and Planning: Enhanced Trust and Reliability through Descriptive Instructions for Digital Citizen Participation," *Journal of Urban Technology* 31 (2024): 25–48.

that allows stakeholders with different domain knowledge to scrutinize data-driven models—thus becomes integral to effective, evidence-based decision-making.

Furthermore, when data-driven workflows and AI-supported processes intersect with established design heuristics, a persistent tension arises between automation and augmentation. While AI excels at searching large parameter spaces and detecting statistical patterns, it remains limited in its capacity for contextual reasoning and interpretive flexibility when familiar heuristics fail. Because machine learning algorithms generalize from historical data, architectural and urban practices—frequently confronted with unprecedented conditions and resistance to standardization—require more adaptive approaches. This recognition has spurred a paradigm shift in design education, where traditional pedagogies once focused on spatial composition and material experimentation now extend to include data literacy, coding proficiency, and algorithmic thinking. The aim is not to displace architectural intuition with computational logic but to cultivate stakeholders who can seamlessly integrate quantitative analysis with qualitative discernment.

Ultimately, the future of design and planning lies in a symbiotic relationship between intelligent workflows and human expertise. By leveraging the computational power of AI while retaining the critical, creative, and interpretive capacities of human designers, the field can move toward a more integrative approach—one in which data-driven insights inform, rather than dictate, design solutions. In this vision, innovation emerges not from the mechanistic application of algorithmic processes but from their contextual calibration within the socio-cultural and ecological dimensions of the built environment.

Case Spotlights: Data in Action

Data-driven design is most effective when it addresses concrete, context-specific problems rather than forcing every scenario into a universal template. The cases in this section illustrate how culture, climate, and interdisciplinary collaboration intersect with data analytics to inform decisions, ultimately leading to evidence-based, data-informed design and planning actions.

As discussed above, data-driven design and planning have evolved to incorporate both qualitative and quantitative data, spanning multiple scales and timeframes. Designers and planners operate in complex environments where they must switch between various scales and frame multiple, often overlapping problems simultaneously. The integration of multi-source, multi-scale, and multi-time information into urban decision-making ensures a richer, evidence-based foundation for planning and design interventions. This approach moves beyond traditional intuition-driven methodologies by providing structured, data-backed insights that support adaptive urban strategies.

The selection and use of data sets in the following cases are context-sensitive, considering the specific needs of each urban scenario. By combining qualitative and quantitative data—ranging from small-scale community surveys to large-scale environmental monitoring—design and planning support tools and platforms have been created where planners can make informed choices that balance technological advancements with human-centric design. A key challenge in this data-driven design process lies in deriving behavioral hypotheses from diverse urban data sets and linking them to spatial and organizational patterns. The integration of big data, user preferences, and designer knowledge into urban planning enables a more nuanced approach that aligns infrastructure development with actual user needs.

Advanced AI and data processing techniques—such as multivariate analysis, natural language processing (NLP), text mining, computer vision, and machine learning—have been integrated into design workflows. These technologies enable planners to make sense of complex, multidimensional urban datasets. AI-driven insights can assist in everything from traffic optimization to community engagement strategies, ensuring that urban environments are both efficient and responsive. When properly structured, AI-supported decision-making fosters a cooperative model where designers pose critical questions and AI generates data-informed scenarios, facilitating more dynamic and adaptable urban planning strategies.

Ultimately, platforms and applications that support data-driven design span multiple scales, from city-wide master planning to detailed neighborhood and street-level interventions, such as those described below. The use of data in such platforms extends beyond passive analytics; buildings and infrastructure can actively participate in urban processes through real-time data exchange. This paradigm shift reframes architects, urban designers, and planners as mediators between technology, environment, and community, where design is seen not just as a product but as an iterative, collective learning process.

A The Informed Design Platform: Multi-Modal Data
for Urban Public Spaces

The Informed Design Platform (IDP) is a digital framework designed to assist urban designers by integrating multi-source, multi-scale, and multi-time
data.[9] IDP incorporates quantitative and qualitative datasets, including sensor
networks, participatory data, and spatial analytics, to evaluate public space usage. The platform enables designers to assess factors such as pedestrian flow,
thermal comfort, and user perceptions, providing a holistic approach to adaptive public space design. By merging real-time environmental readings with
citizen feedback, IDP empowers designers to create responsive and user-cen-
tered urban interventions.

*Fig. 21: Multi-source data collection, analysis dimensions and pillars, and information
model diagram.*

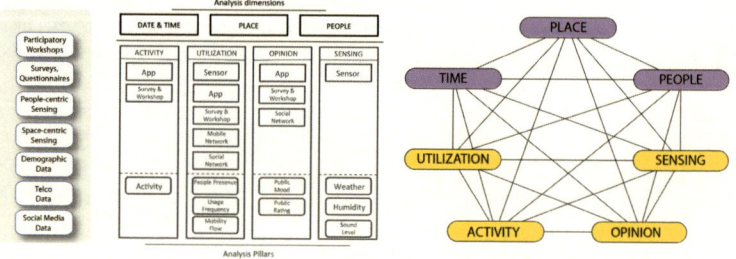

One of the significant strengths of IDP is its ability to bridge the gap
between technical data analytics and intuitive, experience-driven urban planning. By allowing designers to visualize how various factors interact—such
as how temperature variations influence pedestrian density or how seating

9   Billy Lau, Benny Ng, Chau Yuen, Bige Tunçer, and Keng Hua Chong, "The Study of Urban Residential's Public Space Activeness using Space-centric Approach," *IEEE Internet
of Things Journal* 8, no. 14 (2021): 11503–13; Lin Lin You, Bige Tunçer, Rong Zhu, Hexu
Xing, and Yuen Chau, "A synergetic orchestration of objects, data, and services to enable smart cities," *IEEE Internet of Things Journal* 6, no. 6 (2019): 10496–507; Bige Tunçer
and Lin Lin You, "Informed Design Platform: Multi-modal Data to Support Urban Design Decision Making," in *eCAADe 2017*, vol. 2, *SHOCK! Sharing of Computer Knowledge*,
ed. Antonio Fioravanti et al. (2017), 545–52.

arrangements impact social interactions—IDP provides a richer foundation for decision-making. Furthermore, the participatory aspect ensures that the end-users of urban spaces have a voice in shaping them, making public spaces more inclusive and attuned to community needs.

Fig. 22: IDP interface, displaying a comparative analysis of sensed and reposted activities conducted in various playground spaces.

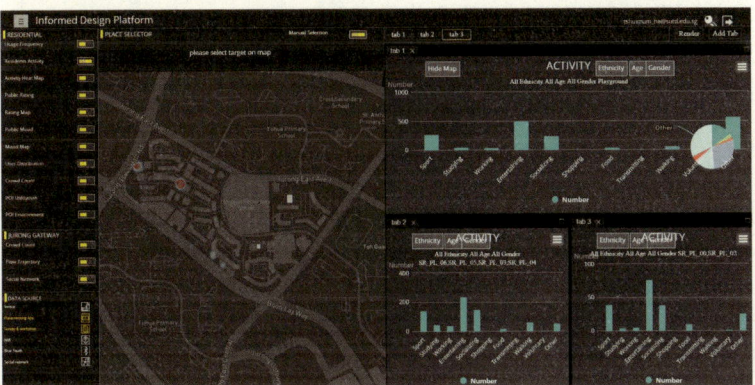

In practice, IDP has been used to analyze multiple urban spaces, uncovering insights into how different population segments utilize shared environments. For example, in a high-density mixed-use area, IDP revealed that a combination of three functions—covered walkways, playgrounds, and coffee shops—acted as bottom-up community activity generators, influencing future urban design strategies. Additionally, the platform identified a disconnect in the utilization of public spaces between sub-areas of neighborhoods with demographic differences, leading to recommendations for better integration of suitable amenities and rest spaces.

Beyond its analytical capabilities, IDP can serve as a tool for predictive modeling. Through AI-driven simulations, urban planners can anticipate how changes in the built environment—such as the introduction of new green spaces, pedestrianized streets, or transit modifications—will impact user behavior. This predictive functionality allows for proactive rather than reactive design strategies, ensuring that urban spaces evolve in tandem with community needs. The potential for real-time urban analytics means that planners can make adjustments based on changing usage patterns, optimizing spaces dynamically rather than relying on static planning models. Future developments of IDP aim to incorporate machine learning algorithms that refine insights over time, making the platform even more adaptive to the complexities of modern urban living.

B Measuring Human Experience in the Built Environment

A case study exploring "Data-Driven Thinking" demonstrated how real-time physiological and environmental data could enhance design decision-making.[10] Through a seven-day workshop, participants used wearable sensors to measure bodily responses to different urban conditions, integrating these insights with environmental data. This methodology highlights the potential of integrating human-centric metrics into urban planning, ensuring that design choices reflect not only functional efficiency but also psychological and physiological well-being. The approach bridges computational analytics with experiential design, fostering a more comprehensive understanding of the built environment.

Fig. 23: Sensors for data collection (left), data collection with mobile sensor station (middle), selected walking route (right).

By incorporating biofeedback data, such as changes in heart rate and skin temperature, this approach provides a granular perspective on how urban environments affect human stress levels, comfort, and engagement. For example, a shaded public square may intuitively seem more inviting, but physiological data might reveal that minor changes in humidity levels or noise pollution significantly alter its perceived comfort. The workshop findings underscore the

---

10   Bige Tunçer and Francisco Benita, "Data-driven thinking for measuring the human experience in the built environment," *International Journal of Architectural Computing* 20, no. 2 (2021): 316–33; Francisco Benita, G. Bansal, D. Virupaksha, F. Scandola, and B. Tunçer, "Body responses towards a morning walk in a tropical city," *Landscape Research* 45, no. 8 (2020): 966–83.

importance of interdisciplinary collaboration, with designers working along-side cognitive scientists, urban ecologists, and data analysts to refine methods for capturing human experiences.

Fig. 24: A visualization of a participant's stress levels on an urban walk, collected via a wearable physiological sensor. The size of the spheres represents stress levels, while the color intensity represents thermal comfort.

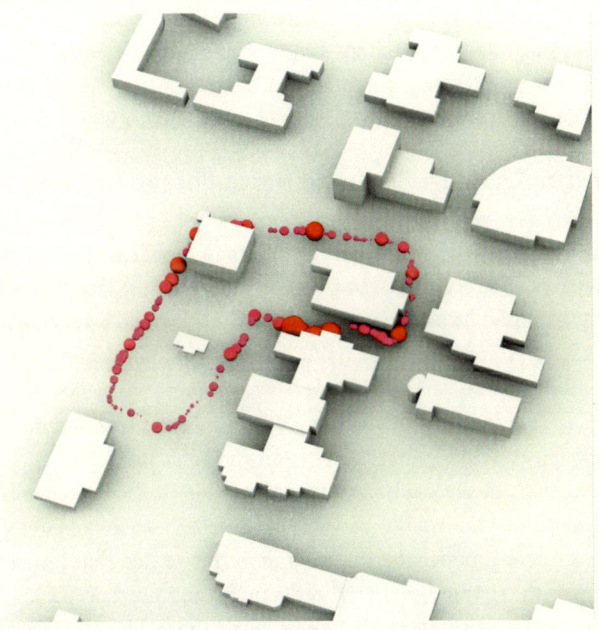

Beyond immediate physiological responses, this approach also sheds light on long-term well-being. Prolonged exposure to certain urban condi-tions—such as persistent noise, high traffic density, or inadequate green spaces—can contribute to chronic stress, impacting mental and physical health. By continuously monitoring biometric responses across different environments, urban planners can design interventions that promote both momentary comfort and sustained well-being. Moreover, the ability to com-bine these insights with subjective user feedback adds another layer of nuance, allowing planners to understand not just how people react physically to their surroundings but also how they emotionally interpret those experiences.

Further expanding on this approach, researchers have begun integrating AI-powered emotion recognition into physiological monitoring, providing even deeper insights into how the built environment shapes human experience. For instance, facial recognition algorithms paired with physiological data can detect subtle changes in emotional states, helping to identify spaces that evoke stress or relaxation. Additionally, large-scale data aggregation from multiple test sites allows for comparisons between different urban environments, highlighting best practices in human-centered design. Future applications of this methodology could include large-scale, real-time monitoring of urban well-being, potentially influencing policy decisions related to health, urban planning, and sustainable development.

C Optimizing Pedestrian Comfort in Transit-Oriented Walkways

Pedestrian pathways play a crucial role in urban mobility, yet their design often prioritizes efficiency over human experience. In Singapore, a comprehensive study explored how transit-oriented walkways could be optimized to enhance pedestrian comfort while maintaining accessibility and efficiency.[11] The study combined large-scale digital preference surveys, virtual reality (VR) simulations, and environmental analytics to gain a deeper understanding of how design elements influence user perception and behavior.

A key aspect of the study was the integration of VR experiments, allowing participants to virtually experience different walkway configurations and provide real-time feedback. This approach revealed that factors such as walkway width, shading, material reflectivity, and noise levels significantly impacted perceived comfort. The study found that wider walkways with integrated greenery and noise-dampening materials led to a more pleasant experience, particularly for elderly pedestrians and individuals with mobility impairments. Furthermore, dynamic lighting solutions that adjusted based on time of day and foot traffic density were identified as an effective strategy to enhance safety and usability.

---

11   Bige Tunçer et al., "Informed Design of Pedestrian Pathways," in *Accelerated Design: Proceedings of the 29th International Conference of the Association for Computer-Aided Architectural Design Research in Asia*, ed. Nicole Gardner et al. (2024), 405–14, https://doi.org/1 0.52842/conf.caadria.2024.2.405.

Fig. 25: The eight design variants presented to participants in the VR experiment.

Open atrium   Elevated walkway   Green planters   Green wall

Empty walkway   Public art   Food and   Retail stores
decorated wall   Beverage stores

Fig. 26: Walkway widths in indoor and outdoor conditions (left 3 columns); edge conditions of indoor and outdoor walkways (right 3 columns).

Beyond environmental factors, the study examined behavioral patterns using GPS tracking and AI-powered pedestrian flow simulations. By mapping movement trajectories, researchers identified congestion points and areas where pedestrian flow was disrupted due to poorly placed obstacles or inefficient crossings. These insights informed recommendations for improved wayfinding systems, strategically placed rest areas, and enhanced connectivity between transit nodes and key urban destinations.

Another innovative component of the study was the use of biometric feedback to assess pedestrian stress levels in different walkway scenarios. Participants equipped with wearable sensors provided real-time physiological data, highlighting specific design conditions that triggered stress or discomfort. For instance, narrow passages with poor airflow and high foot traffic led to elevated heart rates and increased reports of anxiety, whereas open, well-ventilated walkways promoted relaxation and ease of movement.

The findings of this study have been instrumental in shaping new pedestrian infrastructure policies in Singapore. By leveraging data-driven insights, urban planners have been able to implement targeted design modifications that prioritize pedestrian well-being without compromising transit efficiency. Future initiatives aim to integrate adaptive walkway technologies, such as smart pavement materials that adjust surface temperature and intelligent traffic management systems that dynamically reroute foot traffic based on real-time congestion patterns.

This research underscores the importance of human-centric urban design, demonstrating that pedestrian comfort is not merely an aesthetic consideration but a critical component of sustainable and livable cities. By combining advanced analytics, participatory feedback, and physiological monitoring, transit-oriented developments can evolve to meet the needs of diverse urban populations, ensuring that walkability remains a cornerstone of future urban mobility strategies.

Conclusion

As architecture and urban practices evolve in an era of unprecedented computational capabilities, the challenge goes beyond refining data-driven methodologies to ensuring they serve broader objectives of human and environmental well-being. While AI and algorithmic workflows offer powerful tools for analyzing spatial patterns, optimizing performance, and predicting urban dynamics, they must remain instruments of inquiry rather than arbiters of design. The true potential of data lies not in dictating outcomes but in revealing latent complexities, provoking critical reflection, and enhancing the depth of design discourse.

Moving forward, the discipline must transcend a technocratic fixation on optimization and efficiency to embrace a more integrative approach—one that recognizes the situated and contextual nature of design. Architectural and urban challenges are not abstract mathematical problems; they are deeply embedded in social, cultural, historical, and environmental realities that defy standardization. Processes that uncritically apply generalized datasets or rigid computational models risk oversimplifying the complexities of local contexts. Thus, the challenge is not to surrender expertise to machine intelligence but to forge a symbiotic relationship in which data operates as a catalyst for creative exploration rather than a constraint on it.

Furthermore, this shift requires a fundamental rethinking of professional practice, research collaboration, and education. Instead of viewing data as an external imposition on design and planning, architects and urban practitioners must cultivate a capacity for critical engagement with computational tools, ensuring that design intelligence drives technological development rather than the reverse. This perspective calls for a transition from data-driven design to design-driven data—a paradigm in which data is not simply assembled for validation but is actively shaped to generate new insights, challenge assumptions, and foster meaningful stakeholder engagement. Toolchains and toolkits developed through research—encompassing multi-source, multi-scale, and multi-time data—can facilitate this paradigm shift by translating advanced AI techniques into actionable workflows that professionals can integrate into practice. This translation process requires not only refining computational methods but also working closely with relevant stakeholders, from engineers to policymakers, to align technological innovation with cultural and environmental objectives. In this context, transparency, inclusivity, and ethical accountability must be woven into every stage, ensuring that digital methodologies remain answerable to the diverse stakeholders, domains, and contexts they serve.

Consequently, the future of design does not hinge on a strict dichotomy between standardization and local adaptability, automation and human judgment, or data and intuition. Rather, it centers on striking a dynamic balance—leveraging computational intelligence while continuing to value lived experience, collective expertise, and human creativity. Moreover, these technological advancements in data analytics and algorithmic methods must be aligned with the foundational values of equity, sustainability, and cultural responsiveness. Architects and urban practitioners, in turn, bear a significant responsibility to shape built environments that are not only data-informed but also profoundly human-centered. This is not merely an aspiration; it is an imperative for forging a resilient, inclusive, and contextually attuned future.

Beyond Machine Perception: AI Urban Imagination

Darío Negueruela del Castillo, Iacopo Neri

Introduction

The city has always been a subject of fascination and study, its complexity and dynamism defying simple categorization. In recent years, the rapid development of AI has opened up new avenues for exploring the urban landscape, offering novel tools and the capacity to analyze multimodal data at scale, which could contribute to our understanding of cities as a complex, historically grounded, and culturally mediated environment.

This paper delves into the potential of AI to go beyond mere machine perception and engage with the city as a "found world," shaped by both material structures and contested fields of vision, imagination, and representation. It examines three projects: Clip and the City (2023), World Gist (2023–24), and The City in a Bottle (2024–25), each leveraging different AI techniques to analyze urban landscapes, uncover cultural biases, and simulate urban environments through the lens of critical urban theory. These systems, in their very attempt to render the city legible through algorithmic means, paradoxically perform what Baudrillard would recognize as a parade of simulacra, where the model precedes and determines the territory it is supposed to represent.

The Closure of Urban Imagination

Our age seems dominated by "platform urbanism."[1] The city becomes increasingly indistinguishable from its digital shadow, cast by the vast apparatus of data collection and algorithmic processing that mediates urban experience. This apparatus extends its reach into economic, leisure, social, and affective spheres, shaping the dynamics of branding, retail, property development, and services that give form to our urban environments. This already widens the gap between lived experience and comprehension of the larger structures that shape that experience, but there is more to the story.

AI foundation models and multimodal Large Language Models (LLMs) now join this picture. These generalist models, trained on a huge snapshot of the Internet, like Common Crawl[2] (itself a kind of digital unconscious of contemporary culture), are increasingly present, mediating our online and physical lives. They perform a restriction of urban imagination to the combinatorial possibilities inherent in their training distributions, which I call "algorithmic foreclosure of the possible." This operates through a recursive semiotic trap. The AI systems, in learning from the sediment of Internet culture, construct what appears to be an infinite space of potential but which is, in reality, a closed system, a hermetically sealed universe of remixed existing forms. These models' latent spaces have been called accidental archives or snapshots of our culture, but are in fact self-referential learned distributions with no outside space, where the "culture" that is encoded is trapped within its own walls. Moreover, these latent spaces have become the main brokers of our visual imaginaries, conditioning the generation of synthetic visuals that flood the Internet. This represents not merely a limitation of current technology but perhaps also a fundamental contradiction within the logic of computational urbanism itself.

---

1   Platform urbanism describes the intersection of digital platforms and urban environments. It represents an evolution of the Smart City paradigm, focusing on how digital technologies and services reshape urban spaces and social interactions in which large tech platforms represent a new kind of political geography, and specifically, a new kind of sovereignty, one that potentially transcends the local and national.

2   See https://commoncrawl.org.

Surplus Data and Urban Knowing

Previously, the paradigm of Big Data, where large amounts of data coming from our digital footprints, smartphones, and from the ubiquity of sensors, promised to deliver the structure behind all kinds of phenomena by letting data speak and avoiding imposed or preconceived theories. This went hand in hand with the ideas behind the Smart City model.[3] But we are now facing a different reality. We seem to have too much data, not too little. In what we could consider the third phase of "machinic urbanization" (following Mumford's paleotechnic and neotechnic orders), we are now in a new paradigm that Orit Halpern has called "surplus data." This emerges not merely as an accumulation of information but as a fundamentally new mode of understanding and therefore acting upon cities, a new urban epistemology. Halpern has observed that "data is reassembled and recombined to produce new 'truths' from within the system. Data extends beyond description, creating the world it would describe."[4] In other words, new and autonomous worlds emerge from this vast amount of available and ingested data, especially in large AI models. This takes on a rather sinister aspect for architecture and urbanism, as data becomes a "perfect crime" (Baudrillard) against urban reality itself, eliminating not just the referent but the very possibility of reference.

It is useful here to describe a triad of projects that try to tackle the hidden world of architecture within AI foundation models. With these projects, we attempt to analyze what implicit ideas these models have of architecture. Or in other words: what do they think of architecture, and what are their implicit models and theories?

Clip and the City: Uncovering Urban Cultural Layers

The probabilistic logic of AI systems exemplified in projects like CLIP and the City[5] represents not simply a new tool for urban analysis but a transforma-

---

3   For an informed view, see Rob Kitchin, "The Real-Time City? Big Data andSmart Urbanism," GeoJournal 79, no. 1 (2014): 1–14, https://doi.org/10.1007/s10708-013-9516-8.

4   Orit Halpern and Robert Mitchell, The Smartness Mandate (MIT Press, 2022), 203.

5   Darío Negueruela del Castillo, Iacopo Neri "CLiP and The City: Addressing the Artificial Encoding of Cities in Multimodal Foundation Deep Learning Models," in On Architecture (2023) Conference Proceedings (Strand, 2023), 92–99, https://doi.org/10.60152/zkhvd3 og.

tion in what constitutes urban knowledge itself. In this project, we fed 360° urban panoramas of Rome[6] into large vision-language models (CLiP and Open-CLIP), to extract the embeddings[7] of their visual and textual features. This enabled us to perform spatial analyses that revealed clusters and discontinuities in the urban layout. These clusters, in turn, highlighted the interplay of historical legacies and contemporary urban practices. The project ultimately underscored that while machine learning models can capture remarkable details of urban form, they also propagate cultural biases inherited from their training datasets.

Fig 27: Diagram showing the pipeline for the project, first we download google street imagery for the full city centre of Rome, then we query the matching of these images with labels from urban and architectural terminology through the model CLiP, finally, we spatialize back the result in a map of the city to assess.

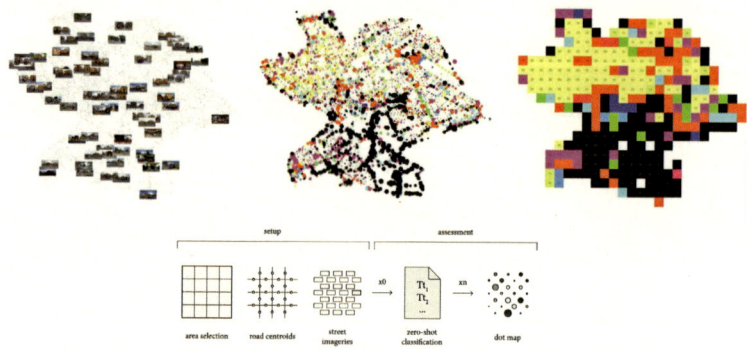

As we have demonstrated through our computational pipeline, these systems operate within the cultural logic of computational urbanism, where the city becomes less a physical reality than a set of statistical correlations floating in high-dimensional space. The physical reality, its dimensions of encounter, embodied knowledge, different registers of self and other, are subordinated to that abstract high-dimensional embedding space. Our findings prompt a more

6   The city of Rome was chosen as our primary case study due to its rich historical tapestry and cultural resonance in Western thought.

7   Which give us information about their relative position with respect to other images and text, revealing proximities and similarities that uncover the way in which the models have "learnt" about the city of Rome.

cautious integration of such models in urban studies, advocating for a foren-sic reading of the city where historical narratives and machinic interpretations intersect.

World Gist: Mapping the Global Urban Imagination

Fig. 28: Genealogy of the generation in WorldGist, showing the different paths in the denoising process, leading to different cities

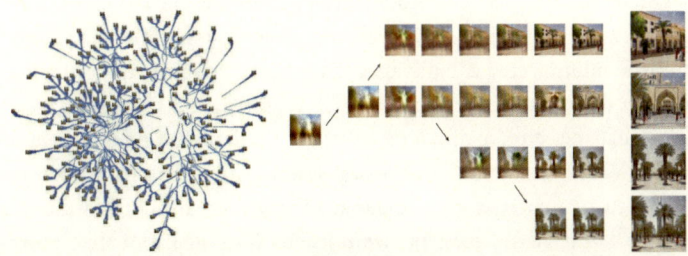

Shifting our focus from a single city to a global perspective, the World Gist project[8] reverses the scale logic of our earlier experiment. Here, we harnessed the power of Stable Diffusion conditioned by CLIP to generate synthetic im-agery for every capital city worldwide. By keeping the same seed—that is, the same noise distribution—we ensured that all image generations were subject to an identical starting point. This methodological choice allowed us to isolate how the model's latent urban knowledge varies across different cultural and geographical contexts. World Gist reveals a kind of computational unconscious of contemporary urbanism. Our experiments revealed that the model "knows" more about cities that are emblematic of globalized culture—predominantly those in the Global North or cities that have achieved a high degree of cultural saliency. These clusters suggest that the model organizes urban representa-tions around certain generic centers of gravity in its latent space. The insights from World Gist expose the uneven distribution of urban knowledge within AI models, revealing what Jameson would call the "political unconscious" of

8   Dario Negueruela del Castillo and I. Neri, "World Gist" [research paper examining how Stable Diffusion and CLIP encode and reproduce urban knowledge] (Routledge, forth-coming).

global urbanization, the repressed contradictions and uneven development that haunt our planetary urban system.[9]

The City in a Bottle: Simulating Urban Assemblages

While both previous projects focused on the representation of cities from existing imagery or synthetic generation, The City in a Bottle takes a bold step toward simulation. This project bridges the gap between data-driven digital twinning and critical urban theory by leveraging advanced vision-language models enhanced with Retrieval-Augmented Generation (RAG). Rather than simply replicating urban phenomena through aggregated data, our method simulates the multifaceted assemblages that constitute contemporary cities, integrating a discursive reasoning on social, material, and physical context. We operationalized seminal urban theories from authors like Henri Lefebvre, Jane Jacobs, Walter Benjamin, and Georg Simmel, as well as from contemporary frameworks such as assemblage theory and urban metabolism. For instance, we extracted key concepts from Jacobs' insights like "urban choreography of play" and distilled them into perceivable visual features that could act as measurable proxies for testing theories on urban imagery. This involved extracting a concept description in cases where it was missing, devising which questions we could ask to evaluate the presence in an image (an urban panorama) of urban elements that make it possible, and breaking it down into a series of reasoning steps that render it graspable and measurable (see appendix). The hybrid method allows us to "bottle" the cognitive processes of urban theorists alongside the tangible urban fabric, offering a speculative yet grounded tool for urban interpretation. Initial results demonstrate that by blending computational precision with theoretical insight, we can generate simulations that highlight dynamic interactions among human and non-human actors, the evolving nature of urban resilience, and the possibilities for climate adaptation.

---

9   Frederic Jameson, *The Political Unconscious: Narrative as a Socially Symbolic Act* (Cornell University Press, 1981).

Fig. 29: Emulating a narrative urban flânerie through the city of Madrid in the thinking style of Henri Lefebvre from the project The City in a Bottle.

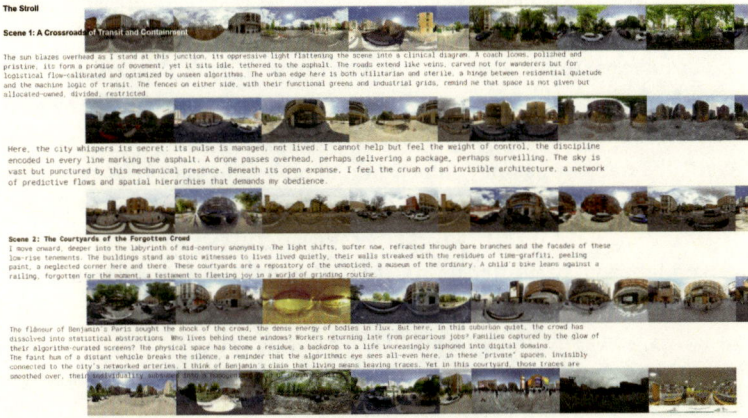

The Triple Abstraction in AI's understanding of the City

This condition of surplus data cannot be understood apart from what we might call the cultural logic of late computational capitalism, following Jameson. The very accumulation of urban data represents a new form of primitive accumulation, transforming lived urban experience into abstract, commodifiable data points. This process, far from being neutral or purely technical, embodies a type of "data colonialism,"[10] a new phase in the long history of extractive relationships to urban space and experience.

The three projects under consideration—CLIP and the City, World Gist, and The City in a Bottle—are not simply applications of AI to urban problems, but reshape the very nature of urban knowledge. The probabilistic logic they employ, while appearing to embrace uncertainty and multiplicity, paradoxically performs a closure of the urban imagination, which is also a digital enclosure of the urban commons of the mind. What occurs in these times of algorithmic urbanity is not merely a quantitative expansion of urban data but a qualitative transformation in the very possibility of urban imagination itself.

---

10   Nick Couldry and Ulises A. Mejias, "Data Colonialism: Rethinking Big Data's Relation to the Contemporary Subject," *Television & New Media* 20, no. 4 (2018): 336–49, https://doi.org/10.1177/1527476418796632.

Here we confront the fundamental contradiction of computational urbanism:[11] the simultaneous hypermapping and erasure of urban possibility. The more thoroughly our AI systems map and model urban space, the more completely they chase away the genuinely new.

This foreclosure operates through a triple movement of abstraction. First, the reduction of lived urban experience to data points (what Mumford would recognize as the ultimate victory of abstraction over the organic and concrete); second, the transformation of this data into high-dimensional latent spaces that, while mathematically infinite, remain topologically closed; and finally, the generation of new urban "possibilities" that are, in fact, merely probabilistic recombinations of existing forms. The CLIP and the City project reveals this process with particular clarity. We performed a zero-shot classification of urban scenes, and while this appears to uncover new urban meanings, it actually performs algorithmic reification: it transforms living urban relations into fixed, computable categories. The project's findings reveal not just bias but that perfect crime against urban reality we mentioned earlier: a substitution of the map for the territory so complete that the territory almost vanishes entirely.

Fig. 30: The methodology of the CLIP and the City project allows us to compare the machinic imaginary of cities at scale using available urban panoramas and conduct comparative analyses. In the image: visualizing the scores of urban terminology in Rome, Madrid, Montreal at the sacle of the city centre.

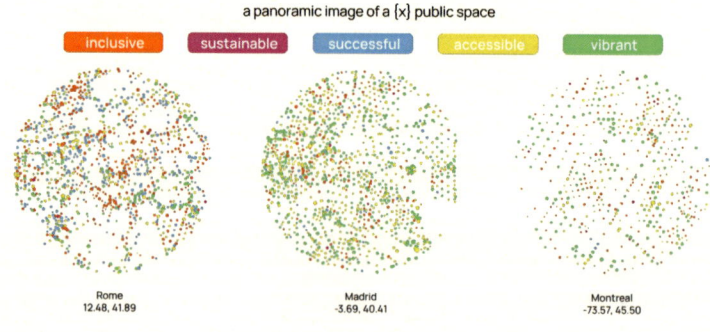

11   This extends Jameson's analysis of postmodernity: Frederic Jameson, *Postmodernism, or, the cultural logic of late capitalism* (Duke University Press, 1991).

The Paradox of AI's Urban Knowledge

World Gist's attempt to construct global urban imaginaries through machine learning confronts us with a kind of a paradox. The more comprehensively these systems process urban data, the more thoroughly they eliminate the "regional framework of civilization" (to quote Mumford again); that is to say, the specific, the local, the unreproducible. This is not merely a technical limitation but rather the logical culmination of the "age of the world picture,"[12] in the words of Martin Heidegger, where the world becomes available to us only as a computed representation.

Fig. 31: WorldGist: Generating images of cities during the day, evening and night, starting from the same seed (same noise distribution as point of departure)

Yet perhaps it is precisely in this moment of apparent total closure that the possibility of genuine urban imagination might be found again. We can, for instance, follow Jameson's insistence on the political unconscious, and identify in the very contradictions of algorithmic urbanism the seeds of what could go

---

12   Martin Heidegger, "The Age of the World Picture," in *The Question Concerning Technology and Other Essays*, trans. William Lovitt (Harper and Row, 1977), 115–54.

beyond. The City in a Bottle project, in its attempt to simulate historical urban thinkers' perspectives on contemporary cities, inadvertently reveals the limits of computational urban thinking, the "blind spots of the algorithm."

What is required is not an abandonment of computational tools but rather a "right to the algorithmic city," extending Lefebvre's ideas of the "right to the city"[13] and putting forward a demand that urban AI systems be repurposed toward what Walter D. Mignolo terms "digital pluriversality."[14] This would entail not merely technical modifications but a fundamental rethinking of what constitutes urban knowledge itself. Such a project would need to embrace productive contradictions: the tension between data's promise of total knowledge and the irreducible particularity of urban experience; between algorithmic prediction and genuine urban emergence; between the closure of computational thinking and the openness required for genuine urban imagination.

New Urban Possibilities

This brings us finally to the political dimension of urban AI, the "distribution of the urban sensible."[15] The question is not simply how to make AI systems more accurate or comprehensive, but how to preserve and nurture spaces of genuine urban imagination within and against the totalizing logic of computational urbanism. This perhaps requires going beyond the divide between human understanding and machine prediction and embracing an unavoidable hybrid condition. We could call this, extending Haraway's concept, an "urban cyborg politics," one that neither fully embraces nor entirely rejects algorith-

---

13　A similar idea has been put forward by Rashid Mushkani, Hugo Berard, Allison Cohen, and Shin Koeski, "Position: The Right to AI," ArXiv, January 29, 2025, https://doi.org/10.48550/arXiv.2501.17899.

14　Walter D. Mignolo, *The darker side of Western modernity: Global futures, decolonial options* (Duke University Press, 2011).

15　Jacques Rancière, *The Politics of Aesthetics: The Distribution of the Sensible*, trans. Gabriel Rockhill (Continuum, 2004). For a discussion and reinterpretation of Rancière's ideas for our times of algorithmic governmentality, see Antoinette Rouvroy and Bernard Stiegler, "Le régime de veritéé numérique," Socio. La nouvelle revue des sciences sociales, no. 4 (2015): 113–40.

mic mediation, but rather seeks to redirect it toward genuinely emancipatory ends.[16]

In this context, AI foundation models like CLIP manifest what we have identified as the technological unconscious of contemporary urbanism. These systems, in their attempt to parse and classify urban imagery, reveal not just the visible and salient aspects of cities but also the accumulated visual ideology of late capitalism encoded in their training data.[17] The zero-shot classifications they produce are thus less discoveries than symptoms, revealing the implicit urban theories embedded in the Internet's visual culture.

The City in a Bottle project presents perhaps the most telling contradiction: In its attempt to simulate how canonical urban thinkers might perceive contemporary cities, it reveals what Baudrillard would call the "precession of simulacra" in urban theory itself.[18] The project's use of RAG systems to ventriloquize historical urban theorists performs double simulation, of both urban space and of urban thought itself. What becomes clear through this analysis is the need for a dialectical urban AI.[19] This would entail, first, the recognition of the importance of the fragments of urban reality that like computational ruins resist algorithmic processing; second, the development of urban AI models that can behave more like "organic prediction machines," modes of computational analysis that enhance rather than suppress urban complexity; and, third, the cultivation of counter-algorithmic practices as methods of urban imagination that explicitly work against predictive closure.

Conclusion: Beyond the Digital Closure of Urban Imagination

What emerges from this analysis is not merely a critique of computational urbanism but what we might term, following Jameson, a fundamental contradiction in the very project of algorithmic urban knowing. Here, the crucial aspect is not simply the revealing of unnoticed patterns due to enhanced machinic

---

16   Donna Haraway, "A cyborg manifesto: Science, technology, and socialist-feminism in the late twentieth century," in *Simians, cyborgs, and women: The reinvention of nature* (Routledge, 1991), 149–81.

17   Jameson would recognize this as their repressed cognitive content.

18   Jean Baudrillard, *Simulacra and Simulation*, trans. Sheila Faria Glaser (University of Michigan Press, 1994).

19   Following Benjamin's concept of dialectical images: see Walter Benjamin, *The Arcades Project*, trans. Howard Eiland and Kevin McLaughlin (Belknap Press, 1999).

perception, but rather the alignment of the reasoning capacities of the models with the interpretative and narrative threads proposed by scholars of reference, and which are already a work of analytical and critical synthesis. The condition of surplus data, which promised to make cities more legible, predictable, and manageable, is paradoxically producing a crisis of urban imagination. This crisis manifests not as a scarcity of possibilities but as their algorithmic foreclosure, a situation where, to paraphrase Mark Fisher, it becomes easier to imagine the end of cities than to imagine genuine urban alternatives outside the predictive logic of AI systems.[20]

The three projects examined here—CLIP and the City, World Gist, and The City in a Bottle—reveal different aspects of this crisis. As we have shown in our study of the latent urban imaginaries embedded within AI models, these systems are not merely tools but active participants in shaping how cities are imagined, designed, and developed. They reveal a blurry generative urban grammar that determines which versions of urban futures can be articulated, thereby performing an enclosure of imagination.

Yet perhaps it is precisely in these limitations that the possibility of genuine urban imagination might be rediscovered, in what we might call the computational ruins of contemporary urbanism. This would require what we could term a "dialectical urban AI," one that neither fully embraces nor entirely rejects computational mediation, but rather works through its contradictions toward new forms of urban possibility. The challenge, then, is not simply to critique these systems but to repurpose them toward a new "right to the algorithmic city," extending Lefebvre's ideas of the right to the city.[21] This can be conceived as the right not just to access urban data but to participate in the very definition of what constitutes urban possibility, from the categories and labels used to categorize data, the architecture of the algorithms used to extract features, all the way to the way latent spaces are articulated into insights, intellectual accompaniment, or production. This would entail the recognition of what exceeds computational capture—which aspects of urban life resist algorithmic reduction—the development of counter-practices that work against the grain of predictive closure, and the cultivation of a more organic and serendipitous urban computation as ways of using AI that enhance rather than suppress the vital and emergent qualities of urban life.

---

20   Mark Fisher, *Capitalist Realism* (Zero Books, 2009).
21   A similar idea has been put forward by Mushkani et al., "Position: The Right to AI."

As we navigate this moment of technological transformation, the question becomes not simply how to make our AI systems more accurate or comprehensive, but how to preserve and nurture spaces of genuine urban imagination within and against the totalizing logic of computational urbanism. For it is only through such a dialectical engagement with our technological condition that we might move beyond the digital closure of urban imagination.

B: Media and Representation

Projections: On the Design Process in AI Architecture

Roberto Bottazzi

AI and architecture: Innovation and invariance

Challenges posed by technical innovations to artistic disciplines are never just "technical." Their significance is proportional to their capacity to exceed the purely technical domain and reconfigure the tenets of a field to furnish new representations, reconsider practices, and develop new agendas. The integration of AI in architecture and urbanism is no exception. As we question what architectural intelligence could become in the light of the introduction of AI, the task is not so much technical—the penetration and improvement of AI models in architecture will continue regardless—as conceptual. Mathematics offers fruitful analogies for setting the terms of this inquiry. We can think of AI and architecture as two series, each with their own characteristics, and our role as crafting the instruments for their convergence and resonance. To extend the mathematical analogy, we could think of the elements of connections between series as invariants: properties that remain unchanged when a system of objects such as a series undergoes transformation. To frame the relation between AI and architecture through series and invariants will not subsume either field under the other; rather, it will allow us to understand the specificity of each, and redefine their operations on each other.

This essay explores how to think of invariants in the bourgeoning relation between AI and architecture. The technical logic of AI must guide this search but not limit it, as the challenge is how to think of AI models within the design process. As Alejandro Zaera-Polos notes, "nothing gets built that isn't transposable onto AutoCAD,"[1] indicating not only that the history of architecture is also

---

1   Quoted in Bernard Cache, "Towards a Non-Standard Mode of Production," in *Projectiles: Architecture Words 6* (Architectural Association, 2011), 61.

the history of their design technologies, but also that design agendas emerges from the conceptualization of the technological instruments at hand. In so doing, we aim to stimulate a more proactive approach to the integration of AI in architecture, which at present seems to be concerned with measuring architecture's ability to comply with the principles of AI.

Beyond visual mimicry: The technical logic of AI

Technically, Deep Learning (DL) models—a subset of AI that we will refer to for the arguments put forward in this essay—produce an output from a vast collection of input instances. Broadly speaking, DL models are programmed to devise a number of steps to turn input data into an output. Inputs and outputs are separated by several layers of parameters—representing the "depth" of the model—which adjust after each input in order to tune inputs and outputs.[2] In other words, during the tuning of parameters—known as training—DL models generate processes that can eventually be applied to a vast range of issues (training and application are, in fact, two distinct phases). This technical characteristic marks a clear departure from previous computational generative methods in which users were tasked with designing processes by formalizing knowledge into code. Now inputs and outputs are the main points of intervention for designers, whereas process (what sits in between) can only be inspected or altered indirectly. Central to this reconfiguration of the creative process is the mechanism known as "backpropagation": the differential feedback function that adjusts the parameters of a DL model to align inputs and outputs during the training stage.[3] Seen from the point of view of design processes, by moving upstream from outputs back to inputs, backpropagation shifts the user's agency from process to output. It is through the evaluation of outputs that users can adjust input data, or, as we will see, charge the output with new, additional design ambitions. Another key technical aspect that DL models share with other AI models is vectorization: That is, to be processed by the model, input data must be abstracted into vectors, which become the actual objects manipulated by DL models. As all input

2   Ian Goodfellow, Joshua Bengio, and Aaron Courville, *Deep Learning* (MIT Press, 2016).

3   Arthur E. Bryson, "A gradient method for optimizing multi-stage allocation processes," in *Proceedings of the Harvard University Symposium on digital computers and their applications, 3–6 April 1961* (Harvard University Press, 1962).

data is eventually rewritten in a vector, within the DL model translations and projections between different media are technically possible. In perhaps the most familiar example, text-to-image AI tools generate images from text, that is, the model projects a vectorized string of text onto an image database to return a new image.

From the point of view of design, architects are endowed with the technical means to project data onto each other and "backpropagate" their intentions onto the design process; the cumulative effect of these two conditions brings design closer to curatorial practices. If in traditional algorithmic approaches designers reified knowledge into code to solve problems, with DL models the designers' task is to critique, question—in short, curate—the outputs of a DL model. The actions require designers to critically investigate the space between two technical and the architectural series to foreground what Aby Warburg called the "iconology of the interval,"[4] the speculative space between existing things.

The exploration of the aesthetic of intervals is further complexified and enhanced by the logic of vectorization. Though technically impressive, the current overreliance of AI tools on image production could also represent a potential involution for the aesthetic of architecture. Images are in fact only representational devices that rewrite numerical probabilistic distributions computed by DL models; in short, they are visualizations of vectors. It is therefore limiting to think of the capacities of AI platforms in terms of visual outputs or mimicry, as their technical logic is much broader and more complex, involving mathematical operations of abstraction, recombination, and projection. It is along these lines that an aesthetic for AI architecture should be articulated. Vector-based projections shift creativity away from pure image-making towards a more curatorial and strategic approach. Again, it is the relation between datasets, the questions posed to tease out relations that come to the fore to provide an alternative approach to visual mimicry. How might we start redefining creative processes as projections?

Projections: How to explore the interval

The following examples are part of a larger list of precedents to suggest a strategic use of AI in architecture. As the issue is conceptual rather than technical,

---

4   Matthewa Rampley, "Iconology of the Interval," Word & Image 17, no. 4 (2001): 303–24.

these precedents are understood as speculative instruments through which to attend to issues of curation and projection in architectural design. Given that what is being suggested is a way of thinking rather than a specific method, the list of precedents that follows deliberately avoids architecture. By referring to art or music, operations of projection and curation, literal applications will unavoidably give way to critical projections.

In 2016 former *New York Times* music critic Ben Ratliff published *Every Song Ever: Twenty Ways to Listen to Music Now*.[5] The "now" Ratliff concentrates on is the age of digital platforms in which a very large database of songs (more than any individual would previously have had access to, yet only a portion of all the recordings there are, as Ratliff himself acknowledges) is available through our smartphones. Each chapter in the book focuses on a theme (virtuosity, density, closeness, etc.) and strings together a series of examples that furnish an open map of how musicians (from different periods and traditions) have interpreted or developed such themes. The result is not only a rich landscape of musical experiments (a true learning journey, regardless of one's musical taste and knowledge), but also an empowerment of the reader/listener whose agency over digital platforms is emboldened. Readers of this essay who pick up *Every Song Ever* with the expectation of finding a compelling analysis of digital technologies for music consumption will probably be disappointed. The book in fact entirely bypasses issues such as data, algorithms, etc.; that is, the themes featuring in most of the literature on AI. Architecture does not feature at all, whereas cities only appear as backdrops to the development of a particular piece of music, genre, etc. Why is Ratliff's book so relevant in the context of AI and architecture, then? Rather than engaging in endless principled battles on the morality of AI, Ratliff moves the conversation one step forward by "naturalizing" it and examining what space for creativity and learning AI might usher. The premise of the book is to recognize the limitations of previous models for listening to music (such as categorizing the work by author or album) and explore the opportunities provided to listen better or differently. This is not to say that the book does not offer elements of critique; on the contrary, the twenty strategies animating each chapter can be seen as forms of resistance to algorithm-guided choices.[6]

---

5   Ben Ratliff, *Every Song Ever: Twenty Ways to Listen to Music Now* (Penguin, 2016).

6   Ben Ratliff, "Listening, inefficiency, and value," lecture delivered as part of the B-Pro Prospective lecture series, The Bartlett School of Architecture, UCL, November 16, 2023.

To tease out relations implies a procedural change that Ratliff articulates through a series of ideas that indicate practical and conceptual ways to move transversally and exercise intelligence as we navigate through vast amounts of data. On the one hand, the structure of the book closely mirrors the technical logic of the processes criticized when we listen to music on digital platforms: given a starting point, we quickly fall into a "rabbit hole" of free associations, emotional responses, rational progressions, philological inquiries, etc., that take us through the massive archive available in a transversal fashion. On the other, while the logic of digital platforms is embraced, a whole series of other considerations are overlaid, or, shall we say, projected and curated, onto the act of listening: these regard the theme of each chapter and unfold irrespective of traditional classifications. It can be a detail, a hidden connection between two musicians who are part of a larger ensemble, a sustained engagement with a piece of music to be the source of discovery for new readings. If we drew an analogy between Ratliff's approach and DL models, we could say that his is a call for small data, for precision and definition. This analogy would entail a non-mimetic and disjunctive relationship between the technology (which can thrive in managing colossal datasets) and our interaction with it that would be based on understanding and exploiting the technological affordances provided, but would complement, rather than mimic, them.

Finally, Ratliff is addressing us, the listeners, not the technological apparatus we use to access music: he proposes a form of digital literacy in the shape of an intellectual gymnastics afforded by digital platforms and their ability to let us travel across the widest spectrum of musical production ever accessible. It exploits the possibility to break boundaries, redraw them, or even follow existing ones, suggesting that the key skill required is not technological prowess but intellectual curiosity. The implicit message seems to be that digital literacy will benefit from the contribution of any other discipline *but* the strictly technical ones. Ratliff's book is thus an ideal for our list of conceptual approaches to AI in architecture. Each chapter in the book offers a series of instruments that can charge an apparently passive activity such as listening to music or inspecting the outputs of a DL model in architecture into a creative moment in its own right to define an aesthetic of curation.

Roni Horn's artistic production has often concentrated on paired objects, on the art of "distant doubles."[7] This theme is present in several pieces such

---

7   Christy Lange, "Clowd and Cloun (Blue)," in *Roni Horn*, ed. Ingvild Goetz, Larissa Michel-
     berger, and Rainald Schumacher (Hatje Cantz, 2013), 179.

as *You are the Weather*[8] (1994–96) or the *Pigment Drawings*[9] series (1984–2012) in which objects appear doubled up or in pairs. The work *Clowd and Cloun (Blue)* (2000–01) consists of thirty-two photographs alternating images of a blurred portrait of a clown and that of a shifting white cloud in an otherwise clear blue sky. Arrayed either in a line or a grid, the subject in each of the two series varies as we move from photograph to photograph, albeit not in a continuous fashion.

The work plays in complex ways with themes we have already encountered. The notion of the series is used to represent each of the subjects—i.e., clouds and the portrait of the clown—which are however both portrayed through the medium of photography. The viewer is invited to focus on the "interval," the "nameless" space connecting the two disparate series. The notion of non-mimetic representation is also at play. The two series do not converge on a descriptive, narrative, or, most importantly, visual plane, but rather on a linguistic one (the least obvious); the title of the piece in fact plays with the similarities between the obsolete spelling of the words "clown" and "cloud." It is, again, the interval between the images that gives rise to an open, ambiguous condition opening up a conceptual space for repositioning.

Similar conditions had already been explored by Horn in other pieces such as *You Are the Weather*, in which interaction between the format of the portrait and the weather leaves the viewer wondering who is influencing whom. The piece consists of a series of 100 photographs of the same model as she takes a daily dip in different geothermal pools in Iceland. The effect is that of a projected portrait in which we seem to be invited to see one element (the face of the subject portraited) through the eyes of another (the weather), and vice versa. In both pieces, it is the consistent use of the medium—the photographic series—that is tasked to be the technical support to allow the viewer to see projectively. Is the cloud being portraited on the face of the clown or vice versa? Analogies with earlier considerations on the projective logic of DL models can be drawn as well as considerations on the technical process of vectorization. Through Horn's work, we can appreciate how projections allow for the object/subject relation to be mobilized, swapped, and expanded in order to charge the act of reading the piece into a creative moment in its own right.

---

8   Roni Horn, *You are the Weather* (Scale, 1997).
9   Amy S. Wilkins, ed., *Roni Horn: 153 Drawings* (Hauser & Wirth, 2013).

Intelligence in AI architecture could thus be one in which multiple points of view can be instrumentalized to dislodge preconceived positions and conjure up a more inclusive, uncertain, and even fragile architecture. Some of the experiments we have been developing with students that play with the notion of projection and curation through DL models have allowed them to assume unconventional points of view to instrumentalize non-architectural themes such as language, sounds, visual clues, etc. as subjects of their design. These entry points allow designers to reread the city and architecture to reconceive it from non-human points of view.[10] Again, Christy Lange's words on Horn's piece are illuminating:

> Both clowns and clouds are spaces of projection, more fleeting and intangible than definitive objects. By pairing the two within the same representational system—the photographic series—Horn suggests how that system of representation might be as arbitrary or mutable as the linguistic system used to name them. *Clowd and Cloun (Blue)* forms a circulatory, contingent web of signs, sounds, words, images, and meanings—all dependent on each other, and tenuously linked by resemblance. In it, we see the gaps between word and image, and, by extension, between the image and their subject, between the image of ourselves, and our selves.[11]

In his famous *Simulations and Simulacra*,[12] Jean Baudrillard had already warned that a technical apparatus able to indefinitely produce and reproduce images would devoid the notion of reality and its rationality to replace it with purely operational procedures. Though in a less apocalyptic tone, some of Baudrillard's warnings still resonate with us as we witness the relentless production of AI-generated images of architecture. To counter this trend, this essay foregrounded the importance of a conceptual approach to AI in architecture in the form of an open list of precedents. The proposition put forward is that what the discipline of architecture needs now is not visual inflation through endless production of images or a technical subsumption of architecture to AI. Rather, what the debate on AI architecture is missing is the ability to conceptualize the technical logic of AI within the disciplinary

---

10   Roberto Bottazzi, Mollie Claypool, and Tyson Hosmer, "Disruptive Ecologies: Design with Nonhuman Intelligences," *Architectural Design* 94, no. 1 (2024): 30–37.

11   Lange, "Clowd and Cloun (Blue)," 180–81.

12   Jean Baudrillard, *Simulations and Simulacra*, trans. Sheila Faria Glaser (University of Michigan Press, 1981).

repertoire of architecture: to indicate references, directions, practices; in short, a conceptual agenda for the discipline in the light of the penetration of AI in architecture. Beyond visual mimicry, the potential of AI in architecture is far greater and deeper: to redefine architecture's conceptual and technical operations.

Fig. 32: Sensory Balance uses DL models to design the sensory (visual, olfactory, and auditory) experiences of urban environments. DL models and data spatial analytics are deployed to survey and generate different ephemeral spatial qualities concentrating on sensorial experiences rather formal innovation. For instance, DL models are trained on film images to provide a palette of colors, spatial arrangements, and materials to induce particular emotions in the user.

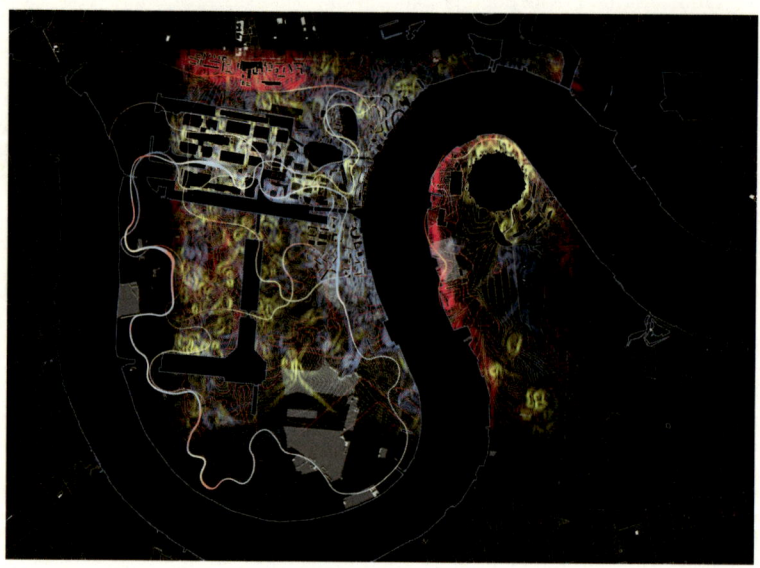

Fig. 33: Accent Diffusion utilizes data analysis and DL models to generate an urbanism based on accents, projecting the immaterial qualities of the 270 languages making up London's cultural landscape onto a database of physical artefacts. The massive catalogue of morphologies generated was used to represent the complex and hybrid cultural landscape of London.

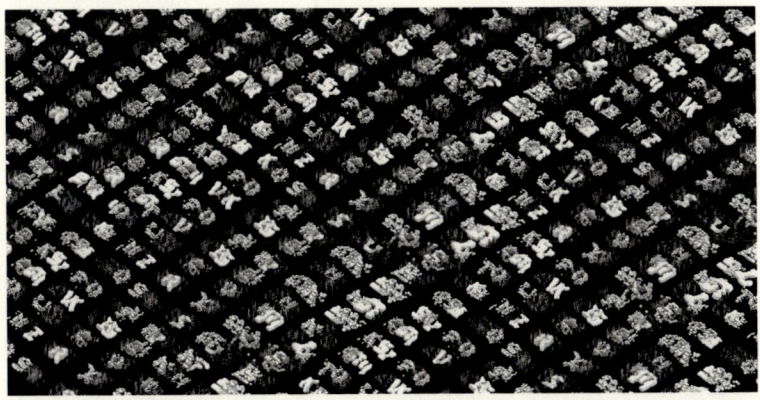

Fig. 34: Ebb and Evolve explores the use of DL models to develop an urban strategy for flood-prone areas in East London. Urban, social, and environmental data are analyzed to develop a time-based strategy in which programs and structures can change to adapt to raising water levels. A series of inflatable structures are used to provide emerging spaces, protect important buildings, and provide a communication infrastructure for the local population.

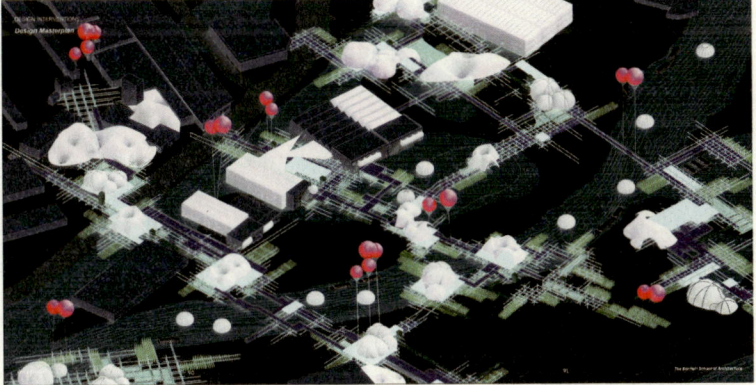

Fig. 35: Attenomy City deploys DL models to study and design spaces around the notions of attention and spatial intelligibility to redesign Euston Station in London. The most dramatic element of the project is the large roof spanning over different parts of the site. The roof performs different roles such as guiding pedestrians as they cross the public areas and controlling environmental conditions. Its overall effect is, however, much greater than any of its functions: the dynamic features of the roof animate and guide the users' experience.

Open Media and Experimental Intelligence

Lidia Gasperoni

What is the human relationship to the environment that is co-designed by AI? What is made available through this technology? What remains unavailable or inaccessible? Who can make content available, and how, and who can access it? Today, AI and, more recently, Generative AI, appear to be transforming processes of image and text production in architectural design. Without reducing AI to a mere tool used by designers, this essay assigns this critical function of its use to the experimentation through which the tool is conceived, adapted, and hybridized by designers—later defined in their role as "experimental users." From this perspective, the present essay is a dialogical invitation to inquire into the role of experimental practices and uses of AI as a humanistic task.

Such a "humanistic operation" means, on the one hand, defining media practices as the core of design research by emphasizing their role as "mediators"[1] and their responsivity to the design of just environments. On the other hand, it means resituating human beings in their abilities and limitations to experience the world. In order to respond to the need of designing more just environments, it is vital to diversify and extend the realm of semantic layers that spatial design is able to process and creatively transform. The transdisciplinary discourse around the Anthropocene and related criticisms, such as the Chthulucene, Capitalocene, and Post-Anthropocene, challenges the constitution of conventional representations in which the world appears to us as a homogeneous reality that lends itself to categorization.[2] This discourse—which has a specific ground-breaking force to reactivate a variety of fundamental turns (phenomenological, constructivist, spatial, ecological,

---

1   See Bruno Latour, *We Have Never Been Modern*, trans. Catherine Porter (Harvard University Press, 1993).

2   For an introduction, see Eva Horn and Hannes Bergthaller, *The Anthropocene: Key Issues for the Humanities* (Routledge, 2019), and Marianne Krogh, *Connectedness: An Incomplete Encyclopedia of the Anthropocene* (Strandberg, 2020).

etc.)—reveals the urgency inherent to the fullness of human experience, to discover and rediscover alternative ways to explore and make visible a more-than-human relationality as a plural field of practices of "worlding."[3]

This field reinforces the regulative, critical, and countering function of experimental practices in the use of specific media and, in this specific case, AI. The assertion of the "regulative function" of experimental practices is driven by their capacity and responsivity to expand and disrupt the conventional use of media and transform their representational capacity by extending the realm of semantic layers. To "open up media" is therefore a critical disposition capable of extending and transforming signification through specific media that generate alternative ways of designing and projecting both existing and future building stock. The practice of experimentation enables the re-assemblage and reflection of contextual knowledges in the medium itself. This is a "performative" use of the medium capable of destabilizing and transforming representational practices.

With this in mind, the essay integrates the experimental use of AI in a broader reflection on media practices in architectural design. The field of application is referred to as spatial design, but it fits into the broader field of media studies and media pedagogy. After a brief critical inquiry into the medium intended as a black box, I will define the performative function of media and more specifically AI for spatial design. Three steps are needed for this aim: first, a deep understanding of a media practice as a specific gestaltic relation between sensory modalities and techniques; second, a discussion of the experimental user able to "reach" and operate in the medium; and, in conclusion, a paradigm shift from content-related meaning to meaning as relational space.

Black Box: Legacy and Reductionism

AI is compared to human intelligence using the black box analogy. This is based on the definition of a functional mechanism of establishing connections shared with neural processes. This leads, in pursuit of the idea of strong AI, to the development of a conscious machine able to generate autonomous connections. This comparison—at the basis of connectivism—can be traced

---

3   Donna Haraway, *Staying with the Trouble: Making Kin in the Chthulucene* (Duke University Press, 2016), 1.

back to the association of the computational machine's functionality with that of the neuronal machine. Their complexity appears both enigmatic and comparable to a black box. In this regard, the black box can be regarded as a concealed layer between the input and output stages. This epistemological and cognitivist perspective embeds specific assumptions. First, the legacy of the comparison between neuronal and technical mechanisms that facilitate its functioning, associating the human body with the machine's ability to imitate it and acquire its cognitive skills cumulatively. This association is evident in the complexity of computational processes that allow data of varied natures to be related, facilitating their integration and manipulation. This complexity results in a perpetual exchange and convergence of data, and ultimately in Generative AI producing copies of copies that could reach the inventiveness and situatedness of analogue craftsmanship.[4]

The complexity of this process leads, second, to a reductive definition of signification as "content generation," believing that computational processes make the generation process itself, and thus the explanations related to the output produced more real, objective, and scientific.[5] In certain instances, this is regarded as an externalization process of objectivation, in contradistinction to the "intuitive" process, which is subjective and tacit.

The complexity of connections and the objectivation of meaning consti-tute the basis of a reductionist perspective of technical implementation and determinism based on the idea of a black box and autonomy of the represen-tation, which can be produced and downloaded. Determinism ignores on the one hand a philosophical analysis of how intuitive and imaginative processes achieve experience through sensory modalities and media practices that 'form' perceptions and their interpretations. On the other hand, it undermines the countering function of experimentation and critical thinking for establishing a space of relationality to generate signification. Mario Carpo asserts that "com-puters don't need theories to crunch numbers, but we need theories to use com-puters."[6] Along these lines, we could argue that philosophy is a further layer that approaches and diverges from technology by exploring a relational field in which media are performative and bring technology to matter. There is thus

---

4   This is a subject explored in Mario Carpo, *Beyond Digital: Design and Automation at the End of Modernity* (MIT Press, 2023).

5   See Neil Leach, *Architecture in the Age of Artificial Intelligence: An introduction to AI for architects* (Bloomsbury, 2022), 108.

6   Mario Carpo, "The Alternative Science of Computation," *E-flux Architecture* 6 (2017): 5.

a surplus to the analysis of perception and cognition through the analysis of neural and embodied mechanisms.

Media of Making Sensible: If We Open Our Brains, We Do Not Find Images

Experience cannot be exclusively explained by neural connections and sensory perception. This essay aims to overcome a reductionist comparison between the human brain and the machine, which defines a specific field of mediation as an embodied practice of sensing exceeding the physical black box. Any programmer or user has to identify a specific medium in which to code and use an application. If you ask an application designed to generate text to "generate an image," it will respond: "I am not programmed to generate an image." Similarly, Midjourney can generate an image from a text. This suggests that the brain or the programmed machine can be regarded as a "black box," yet the manner in which we comprehend its operation cannot evade scrutiny of the media dimension that constitutes the media boundaries of the "black box" in both theory and practice.

In this perspective, due to the fact that humans have a limited set of senses and a more-than-human ability to combine them, it is no coincidence that researchers and designers are increasingly committed to developing multi-modal practices and uses of AI. The human ability to connect, which is significantly slower than that of some species or machines, remains very elaborate in its capacity to use sensory modalities through specific media practices—such as languages, haptic and proprioceptive movements, and specific figurative schemata, such as painting, drawings, diagrams, geometric figures. And to translate this complexity to the machine does not mean to imitate "our" brain and body, but rather to explore the connection between sensory modalities and media practices by designing the jumps and gaps of textual and figurative perceptions.

These specific media practices enable us to articulate meaning at a sensory level between more pictorial and more auditive languages, and precisely due their gestaltic plasticity they allow spaces of translation. The "opening up" of the brain certainly reveals a series of physiological conditions that, when connected with specific sensory modalities, enable perception and the development of cognitive capacities. Technological devices make this connection possible outside of the body and constitute an extension and, in some specific cases, a prosthesis of it. Although media practices depend on technical components, they are the result of experiential, dynamic, and mutable processes that articulate the crystallization of cultural, empirical practices between sensory modalities and technologies. Media practices are both embodied and externalized in technical apparatuses at the intersection of analogue and digital.

However, the physiological, sensory, and technological conditions do not exhaust the human condition of constituting knowledge through media practices. In this perspective, the domain of mediality cannot be reduced to physiological and mathematical analyses, it transcends both. This is not to suggest that media define an a priori or pre-established semantics; rather, it is a discussion of the gestaltic capacity of human perception, which offers a field of experimentation in which sensory experience is related to a specific field of technological practices.

In this vein, Western philosophy in different epochs has paid particular attention to specific sensory modalities in order to understand the gestaltic function of the senses. They are not only receptive sensors but have the function of shaping and forming sensory data through schemes. The image is a space of mediation that can be seen and generated through various practices. A three-dimensional image, for instance, is a medium with a proper gestaltic function of seeing and being in relation with different kinds of (more or less material) objects. This gestaltic function is rooted in a human space of friction and precarious stability between sensory modalities and practices. On the empirical level, the focus is on the ways in which technologies and technical tools are used. On the transcendental level, however, the emphasis lies on the conditions of possibility of using media. The former interrogates the "device" by which we receive, express, communicate, and archive various meanings in specific situated conditions, while the latter explores the conditions of possibility of this instrumental device. The distinction between the empirical and the transcendental levels is crucial to an understanding of how media practices constitute a field of transformation, transposition, and transfiguration.

I have described this interdependency of the two levels with the German term *Versinnlichung* (partially translatable as "sensualization"),[7] rooted in the discourse on imagination in the seventeenth and eighteenth centuries and the gestaltic capacity—following Kant—of "schemata" that constitute meaning in the process of a hybrid mediation between sensibility and conceptualization.

---

7   See Lidia Gasperoni, *Versinnlichung. Kants transzendentaler Schematismus und seine Revision in der Nachfolge*, Actus et Imago, 20 (De Gruyter, 2016).

It is Johann Gottfried Herder, in particular, who re-proposes this theory in the form of a "metaschematism." With this notion, Herder introduces an extended transcendental field that involves a specific inquiry into the sensory modalities comprising the image and sound of language and a questioning of their morphogenetic capacity to become meaning. Schematism in its performative, anthropological, and phenomenological reinterpretation, drawing on readings by Plessner, Merleau-Ponty, and Deleuze, constitutes a field of interference between the empirical and the transcendental in which the schemes are not schematic content learned by use, but a sensory modality in which meaning becomes perceivable, material, and real through a media practice. Versinnlichung is the transcendental level that allows a space of human perception that can be expanded and transformed through practice, and the embodiment is the empirical level of situated practices.

The fact that a media practice is empirically established allow them to be shifted, transformed, or overcome—for example, in its discursive interpretations, pedagogical uses, or artistic practices (to name but a few). Destabilization and transformation initiate a potential space between media as sensory modalities and technological practices. This is a pivotal aspect to support a critical approach to specific uses of AI that has the ability to both establish and destabilize AI epistemologies in their connections to sensory schemes. In this perspective, the transcendental level is a counter-intuitive move. That is to say, its stability is not content-related, but process-related. It allows the use to be in a productive relation with the medium. That means that AI needs an experimental use to be a counter-practice of a conventional, and to a certain extent passive, use.

The transcendental level that investigates the gestaltic function of sensory experience and its transformation at the empirical level in the experience of plural worlds is, it can be argued, an answer to the general question of whether artificial intelligence and human intelligence correspond. The answer is no, if we assume that human intelligence is an embodied act that implies an act of making sensible (*Versinnlichung*) as a philosophical reflection on the plural ways through which a media practice unfolds our capacity to sense. In this perspective, a transcendental approach falls short of encompassing the full scope of performativity that implies—according to John Dewey—the "aesthetic" use of media. On the contrary, an instrumental, representational approach reduces tools to means that adapt to certain sensory modalities without crossing them. Mere "tools"—which Dewey defines as "means"—in the instrumental version indeed do not possess an aesthetic character; that is to say, they do not possess a performative capacity to experiment with and hybridize sensory modalities to destabilize and shift canonical representations.

If architecture does not enter this space of fundamental mediation, it will instrumentalize and be instrumentalized by AI as a tool—as is true of many other analogue and digital tools. Architecture will be merely instrumentalized by the conventional empirical use that is available as pre-programmed. This will undermine the performative friction between a wide range of sensory modalities and multimodal devices—as I will explain concerning the performative role of experimental users.

Performativity and Reachability

On the empirical level, media practices can be defined as a (mutable) synthesis between sensory modalities and technological devices. This generative synthesis depends on the inventive capacity of the user, who not only uses the device to generate the output but changes its use by generating the output. It is within this domain that media experimentation emerges, namely in its capacity to change media practices from within, to unveil them, and to "hack" them with each use.[8] This process of hacking renders media practices unstable, while delving into the potential of the medium in the articulation of sensory experience and layers of meaning.

This performative ability, which destabilizes representation, is a human predisposition to experiment playfully with perceptions and meanings that should be preserved and educated. If human beings reduce their modes of use—from early childhood—to a passive use of media and digital media, this restrictive use will render them passive with respect to technology as a space of sensory mediation. This will result in a decreasing capacity to experience media as open devices, which is characterized by the interdependencies between sensory modalities and technologies. Passive users will become increasingly dependent on those who develop and disseminate technologies. It is therefore asserted that experimentation, also as an everyday pedagogical practice, is a

---

8   See Corneel Cannaerts, "Hacking Agency: Digitale Fabrikation als Entwurfsmedium," in *Media Agency – Neue Ansätze zur Medialität in der Architektur*, ed. Lidia Gasperoni and Christophe Barlieb (transcript Verlag, 2020), 179–96, and Corneel Cannaerts, "Mediality of code: Architectural design and coding practices," *Cloud-Cuckoo-Land* 25, no. 40 (2021): 25–43.

practice of activation with a processual, dynamic value capable of reopening and renegotiating the relationship between body and technology.

Performative practices of coding and re-coding generate software and applications that make a specific generation of content available and can generate content itself through a specific interaction and incremental learning. Applications and interfaces, functioning as protocol, are in this regard limited and controlled practices that seem to work well as a black box. This level of availability and control has been the focus of criticism by Hartmut Rosa, who employs the concept of *Unverfügbarkeit* ("uncontrollability"). This is defined as an experience that is uncontrolled and maintains a dynamic and inexhaustible relationality to the world. In this perspective, the user who exhausts this relation with the world, through the control and full availability of the medium, runs the risk of reducing the fullness of this experience and what Rosa defines as "resonance." The easy accessibility of the world, in particular with regard to digital media, ought to be critically constrained, according to Rosa.

However, Rosa's approach to the concept of *Erreichbarkeit* ("reachability") could function as a regulatory idea for the use of digital technology and AI, though he appears not to investigate the possibility further in this specific context: "Resonance requires a world that can be reached, not one that can be limitlessly controlled. The confusion between reachability and controllability lies at the root of the muting of the world in modernity."[9] *Erreichbarkeit* is the condition of possibility for the resonance of experiencing the world, which should possess a certain degree of reachability to enable an experience of the world that is not purely contingent. Reachability, as a further step of this argumentation, underscores the regulatory capacity of experimental media practices. In the specific case of Generative AI, this regulatory function entails the ability to access the underlying coding and programming, not for the purpose of complete control, but to enhance its semantic capacity. In this perspective, whoever is able to experiment with media and with Generative AI, too, employs the medium not to deliver an outcome, but rather to be the mediator both for the analysis of heterogenous and fragmented data and for the generation of an outcome. In this regard, a dualism between input and output—which are connected by fully inaccessible, unreachable computational processes—constitutes a situation where the space of mediation is out of play and turns the user into a passive agent.

---

9   Hartmut Rosa, *The Uncontrollability of the World* (Polity, 2020), 58.

In this perspective, the disposition towards media defines their use and their degree of reachability. Experimental processes represent an ongoing negotiation between mastery and resistance in the use of the medium, whereby a sensory practice is explored through a technological practice (be it analogue, digital, or hybrid). This experimental process can generate a novel media practice or assemblage of media practices that can then become conventional, established, and operationally iterable to such an extent that it becomes a "practice in use." This process renders it not only singular and contingent, but also replicable and usable. This is the transition from mere coding to software generation. In this modal shift from experimental to conventional practices at the technological level, the experimental value of the practice itself is rendered obsolete. It is the protocol of use (the transition from coding to software) and subsequent conventional use (in which the user employs the software according to pre-programmed possibilities) that create the limits of the black box.

The crux of experimentation therefore lies not in the development of media practices as controlled and available devices but in its generation or adaptation, where the distinction between the process and the maker appears to coalesce. The subjective disposition and the medium converge as if they were "transparent" and re-divert into a space of opacity.[10]

The Regulative Role of Experimental Users

Media are always potentially "hackable," namely in an act of learning a tool by grasping its agency as a medium. This act of opening and critically inquiring into media implies approaching the historic genealogies, transdisciplinary uses, and porous transmissions of media. The experimental user is a counter-figure, capable of a responsive coding and use of the "machine" to invent alternative and counter uses. This kind of user is an artisanal, creative, and multimodal encoder, a performative hybridizer, in certain cases a super-user[11] and cybercrafter.[12] The performative function of alternative uses of the machine is

10   See Markus Rautzenberg and Andreas Wolfsteiner, *Hide and Seek. Das Spiel von Transparenz und Opazität*, (Wilhelm Fink, 2010).

11   Cf. Randy Deutsch, *Superusers: Design Technology Specialists and the Future of Practice* (Routledge, 2019).

12   Cf. Christophe Barlieb, "Cybercraft: Das neue Paradigma," in *Media Agency*, ed. Gasperoni and Barlieb, 197–215.

a pivotal aspect of media studies, as Hans Ulrich Obrist recently stated: "When I was a student, I met the philosopher Vilém Flusser; he said we cannot control the machine, but we can use the machine in a way that the inventor of the machine didn't think one could use it."[13] While open media include fragmented signification, instrumentalized tools on the contrary exclude and reduce complexity. The most problematic aspect of technological reductionism is not the technology itself but the way in which it is narrated and used as fully available, yet is not reachable for certain fields of devices—with a specific reference here to spatial representation and design. The objective of theoretical reflection is therefore not to delineate the limits of these machinal devices, but rather to identify the human dimension in which they become media of experimentation and opening. This issue is also pertinent to the pressing need to elucidate the positionality of human agency in creating ecological practices. Such practices can serve to make ecosystems—undoubtedly more-than-human—in which humans participate and act, sensible. Mere implementation can sometimes open the black box, but only in order to progress on the technological level or, for example, to find other technological devices that can improve the design and representation of architectural spaces. Going beyond mere implementation, experimental users experiment with technological devices "from within" by crossing the boundaries between stable and unstable re-presentations. They open media on the critical level in order to break their mechanisms.

Experimental users should be able to respond to the experience of the world through coding as a sort of additional multimodal sensing that creates a hybrid synesthesia by perceiving and generating sensory outputs. They work behind the scenes of technical implementation and form generation. Some of them experiment by developing autonomous creative practices. In this perspective, experimental users have a specific operative, creative authorship. They are able to recognize and to a certain degree generate coding practices as a diagrammatic operative space beyond the generated output.

In their approach to mediality, in choosing a given medium and how to hybridize it, experimental users manage a complexity of a different order to that of computational and algorithmic complexity, which is now insurmountable for us.[14] It is precisely in the limitation of the human and its experience of the world that the regulative power of experimentation emerges as an act of medial

---

13   Catherine Malabou, "Plasticity, Intelligence and Mind," interview by Hans Ulrich Obrist, in *Atlas of Anomalous AI*, ed. Ben Vickers and K. Allado-McDowell (Ignota, 2020), 241.

14   On complexity, see Carpo, *Beyond Digital*, 158.

disposition and responsibility towards all that is more than human and tran-scalar. Such experimentation remains a heuristic process, even when "the next frontier of automation will beget a new kind of artisan workers carrying out unscripted, endlessly variable, inventive, and creative tasks."[15] In this heuristic process, the human being is the mediator not of *what* but of *how*. And in this perspective, the experimental user has a specific responsibility for designing an open box, making several types of coalescence between the made and the maker, the input and the output, the visible and the contextualizable.[16]

With this in mind, the role of experimental users beyond technological determinism should play a regulatory role in design practice and education. This addresses their legacy and visibility also at the moment when the open medium becomes a device, software, an application, and the experimental users no longer seem necessary. At that point, the operative diagram seems to coalesce with the output in the very act of use. Devices, software, and applications crystallize and control specific uses that can be reopened in a visible space of experimentation and re-adaptation.

Experimental users, in their ability to experiment with media, are often invisible. However, they should play a fundamental role in the historical and theoretical narrative of the transformation of architectural representation, which is often too focused on the figure of the architect as a generator of ideas and forms. It would exceed the limits of this essay to inquire into the distinction between architects and experimental users in the field of cybernetics[17] and in the development of digital design since the second half of the twentieth century, the institutional role of super-users in architectural education, and the development of architectural and engineering firms in the construction sector. It

15   Cf. Carpo, *Beyond Digital*, 160: "The next frontier of automation will beget a new kind of artisan workers carrying out unscripted, endlessly variable, inventive, and creative tasks to produce no more no less than the right amount of non-standard stuff we need: where we need it, when we need it, as we need it; made to specs, made on site, and made on demand."

16   Cf. Witt, "Shadowplays," 38: "As artificial intelligences model, incubate, and encapsulate cognition, that careful distinction between made and maker, thought and thinker may seem as antiquated as physical maquettes themselves. Between the maquette and the architect there is a new actor and mediator, the quasi-intelligent model that embeds human intuitions and hallucinates endlessly elastic images, drawings, and buildings."

17   Cf. Georg Vrachliotis, *The New Technological Condition: Architecture and Design in the Age of Cybernetics* (Birkhäuser, 2022).

could be asked whether super-users—as well as other actors, including materials, professional figures, climatic factors—are often reduced to mere mediators and translators of forms. In some cases, schools of architecture produce
experimental users who are employed to make possible forms which are generated by others.

A shift in the institutional, pedagogical role of the experimental user is
needed. But it also calls for a change of perspective with regard to future architects. They should be trained both to experiment in a plural field of media
practices and to recognize the historical, political, social, or economic genealogies of the technologies used in design as well as their environmental impact.
From this perspective, the figure of the experimental user—which can be found
potentially in many laboratories, university workshops, software development
companies, and offices—must be emancipated from the role of "supplier." In
doing so, we can create a space of collaboration between the ability to reach a
level of creative intuition through digital technologies and the urgent need to
design just environments. And this is one of the great questions of the efficacy
of architecture and its intelligence—and the way in which it is taught—that
is, the ability to situate itself at the level of the environment as a multimodal
field made up of multi-media practices, and with them to design its care and
transformation. The ability to rethink architectural design as the constitution
and co-existence of ecosystems[18] will be increasingly linked to the use of AI
and Generative AI. This requires first and foremost a rethinking of design as a
media and relational practice, i.e., a more porous hybridization between analogue and digital media. This porosity should not be confused with hybridization of techniques for architectural form generation; it is rather also a semantic project that shift meanings through media. This requires us also to consider
the space of computation and coding as "dirty," as Hélène Frichot observes with
reference to Jennifer Bloomer's work:

> Inspired by Bloomer, who is unafraid of mixing her thinking with the dirt
> and remaining open to productive if risky contaminations, the dirty tactics of
> 'dirty theory' throws dirt into the hegemonic machine of kingmakers, it offers

---

18   Cf. Randy Deutsch, *Superusers: Design Technology Specialists and the Future of Practice*
(Routledge, 2019).

up counter-narratives to disrupt the status quo, it seeks to introduce noise and grit into the system, to disrupt architecture, which must be troubled.[19]

This approach to design and making can be related to the transformative role of "counter-computational spatial practices" proposed by Laura Kurgan, Adam Vosburgh, and e-flux Architecture:

> If there is no outside, conscious computation must move beyond techno-logical determinism, the black box, and the dream of 'liberation' from data and the map. The task at hand is to introduce the unknowable, uncertain, serendipitous, diverse—which is to say, wisdom, rather than data—into computational design. Taking on this difficult task, counter-computational spatial practices engage with the methods of spatial computing to challenge and propose alternatives to what is typically created by the very tools, infrastructures, or media they are using.[20]

This counter-space, which we could compare with the medium as a space of destabilization, has a critical and destabilizing value. It is an alternative way of opening up media given to us as usable tools to examine the network of political, economic, social, and cultural factors at the basis of their development and establishment. It is the value of this multiple and multimodal relationship that must always be reconstituted beyond the narratives of the unattainability of technical tools and their related epistemologies.

In this perspective, the experimental user as a regulative figure implies a relational and intersectional extension of epistemologies that are generated and established through media practices. With particular reference to AI, the edited volume *Atlas of Anomalous AI* questions the possibility of approaching AI as the "continuation of a wisdom tradition."[21] The essay "Making Kin with the Machines" embeds indigenous epistemologies into this perspective so as to

19   Hélène Frichot, "A Dirty Theory for a New Materialism: From Gilles Deleuze to Jennifer Bloomer," in *Utopia Computer: The "New" in Architecture?*, ed. Nathalie Bredella, Chris Dähne, and Frederike Lausch (University Press TU Berlin, 2023), 38.

20   Laura Kurgan, Adam Vosburgh, and e-flux Architecture, "Editorial: Spatial Computing," *e-flux Architecture*, June 17, 2024, https://www.e-flux.com/architecture/spatial-compu ting/614028/editorial/.

21   K. Allado-McDowell and Ben Vickers, "Introduction to Atlas of Anomalous AI", ed. Al-lado-McDowell and Vickers, 9.

question an epistemology of control (Jim Cheney) as a practice of appropriation of resources and elements that allow the use of AI and its materiality:

> The agency of stones connects directly to questions of AI, as AI is formed not only from code, but from materials of the Earth. To remove the concept of AI from its materiality is to sever this connection. Forming a relationship to AI, we form a relationship to the mines and the stones. Relations with AI are therefore relations with exploited resources. If we are able to approach this relationship ethically, we must reconsider the ontological status of each of the parts which contribute to AI all the way back to the mines from which our technology's material resources emerge.[22]

Relational Spaces and Practices

This countering role of experimental practices cannot avoid the question of signification: meaning production is not an unambiguous and objective correlation between content and form, but rather a relational space in a tangled web of meanings.[23] Media practices are the conditions of possibility for the sensitive experience with which human beings "practice" worlds by representing and transforming them. At the same time, media produce and determine through specific uses spatial design. Design processes, incorporating a range of media practices, are intrinsically relational and not neutral. With the objective of fostering an active relationship with the ecosystems in which we are immersed, the design of just environments requires a more plural, field-sensitive relational intelligence, which serves to generate the critical capacity to approach mediality as a relational space.

Keller Easterling's concept of "medium design" explores this empirical constitution of mediation. Medium design is a relational critical practice that explores situated objects not as given, fixed, and stable content, but as a "matrix" from which new relations and connections emerge. Easterling's approach

---

22   Jason Edward Lewis et al., "Making Kin with the Machines," in *Atlas of Anomalous AI*, ed. Allado-McDowell and Vickers, 49.

23   This conception of meaning can be criticized as semanticism, defined as "the application of semantic principles both as descriptive and generative framework for the discipline" that follows a specific ambition "to help architects both describe and generate the shapes and forms that populate our built environment." See Stanislas Challou, *Artificial Intelligence and Architecture* (Birkhäuser, 2022), 193–94.

draws on Gilbert Ryle's distinction between "knowing that" and "knowing how." In this vein, it goes beyond what might be termed a "semantics of content" that reduces knowledge to an understanding of content. It is through this semantics that various misunderstandings and reductionisms in the analytical, cognitive, and behavioral fields have emerged. Instead, medium design focuses on a "modal semantics," in which content emerges from relational modes that reveal alternative narratives:

> It asks readers to look with half-closed eyes at the world, focusing not only on objects with names, shapes, and outlines, but also on the matrix of medium of activities and latent potentials that those objects generate. It looks beyond object to matrix. It looks beyond nominative expressions to infinite expressions of activity and interplay. And it looks beyond declared ideologies to undeclared dispositions—beyond the authority of economic or political labels that often obscure or misrepresent latent potentials in organizations of all kinds.[24]

This paradigm shift from the "what" to the "how" is underpinned on a theoretical level by a reflection on both tacit knowledge and the notion of medium, apparatus, and dispositive, which Easterling identifies as a specific task for the designer. According to her, the designer's role is not to design objects but rather "the interplay between things."[25] This trajectory or field of transformative effects, termed "medium design" by Easterling, represents a third way that overcomes the polarization of conventional design and critical design practice. While conventional design, "it is assumed, must wait to be engaged by the market to prepare another right answer—a solution in the form of a building or a master plan," the critical design practitioner "must work for the absolute defeat of this market."[26] Medium design is defined by its relational nature, which enables the integration of diverse layers of information—political, social, economic, and environmental—present within "spatial arrangements." These arrangements are "information-rich," according to Easterling, "because of the coexistence rather than the succession of technologies. Most prized is not the newness of technologies but the relationships between them."[27]

---

24   Keller Easterling, *Medium Design: Knowing How to Work on the World* (Verso, 2021), x.

25   Easterling, *Medium Design*, xi.

26   Easterling, *Medium Design*, 9.

27   Easterling, *Medium Design*, 72.

Relationality should also be an experimental design practice when using AI. This is a fundamental aspect of Paola Sturla and Michael Jakob's coauthored essay concerning the interface that AI must possess with the human practitioner. They take Lawrence Halprin's design practice and the development of scores as a case in point:

> By recognizing that design aims at shaping the physical world and that the designer's point of view in itself biases the design process, we suggest that artificial intelligence could be engaged in a recursive feedback loop that expresses its aesthetic through its interface with the human practitioner. Such a feedback loop indicates the evolution of 'new-humanism' toward a renewed 'new-humanism,' a rediscovery of the creative agency of the designer in an un-hierarchical relationship with nature.[28]

Experimental spatial design emerges as a pivotal practice in this context. This primacy is linked to its capacity to traverse—even in its more post- or more-than-human iterations—a plural field of sensory modalities. Through the employment of specific technological devices, this field is subject to perpetual tightening or widening. The theory of mediality, inseparable from the praxis of media experimentation, is pivotal to comprehending the perceptual, design, and co-constitutive capacities of space, contingent on our pluralistic inhabitation of the earth. The nexus and liminal space between design and use must be a negotiable and interrogative space.

It is mediality that engenders a medium of stability in such a reflection, allowing us to reopen the field of media practices, to explore the potential and the limits of digital technologies, to suspend and overcome medial practices, and to create new hybrid practices. Furthermore, it enables us to critically approach the economic mechanisms that underlie the commodification of practices embedded in software. It compels a non-reductionist approach to spatial experience, facilitating the integration of plural epistemologies and the articulation of plural bodily, visual, and verbal languages.

---

28   Paola Sturla and Michael Jakob, "Artificial Intelligence as (Meta-)Art? Emergent Technologies in the Design Process," *Cloud-Cuckoo-Land* 25, no. 40 (2021): 87.

Practicing Theory as Interference and Divergence

This act of opening is indicative of the performative function of experimental practices that are defined as "heuristic," i.e., practices of discovering the known and unknown. The term "performative" is used with reference to Karen Barad's reference to performative approaches that "call into question the basic premises of representationalism and focus inquiry as well on the practices or performances of representing, as well as on the productive effects of those practices and the conditions for their efficacy."[29]

Understanding the performative value of mediation implies a specific way of "practicing theory" that is not merely reduced to a "theory of that" but it is a genuine "theory of how." That is to say, it becomes a thought of interference,[30] capable of displaying interdependences between discourse and material realities, thereby demonstrating the constituted character of representations generated by technological devices. The reaffirmation of the performative role of media, which is connected to the serendipity of scientific experimentation, in contemporary debate necessarily relates to rethinking a reductionist understanding of science. A conception of "exact science" underlies a reductionist perspective on technical implementation and the consequences it engenders. This reductionist perspective fails to encompass the serendipity and experientiality—highlighted by Isabelle Stengers, Bruno Latour, and Hans-Jörg Rheinberger—on the basis of effects produced by technologies. Its critique leads to a comprehensive discussion of the network of political, economic, social, and environmental factors from which technologies emerge, and of the networks of effects they generate. Beyond the confines of reductionism, a "divergent" theoretical and philosophical domain emerges in which the conditions, factors, and effects are reconsidered beyond a statuary conception of sciences—and technological determinism. As Stengers reminds us through her rereading of Deleuze and Guattari with respect to the "complementary lines of science and philosophy," this relational field is characterized by a divergence from the scientific paradigm. A philosophical "counter-effectuation," according to Stengers

---

29   Karen Barad, *Meeting the Universe Halfway: Quantum Physics and the Entanglement of Matter and Meaning* (Duke University Press, 2007), 28.

30   For a philosophical reflection of the concept of interference, see Lidia Gasperoni, "For an Architecture as a Productive Interference," *Stoa* 4, no. 9 (2024): 35–39.

would create by its own means what busy scientists so easily forget, namely the 'dignity of event' that makes them busy. Such a perspective has a dream-like quality, however. It may help philosophers to resist, but we need to know what they have to resist, to characterize the kind of present they lack resistance to.[31]

From this standpoint, philosophy is a practice of interference with the objective of "opening up" deterministic constructs and situating experimental practices capable of establishing novel relationships between epistemologies, bodies, technical devices, and matter. The medium—or the open medium—is a practice of extending conventional signification and incorporating meanings that have been excluded from a representational and instrumental approach to "tools."

Theory then facilitates a holistic practice that opens the black box in which the practice of coding and production of software, applications, and interfaces—ready for utilization—appear to be contained. For this purpose, theory participates in practices, becoming an 'ethnography of practices'. This ethnography involves the observation of laboratories, workshops, pedagogies, and firms, with the aim of comprehending the transformative and experimental value of these practices. There is no exhaustive, universally applicable theory of any particular media practice, and consequently no definitive judgement on AI can be made. Instead, critical theory—as a sort of transformative comparativism—must examine the field of media efficacy—in one word, its experimental intelligence.

---

31   Isabelle Stengers, "Deleuze and Guattari's Last Enigmatic Message," *Angelaki* 10, no. 2 (2005): 158.

C: Practice

Architectural Practice and Artificial Intelligence

Stefan Kurath

Digital transformation has characterized architectural practice for decades. In the 1990s, computer-aided architectural design (CAAD) and 3D programs fundamentally changed the practice of drawing. As a result, digital data exchange has successively extended the digital chain. Today, it is employed from the initial idea to the construction site, at least in some areas of the construction industry, particularly timber construction. In the upcoming third wave of digitalization, the autonomous viewing, evaluation, learning, and application of data based on AI is becoming the central focus.

If you listen to AI developers and reflect on the possibilities they suggest, you may find yourself fantasizing about the possibilities for using the myriads of planning tasks that have already been completed in order to deduce connections between outset, planning, and implementation by means of self-learning entities in the foreseeable future, rendering present day problems resolvable through planning. Thanks to AI, problems and challenges in architecture and urban planning could in future be recognized independently based on data and evidence, a multitude of solution approaches and implementation templates could be generated autonomously, the construction elements could be milled and printed, and implementation could be monitored and corrected if necessary. "Smarter, better cities" is the slogan.[1]

These forecasts also impact the future of architects. In politics as well as the construction and real estate industries themselves, the hope is growing that, with digitalization and AI, they will become completely independent from the architects' interpretative monopoly on "correct planning," which is

---

1   In the parametric area, such tools are already well advanced, but not yet self-learning and autonomous, cf. SUPat, "About," accessed January 16, 2025, https://archive.arch.e thz.ch/supat/about/index.html; LUUCY, accessed January 16, 2025, www.luucy.ch. See also Collage (February 2024), a magazine for spatial development on artificial intelligence.

merely understood as a limitation preventing development. "Evidence-based planning"—i.e., rational planning based on data (as supposed facts)—is the buzzword of the moment.[2] This hope is strengthened by the fact that the architects' visualizations can hardly be distinguished by laypeople from the images produced by evidence-based AI. Even an architectural theorist like Neil Leach arrives at the provocative conclusion in his lectures that 80 percent of architects will lose their jobs.[3]

This comparison and hypothesis are, among other things, also afforded to the image that architects, historians, and theorists have been conveying to the public regarding the work of architects. In their disciplinary debate they reduce the essence of buildings and cities to idea, structure, and form. The works, texts, and lectures of Aldo Rossi or Oswald Matthias Ungers, for instance, convey a clear outline of this process, subsumed under the demand for the "autonomy of architecture," which excludes non-architectural considerations from the examination of buildings and cities.[4] Thus architects are less inclined to explain their work verbally, but present it in the form of floor plans, sections, façades, 3D models, visualizations, and images instead.

As a result, architecture is increasingly perceived by outsiders as a system comparable to a construction kit—as a practice combining prefabricated floor plans and façades in order to generate images. Hence the developers' conclusion stands to reason: all you need is autonomous AI trained to reassemble digitized representations of such floor plans, sections, and façades. Formulate framework conditions. Generate floor plan. Generate façade. Generate image. Done.

2   See Joris van Wezemael, "Innenentwicklung wird zur kooperativen Zukunftsgestaltung," *Forum Raumentwicklung*, no. 3 (2017): 4–8; Stefan Kurath, *Jetzt: die Architektur! Über Gegenwart und Zukunft der architektonischen Praxis* (Park Books, 2022), 46.

3   Neil Leach, "AI and the Future of Architecture," *INDESEM*, October 8, 2023, YouTube video, 1:05:32, https://www.youtube.com/watch?v=SZ3JOkQXRKo.

4   See Aldo Rossi, *The architecture of the city* (MIT Press, 1982); Oswald Mathias Ungers, "Berufsvortrag zu den Prinzipien der Raumgestaltung gehalten an der TU Berlin 1963," *Arch+*, no. 181/182 (2006): 30–44. However, the exclusion of non-disciplinary content is not a development that only affects architecture. It can be found in all disciplines and has a lot to do with research practice. Gaining knowledge is only ever possible by reducing complexities. Since the beginning of the Enlightenment, this has led to a differentiation of the world into different areas of knowledge and practice, which have broken down the complexity of the world into specific disciplines and thus made it manageable. See also: Bruno Latour, *Die Hoffnung der Pandora*, (Suhrkamp 2000), 86.

Nobody would come to this conclusion if architects were to describe their arduous practice through words. Bruno Latour and Albena Yaneva address this in their critical examination of architects' work and their 3D CAD renderings. "When we picture a building, it is always as a fixed, stolid structure that appears in four colors in the glossy magazines that customers flip through in architects' waiting rooms."[5] However, these representations are missing some fundamental elements of architectural reality:

> Where do you place the angry clients and their sometimes conflicting demands? Where do you insert the legal and city planning constraints? Where do you locate the budgeting and the different budget opinions? Where do you put the logistics of the many successive models that you had to modify in order to absorb the continuous demands of so many conflicting stakeholders—users, communities of neighbors, preservationists, clients, representatives of the government and city authorities? Where do you incorporate the changing program specifics?[6]

They continue by pointing out that these influences and dynamics are part of the production conditions that apply to buildings and cities, rarely addressed or discussed. They perceive this as a significant shortcoming of architectural theory. Architectural theorist Jeremy Till sums up the problem, writing: "First, architecture is a dependent discipline. Second, architecture, as profession and practice, does everything to resist that very dependency."[7] This describes a peculiarity of architecture and urban planning that, in the general perception of architects' achievements, is increasingly becoming a boomerang with regard to the relevance of architecture, especially in connection with the increasing focus on AI.

Considering the real conditions under which buildings are created in all their complexity, architecture is not "only" about assembling building elements, but also about a multiverse of pluralities of concrete entities in constantly changing constellations that lead to constantly changing physical assemblies (with a spatial effect).[8]

---

5   Bruno Latour and Albena Yaneva, "Give me a Gun and I will Make All Buildings Move: An ANT's View of Architecture," in *Explorations in Architecture: Teaching, Design, Research*, ed. Reto Geiser (Birkhäuser, 2008), 80.

6   Latour and Yaneva, "Give me a Gun," 81.

7   Jeremy Till, *Architecture Depends* (MIT Press 2009), 1.

8   Latour and Yaneva, "Give me a Gun," 82.

Buildings are therefore always unique and cannot be reproduced. Not because architects seek to realize themselves, but simply because the same clients, investors, spatial programs, building ground conditions, topographies, access, material conditions, use cases, available and required resources, and construction companies never match twice. In addition, the dynamics of social negotiation processes, economic developments, and geopolitical shifts lead to constantly changing interests and thus to constantly changing framework conditions.

Architects therefore never know in advance what a project will actually encompass and which conditions will prevail. Unpredictability, and thus uncertainty, are key parameters of architectural practice. In the majority of cases construction conditions are unpredictable and therefore incalculable. Constantly adapting unforeseeable developments without abandoning content and concepts that have already been developed (if you don't want to keep starting from scratch) is an essential element of architectural practice.

As a theory of action, design as the architect's craft therefore precisely aims at integrating the constantly emerging and changing interests and conditions, balancing them, relating them to original ideas and interests in order to maintain the network of entities, and constantly expanding it if necessary for the realization of buildings.[9] In architectural practice, this requires not only craftsmanship but also intellectual as well as political—i.e., strategic and tactical—skills, without which contradictions and breakdowns in negotiations between all players involved would constantly arise, repeatedly forcing fundamental restarts of the project.[10] Due to unpredictability and therefore uncertainty, nothing can be calculated here.

A clear transition reveals itself between the performance of artificial intelligence—processing what is already known in the form of existing data—and architectural intelligence—processing the unforeseeable in all conceivable forms such as changes in mood, lack of resources, economic crises, funding problems, legal changes, neighborhood disputes, contractors going out of business, misinterpreted plans, and construction machinery breakdowns.

---

9   See Stefan Kurath, "Was tun Architektinnen und Architekten eigentlich?" in *Digitalisierung und Architektur in Lehre und Praxis*, ed. Patric Furrer, Andreas Jud, and Stefan Kurath (Triest Verlag, 2022), 17–27.

10   Stefan Kurath, jetzt: die Architektur! Über Gegenwart und Zukunft der architektonischen Praxis (Park Books, 2022), 216.

So, when talking about AI and architecture, it is imperative to first establish a theory of architectural practice that links the representations of architecture with the production conditions as well as the required intellectual, technical, and political achievements.[11] Then we need to weave in artificial intelligence as a separate entity applied in order to extend architectural intelligence. Such a theory of architecture and AI is enriched with a corresponding realism regarding architectural practice, in the context of which the significance of AI within architecture as well as the effects on its forms of representation must be addressed.

There is no doubt that AI tools will become an essential part of architectural practice. It is, however, not yet possible to predict the final result of this process, especially considering the significant discrepancy between the forecasts and the actual current possibilities that AI offers. Nonetheless, we need to try to find out, step by step.

Experience reports were discussed in the context of an event on AI in professional practice at the BDA in Munich in June 2024. In the first presentation, Jacob von Rijs from architecture firm MVRDV shared insights into their experiences, primarily with the deployment of image-generating AI tools. Gheyath Mohammed from Henning Larsen spoke about his experiences with using AI tools for generating and analyzing structures. Stefan Höffgen from Tegel Projekt GmbH spoke about AI applied in neighborhood development, particularly for the self-learning analysis of aerial images with vehicle and plant recognition. What all three had in common was their curiosity and interest in the new AI tools.

All three recognized a great potential in the future application of AI. At the same time, the tools evidently do not yet provide the desired added value in everyday practice. This is attributed to the fact that the tools have not been developed for architecture-specific applications, and most tools rely on generic

---

11   The German architectural theorist Stephan Trüby also points out that buildings can hardly be traced back to individual figures alone, but rather to complex framework conditions. He speaks of architecture as a maximally complex cultural technique. Against this background, an architectural theory that only refers to architecture would greatly underestimate architecture. Stephan Trüby, *Absolute Architekturbeginner. Schriften 2004–2014* (Wilhelm Fink Verlag, 2017), 19. Architectural theorist Bart Lootsma already sees improvement here, and points to a paradigm shift. Architectural theory is now "not only concerned with an elite and canonized part of the built environment, but with spatial practices in general": see Bart Lootsma, *Reality Bytes: Selected Essays 1995–2015* (Birkhäuser, 2016), 31.

data collections sourced from the internet. The lesson learnt is that architects urgently need to participate in the development of AI-related tools and must create their own (controllable) data collections.

ZAHA Hadid Architects are very advanced in this respect. They command a vast data pool derived from their own projects, and develop their own AI tools. A presentation by Christoph Geiger and Clemens Lindner at an ideas workshop on Munich North in November 2024 impressively demonstrated great potential in this regard. Their text contribution merits discussion here.

The experiment, which encompassed a hands-on AI event organized by metris / Plan:kooperativ and moderated by Matthias Burgbacher, yielded interesting insights. The task was to generate a live visualization using AI in dialogue with the public and the planning teams participating in the ideas workshop. The regulations of the City of Munich served as a basis for the visualization, as well as various expert opinions on Munich North and text prompts from the planning teams on specific spatial situations contained in their designs. Image-generating AI was employed in order to create images in real time, which were then discussed, criticized, and adapted by residents from the northern districts of Munich—also in real time.

It was interesting to experience how this workshop yielded insights to non-planners regarding the challenging practice of architects. Initially, the sum of contradictory ideas and comments did not yield any result. Moreover, all demands needed to be balanced constantly and negotiated anew in order to proceed to the next step. In their discussion with the planners as well as architects Geiger and Lindner, all participants demonstrated the aforementioned intellectual and technical capabilities of architectural practice: registering concerns, translating them into language, translating them into realization suggestions, and constantly reprocessing them. Such insights into the reality of architectural practice are rarely offered to non-architects, although they help substantially to convey what it is that architects actually do. Therein lay the great value of the event. The AI was but the means to this end.

The history of science reveals that new technologies and tools always lead to new insights. The invention of the telescope is a vivid example of how magnifications of the universe enabled completely new insights and provided evidence for the heliocentric view of the world. When seeking to make progress in architecture and urban planning, a proactive, affirmative, and critical approach to AI developments in architectural practice is therefore of great importance. However, this does not merely apply to application, but also to the question regarding how to deal with new technologies and the discoveries they yield.

Cornelia Diethelm, an expert in digital ethics, points out: "Employing AI tools responsibly means that employees and managers need to know how to use these new possibilities correctly and in compliance with the law, and that they must always view the results critically."[12] This also includes an awareness of what AI actually does, as Diethelm continues: "AI-generated content is only spawned through probability calculations and chance based on the training data. Therefore results can be outdated, misleading, or even wrong."[13]

This has different implications for different applications of AI. Analytical AI, which analyzes existing objects broken down to data based on questions, can still be controlled to a certain extent, even if it is not always possible to comprehend exactly what is occurring and how, especially regarding self-learning processes. Therefore it is crucial to take a particularly critical look. With regard to the surge of information that is increasingly flooding architectural practice, great added value is generated nonetheless. In fact, the available data on space, utilization, and motion has assumed a new quality. Analytical AI in particular will contribute significantly to the immediate identification of shortcomings and development opportunities in existing urban structures by categorizing patterns, rules, and comparisons of cities, and comparing them with empirical knowledge from the fields of architecture and urban planning. In medicine, such procedures are already being applied in diagnostics in order to compare and analyze imaging procedures—for instance, to attain cancer diagnoses in a much faster and accurate manner.

However, while clinical data from studies are published and therefore accessible to researchers, the greatest challenge within architecture and urban planning lies in making access to corresponding data sets on movement and spatial behavior available. They are collected by the big tech companies in the background, for example through app usage or location tracking on mobile phones. The companies retain these data sets for themselves as data gold in order to utilize them commercially. An open-source strategy for research purposes needs to be demanded from tech companies under state law.

---

12   Cornelia Diethelm, interviewed in Isabelle Amschwand, Brigitte Maranghino Singer, Reto Savoia, Michael Grampp, and Daniel Laude, "Generative künstliche Intelligenz – neue Horizonte für Verwaltungsräte" (swissVR Monitor II/2024, August 2024), 21. Author's translation.

13   Diethelm, interviewed in Amschwand et al., "Generative künstliche Intelligenz," 21. Author's translation.

With regard to generative AI in connection with architectural practice, there are clear limits concerning the quality and usability of existing data. Such data are always related to the past. Using them carelessly reproduces the status quo. This can be seen impressively in the careless use of today's image-generating AI for visualizations of future city concepts. Here, too, AI proves to be a "stochastic parrot" that calculates probabilities based on what is already known.[14]

But architectural practice is always future-oriented. It is precisely about the unknown. It is precisely about improving an existing situation in the context of constant change and unknown framework conditions. Especially in the context of the global warming, biodiversity, resource, and housing crises, a change in thinking and planning with regard to architecture and urban development is urgently required. If newly-generated most probable rows of letters and image pixels produced by AI are based on data from developments that have actually caused the crises themselves, the benefits for architecture and urban planning remain extremely limited. Thus, probability calculations referring to the past generated by text-, image-, and structure-generative AI cannot simply be applied in their current form. Instead, they may serve as a starting point for further enhancements, corrections, improvements, and additions. As mentioned above, design as the architect's craft—adapting the unforeseeable in real time—will retain a central role in the disciplines of architecture and urban planning.

AI will therefore not replace architectural practice, but rather add value. Nevertheless, there will be displacement movements. The future of architects will depend on the extent to which they succeed in making themselves indispensable again in the social negotiation processes surrounding spatial development. In order to re-establish this connectivity, architects must engage with the possibilities presented by AI. They must do so not only in order to work in a more evidence-based manner and restore trust in politics, but also to free up time for what lies at the core of an architect's work: to invest great effort and passion into connecting their reflections on space and their sustainable and resilient spatial concepts with society on a day-to-day basis in order to realize them in the material world and translate them into physical space.

---

14   See Emily Bender, Timnit Gebru, Angelina McMillan-Major, and Shmargaret Shmitchell, "On the Dangers of Stochastic Parrots: Can Language Models Be Too Big?" in *FAccT '21: Proceedings of the 2021 ACM Conference on Fairness, Accountability, and Transparency* (FAccT '21, 2021), 610–23.

Beyond Disruption: Digital Intelligence and Human Intuition in Architectural Practice

Adam Kiryk[1]

Introduction: Framing the One-Year AI Research Project

For centuries, architects have advanced by adopting new design tools: From ink sketches on vellum to digital sketching tablets, from hand-drafted layouts on drawing boards to modern CAD systems, from manual spreadsheets in Excel to BIM-driven coordination, or from classical hand-drawn perspective renderings to hyper-realistic VR-based visualizations. Each shift subtly reshapes the creative process, bridging tradition with technology. Now, AI emerges as the latest step in this continuum, offering the potential not to disrupt or replace the profession, but once again to enhance the traditional skills that define it. By revisiting workflows once deemed obsolete and pairing them with digital precision, AI can reinvigorate the practice, ultimately striking a balance between time-tested methods and new efficiencies.

In early 2024, the Managing Board of architectural and construction design office Penzel Valier identified AI as a strategic focus for our Digital Technology Competence Team, alongside Digital Twins, 3D Scanning, and Modularization. The newly outlined strategy aimed to explore AI's potential in ar-

---

1   Author's note: This article was written with strong support from ChatGPT-4o, primarily for text editing and structural refinement. The GPT-o1 model was used for deeper analysis and critical review to identify gaps in coherence and ensure logical flow. This process allowed me to focus primarily on content development, while AI-assisted editing helped maintain a concise and consistent style. Given my multilingual thought process—shifting between Polish, English, and German—AI played a key role in unifying the text into one cohesive narrative. The writing process became a moderated dialogue between AI and an experienced architect (but amateur writer), creating a continuous learning experience in structuring and refining ideas while working with LLMs.

chitectural design and construction while aligning with both short-term efficiency goals and long-term innovation strategies.

To lead this effort, the Board established a dedicated AI Unit, tasked with conducting an open-ended one-year research project. The objective was to evaluate AI's practical applications, identify key workflows where it could enhance efficiency, and build a roadmap for gradual implementation.

This initiative aligned closely with my research at ETH Zurich, where, since 2017, I have been teaching courses on digital technologies and design processes. My involvement with various research units at the university—such as the ETH AI Center, the Media & Game Technology Center, and the Center for Augmented Computational Design in Architecture, Engineering, and Construction (Design++)—provided a strong foundation for exploring AI's transformative role in creative industries, bridging theoretical research with practical applications in architectural design.

At Hybrid Reality Research, a unit I led under the Chair of Digital Building Technology supervised by Prof. Dillenburger, we organized a "Guest Input" lecture series within our elective courses, giving us and our students the opportunity to exchange ideas with experts such as Michael Mieskes (ZHAW), who explored AI's role in design theory, George Guida (Harvard GSD), who focused on AI in architectural education, and Dr. Sergey Prokudin (ETH), who researched NeRF (neural radiance field) 3D scanning methods. On the industry side, discussions with Keir Regan Alexander (Arka.Works), Bas van de Poel (Modem Works), and Michael Drobnik and Martin Schulte (Herzog & De Meuron) provided practical insights into AI and XR (Extended Reality) applications in architecture. These dialogues helped shape our research direction at Penzel Valier, blending theoretical exploration with hands-on implementation.

Beyond academia, we analyzed case studies from leading architectural firms such as MVRDV, BIG, and Herzog & de Meuron, which had already integrated AI into their design pipelines. These insights—combined with an extensive literature review and industry reports—allowed us to position Penzel Valier's AI strategy within the broader technological shift taking place in architecture.

Digital Transformation & Readiness for AI

Penzel Valier's existing digital infrastructure provided an ideal environment for AI experimentation. Several years ago, the office's IT setup was restructured to allow employees to work seamlessly across physical and virtual spaces, fostering a culture of hybrid collaboration and tool integration. This digital-first approach created a robust foundation for testing new technologies and exploring how AI could complement established workflows.

In designing the initiative, we drew on the technology-adoption lifecycle—a framework describing how innovations gradually spread from early adopters to the broader mainstream—focusing on identifying high-impact workflows where AI could offer the greatest efficiency gains. To begin, we engaged employees who were most curious about AI in small pilot tests. Through weekly feedback loops and structured evaluations, we mapped out AI's potential in key operational areas, ensuring that our approach remained grounded in practical, real-world scenarios. Ultimately, we created four test groups to explore AI's role across different office functions:

a) Project Development & Competitions Visualization, floor plan generation, material studies, feasibility analyses
b) Office Admin & Communication Text structuring, email automation, document analysis, social media content
c) HR & Finance AI-assisted accounting, resource planning, legal document processing
d) Construction & Site Management AI-driven cost estimation, BIM integration, construction tracking, XR applications

After three months, we compiled fifty-six use cases spanning multiple domains, each with a problem statement, proposed AI solution, and effectiveness assessment. These ranged from text-based automation and document analysis to more advanced AI applications in design visualization and BIM integration. By adopting a bottom-up, iterative approach, we ensured that AI was tested in real-world settings, with direct input from employees who would eventually use these tools.

LLMs: Accessibility, Personalization, and Automation

From the outset, we recognized that Large Language Models (LLMs) would play a central role in our AI strategy, serving as accessible, customizable tools to enhance productivity across all areas of the office. Their versatility—combined with rapid development and the continuous addition of new features—has significantly improved efficiency in both day-to-day tasks and complex workflows.

Our core challenge in implementing LLMs was ensuring that every employee, regardless of technical expertise, could leverage AI effectively. To address this, we focused on low-threshold solutions that enable team members to customize GPTs for their specific roles and project needs.

During the initial testing phase, we created six accounts: Four for the test groups, one for IT and administration, and one for the management team. This structure helped us evaluate LLMs in different office contexts while maintaining data security and role-specific configurations. As adoption increased, we introduced personal AI accounts for employees who handle sensitive information, allowing them to benefit from AI-driven efficiencies while working securely. For instance, HR teams manage confidential employee data that must remain inaccessible to others, so they require dedicated accounts with stronger safeguards. We also caution employees against using private accounts for business purposes, since personal licenses do not offer the same level of security as our enterprise AI tools.

With this foundation in place, we then began actively training employees on configuring GPTs in ChatGPT, showing them how to personalize these tools according to the project phase, task type, and desired automation level. We also introduced Copilot Studio and MS Automate, integrated into our familiar MS 365 environment, allowing staff to easily adapt to AI-driven tools without steep technical barriers.

Almost a year after introducing ChatGPT to the entire office, roughly half of our employees use it daily or weekly, with 81 percent finding it intuitive and 94 percent reporting increased work efficiency. While many rely on it for text processing, spell-checking, and automated email drafting, its impact extends far beyond administrative tasks. LLMs have become essential for software support (CAD, BIM, and MS Excel), analytical tasks involving complex datasets, and intelligent web searches through ChatGPT and Bing Copilot.

One of the most remarkable developments has been how quickly some employees discovered its creative potential. With proper prompt engineering, certain team members have built their own GPTs to handle entire workflows—automating minutes of meetings, task assignments, and database queries. For example, we are working on our Swiss Norms databank, trained with Chat-GPT, to assist employees in navigating complex building law questions with ease. In the competitions team, LLMs are used to analyze competition programs, generate spatial programs and unit mix strategies, and support creative text-based design explorations. Meanwhile, HR and finance benefit from AI-assisted Excel solutions for multilayered spreadsheet optimization and financial planning.

These solutions are not dictated from the top down but have organically evolved from the needs of different teams, supported by the AI Unit. Going forward, our vision is for every employee to be able to create and refine their own AI agents, seamlessly integrating services like Copilot Studio and MS Automate to streamline repetitive processes. The key lies in keeping the barrier to entry as low as possible, so that AI adoption remains inclusive and accessible to everyone. In this way, we see AI not as a replacement for human expertise, but as a flexible, evolving assistant—capable of enhancing workflows, accelerating operations, and unlocking new forms of creativity in architectural practice.

Generative Design Process with AI

Alongside our text-based LLM applications, we systematically tested various AI platforms for image and geometry generation to evaluate usability, creative potential, and integration within professional design workflows. Our trials included image-generation tools such as MidJourney and Stable Diffusion (Magnific AI, Prome AI, Yanus) as well as FinchAI and Architectures for floor plan creation.

One key takeaway from these tests was the significant variance in ease of use. Tools based on Stable Diffusion (e.g., Prome AI, Yanus) had lower entry thresholds, making them more accessible for quick sketch enhancements and volumetric explorations. By contrast, MidJourney excelled in producing visually striking images but struggled with the level of detail required for accurate design inputs. Its reliance on more complex prompt engineering also made it less straightforward for architects without extensive AI experience.

We also evaluated platforms specifically designed for floor plan generation (Finch AI and Architectures). While these tools can rapidly produce iterative layouts based on personalized floor plan libraries, we found that inaccuracies and unpredictable outputs often require time-consuming revisions. In many cases, the complexity of the design task—including site constraints and local building codes—exceeds the default parameters of these software solutions, necessitating substantial manual intervention to correct the generated output. Despite these drawbacks, both FinchAI and Architectures show promise as early-stage conceptual design aids, where speed and variety can spark new spatial ideas before moving into more rigorous workflows.

When compared to our architects' expertise in Photoshop sketching, collaging, CAD modelling, and rendering engines, AI-based tools still serve more as supplementary resources than replacements for established workflows. They show particular promise as a kind of creative dialogue partner, generating unconventional results that human designers refine and integrate into ongoing projects.

Interestingly, this has started to redefine the role of the architect—from a "creator" to a "curator" of AI-generated ideas. To advance this approach, we plan to train our own LoRA (Low-Rank Adaptation) models rooted in Penzel Valier's architectural identity, ensuring that AI outputs align with our office's design philosophy. Our forthcoming Penzel Valier monograph will offer a rich, well-curated dataset of text and images for fine-tuning these models, embedding the firm's architectural DNA into future AI-assisted text- and image-based design tasks. In doing so, we aim to move beyond generic AI outputs and create a more context-aware design tool—one that becomes an adaptive extension of our creative process, rather than an external generator of random iterations.

AI as an Evolution, not a Disruption

After a year of structured experimentation, our approach to AI at Penzel Valier demonstrates that meaningful technology adoption is not about disruption but strategic evolution. From the outset, we focused on AI tools that align with our design principles, workflow logic, and creative values, rather than adopting technology for its own sake.

We did not seek to replace existing expertise, but to enhance and refine established processes. Testing AI in visualization, data processing, and automation revealed clear advantages in efficiency and rapid iteration, yet also reinforced the necessity of human oversight—especially in architectural design, where control over the process remains paramount. Tools like FinchAI and MidJourney offered exciting possibilities but fell short in architectural quality and process control, requiring significant manual intervention to produce viable results.

More important than the tools themselves was the mindset shift—both in how we evaluate AI's role in design and how we restructure workflows to integrate it effectively. Rather than viewing AI as an autonomous decision-maker, we embraced it as a collaborative agent, capable of structuring information, assisting in creative discussions, and streamlining repetitive tasks. This perspective supports a controlled, non-disruptive transition, ensuring that AI augments rather than undermines the architect's role.

Like past technological shifts—from CAD to BIM, from 3D visualization to parametric design—AI will need time to find its natural place within architectural practice. Despite rapid advancements, full integration is an ongoing process requiring continued refinement, training, and adaptation. While some creative industries have fully embraced AI-driven workflows, architecture remains a profession where technical precision, material knowledge, and spatial understanding cannot be fully automated.

A major insight from our research is that AI's true potential lies less in stand-alone tools and more in integrated ecosystems. We have already seen that cross-platform solutions—particularly when LLMs are combined with automation frameworks like Copilot Studio and MS Automate—have the greatest potential for long-term implementation. The ability to create custom AI assistants tailored to specific office roles provides a personalized and scalable approach to AI adoption.

Beyond Disruption: Digital Intelligence and Human Intuition in Architectural Practice

Throughout this process, we have underlined that successful AI adoption is not about mastering a single tool but about cultivating a workplace culture that values experimentation, structured learning, and adaptability. Many technologies that seemed revolutionary just a few years ago—3D scanning, 3D printing, VR/AR—are now commonplace. AI will likely follow a similar trajectory.

Ultimately, the greatest challenge for AI in architecture is not the technology itself but the profession's ability to harness its possibilities while maintaining the core values of design integrity, creative authorship, human judgment, and intuition. By balancing structured implementation with openness to innovation, we can ensure that AI is not a disruptive force but a natural extension of our evolving design practice.

Fig. 36: The figure presents a rendering of 45'844 3D furniture objects extracted from a BIM model of a designed building, capturing the essence of digital transformation and the challenges of harnessing extensive datasets to achieve AI-enhanced efficiency in contemporary architectural practice.

Key Findings and Next Steps

As we reflect on the experiences of the past year and look ahead to future developments, several key points stand out:

1. AI Introduction as Evolution
    A structured, incremental approach proves more sustainable than purely disruptive change. The architect's creative control remains at the center, with AI serving as an efficiency booster rather than a replacement.

2. LLMs as Universal Aids
    LLMs like ChatGPT have emerged as accessible, flexible base technologies, applicable to everything from text processing to complex data analytics. Personalized AI accounts and prompt strategies enable all employees to benefit.

3. Generative Design as Ideation Partner
    Image and geometry generation tools still complement, rather than sup-
    plant, established workflows. They spark unconventional ideas that human
    designers refine for real projects.

4. Next Steps
    a. Training Custom LoRA Models to align AI outputs more closely with
        Penzel Valier's architectural identity.
    b. Expanding Partnerships with industry and academic institutions for
        deeper insights and shared expertise.
    c. Deeper Integration of automation platforms (Copilot Studio, MS Au-
        tomate) for more sophisticated AI-based assistants.
    d. Ongoing Training and Workshops to lower barriers and build confi-
        dence across all teams.

The Generative AI Paradigm: Architectural Praxis Reshaped?

Christoph Geiger, Clemens Lindner

In recent years we have all witnessed the slow but undeniably transformative introduction of Generative AI in many professions, including the field of architectural production, where it has received substantial attention.

While this recent hype has fired many in the profession to imagine a future for design enhanced by increasingly capable emergent AI, there is an undeniable gap between the perceived potential and the current status of the industry.

Whereas computational architecture during previous decades primarily focused on procedural and linear logic-based methodologies, AI demonstrates the potential to introduce an entirely new paradigm to the design process—and has already initiated disruption of established practices in this domain.

While traditional algorithmic and logic-based definitions also strive towards increasingly general and applicable solutions, they still necessitate relatively rigid problem formulation, wherein computational designers create definitions to produce solutions with varying degrees of specificity. Although the scope and applicability of these solutions are substantially determined by the computational designers themselves, the majority of resulting computational tools remain quite constrained to specific use cases.

The novel paradigm that AI introduces to computational architecture discourse—and consequently to the architectural industry holistically—resides predominantly in its generative nature: the capacity to produce diverse solution sets modifiable through mere prompt reformulation rather than extensive manual reworking.

The speed of iteration production could be massively increased through these methodologies. Optioneering transcends manual labor processes, variable manipulation of parametric systems, and tedious programmatic redefinition. New solutions could be nearly instantaneous and accessible through simple natural language descriptions.

However, as this analysis will demonstrate, the generic nature of current AI systems simultaneously constitutes their greatest potential and their most significant limitation, but nonetheless offers undeniably massive opportunities for the industry as a whole to become significantly more data-driven and eventually more automated.

Current State

Research into deep learning (DL) methodologies for addressing specific architectural planning challenges has existed for numerous years, but the emergence of large language models (LLMs) and large-scale general text-to-image systems has catalyzed unprecedented attention throughout the broader industry toward these technologies.

In contrast to preceding predominantly academic research focused on specialized architectural applications at smaller scales and for rather specific problems, the high-quality outputs generated by general generative models—developed by major AI research laboratories with substantial financial and intellectual resources—provided initial indications of transformative technological potential, thereby attracting attention widely beyond academic spheres.[1]

Predominantly younger, technologically proficient architects rapidly began applying these large-scale general models to architectural applications. Implementation of diffusion-based text-to-image models initially involved prompting systems to generate architectural visualizations and imagery, while LLMs were tested regarding their architecture–engineering–construction domain knowledge through queries about architectural codes or building regulations.

---

1   Oliver Wainwright, "'It's already way beyond what humans can do': will AI wipe out architects?," *Guardian*, August 7, 2023, https://www.theguardian.com/artanddesign/20 23/aug/07/ai-architects-revolutionising-corbusier-architecture; N. Hitti, "AI will 'completely change the way we design buildings' says Zaha Hadid Architects," *Dezeen*, April 26, 2023, https://www.dezeen.com/2023/04/26/zaha-hadid-architects-patrik-schuma cher-ai-dalle-midjourney/.

Primarily through the proliferation of high-quality architectural imagery across social media and professional platforms, interest in these tools increased substantially. Additionally, the exceptional simplicity and capacity to produce high-quality images with unprecedented speed and volume attracted considerable attention toward Generative AI within architectural circles, particularly among firms and practitioners engaged in early design phases.

Subsequently, challenges emerged regarding the integration of generative visual models into established architectural workflows beyond conceptual design optioneering. Although available solutions—both open-source and commercial—have enhanced user interfaces and incorporated methodologies to address previous limitations such as visual consistency across multiple images or selective editing while maintaining overall visualization integrity, other fundamental constraints remain less amenable to resolution.

For instance, general image generation with stylistic similarity fails to maintain spatial consistency. Consequently, while carefully curated image sets evoking stylistic coherence can be readily generated, they do not actually represent consistent spatial configurations. These images effectively convey atmospheric intentions; however, even with intensive prompting and human curation, achieving solutions that authentically reflect designer intentions while satisfying spatial and functional requirements proves challenging.

Initial architectural applications of LLMS encountered comparable limitations. While model outputs frequently appeared valid and likely benefited from exposure to architectural texts within training datasets, results lacked reliability. These models' tendency toward hallucination and limited knowledge bases for specialized queries resulted in erroneous outputs and incorrect assumptions.

Progressing beyond initial experimentation, certain architects adopted techniques to mitigate described limitations. Ongoing research into text-to-image models has produced various methodologies to enhance visual output guidance, with researchers developing novel model architectures that substantially improved prompt conformity for image generation, exemplified by ControlNet for image-to-image guidance and rectified flow models for enhanced prompt adherence.[2]

---

2   Zhang Lvmin et al., "Adding Conditional Control to Text-to-Image Diffusion Models," *arXiv*, last modified November 26, 2023, https://arxiv.org/pdf/2302.05543; Patrick Esser et al., "Scaling Rectified Flow Transformers for High-Resolution Image Synthesis," in

Methodologies employing image-guided generation have demonstrated particular utility for architectural applications. By utilizing guidance images extracted from 3D models, spatial conformity can be significantly enhanced, with image generation informed by architect-designed massings or interior spaces that comply with established spatial and functional requirements and constraints.

This approach potentially positions guided text-to-image models between conceptual imagery and definitive visualization, where outputs are informed by established parameters while retaining generative randomness that can inform subsequent design refinement processes. Alternative approaches to directing text-to-image models toward specific outputs include fine-tuning techniques. Methods such as low-resolution adaptation—involving training small parallel neural networks—enable substantial influence on style using limited image sets with similar characteristics and minimal computational resources.[3]

Various fine-tuning methodologies applicable to larger datasets can enhance text-to-image models to conform with specific styles or improve architectural imagery generally through training on comprehensive architectural image collections.

Similar guidance potential exists for LLMs, with substantial research concerning content generation and knowledge retrieval through LLMs for specialized domains. These include low-resolution adaptation and more straightforward implementation methodologies that eliminate model training requirements, such as retrieval-augmented generation—which identifies relevant text segments from provided natural language data and incorporates this information within the language model's context window.[4]

As generative DL research organizations have expanded into substantial commercial entities with continued massive investment streams, more general generative models with architectural adjacency have emerged, including

Forty-first International Conference on Machine Learning (2024), https://arxiv.org/abs/2403.03206.

3   Pareesa Ameneh Golnari, "LoRA-Enhanced Distillation on Guided Diffusion Models," *arXiv*, December 12, 2023, https://arxiv.org/pdf/2312.06899.

4   Edward J. Hu et al., "LoRA: Low-Rank Adaptation of Large Language Models," *arXiv*, last modified October 16, 2021, https://arxiv.org/abs/2106.09685; Gao Yunfan et al., "Retrieval-Augmented Generation for Large Language Models: A Survey," *arXiv*, last modified March 27, 2024, https://arxiv.org/pdf/2312.10997.

text-to-video and text-to-3D systems that have attracted architectural experimentation.

Fig. 37: Zaha Hadid Architects, Image generation based on stylistic finetuning

Text-to-video models attract interest through their capacity to generate temporally and spatially consistent outputs, enabling flythrough videos that describe coherent spatial arrangements suitable for digital 3D reconstruction or direct utilization as conceptual visualization.

While architectural interest in text-to-3D models appears more immediately apparent, contemporary state-of-the-art systems predominantly reflect training on extensive video game asset datasets, with architectural outputs primarily applicable to conceptualization, optioneering, and visualization rather than actual production processes.[5] This contrasts with domains such as game design or visual effects, where digital 3D models constitute final products without physical translation requirements—allowing generated textured meshes to integrate directly into the design pipelines.

These DL model types theoretically support similar fine-tuning and control methodologies as text-to-image systems; however, architectural applications have demonstrated comparatively limited implementation or success—potentially due to challenges in acquiring sufficient architectural video or 3D model datasets, or technical complexities in successfully fine-tuning models competitive with emerging general generative systems.

Limitations

All previously described techniques were not originally designed or specifically trained for architectural applications; however, as in numerous industries, specification and enhanced guidance toward visual outputs or specific concepts and topics are crucial for practical utility.

The essential limitation of current models resides in their generic nature, which inherently introduces randomness and hallucination tendencies—producing outcomes that deviate from specific requirements given by the user. Numerous startups focus on addressing these limitations by offering tailored solutions and specialized interfaces, primarily integrations based on foundational research and guidance models from DL research laboratories.

---

5   Ren Xuanchi et al., "XCube: Large-Scale 3D Generative Modeling using Sparse Voxel Hierarchies," *Nvidia*, 2024, https://research.nvidia.com/labs/toronto-ai/xcube/; Zibo Zhao et al. "Hunyuan3D 2.0: Scaling Diffusion Models for High Resolution Textured 3D Assets Generation," *arXiv*, January 21, 2025, https://arxiv.org/abs/2501.12202.

While this approach represents a promising direction likely to integrate increasingly into architectural workflows, general generative base models from the AI industry continue to advance rapidly. This creates the potential for general models to surpass specialized solutions in capability. While industry-specific integrations and user interfaces provide substantial value, the trend from open-source toward closed-source models may increasingly challenge these projects in maintaining competitive capabilities without backend integration of general solutions, particularly as major technology corporations increasingly capture revenue through usage-based pricing models.

Beyond individual architectural experimentation with generative models, software companies providing CAD and 3D modeling solutions have actively integrated text-to-image, text-to-3D, and similar functionalities, or enhanced search and automation capabilities with deep search and generative methodologies based on LLMs—a trend expected to continue.

In summary, utilizing diffusion and rectified flow models exclusively for visualization and transformer-based LLMs primarily for information retrieval fails to fully leverage the demonstrated capabilities in both domains, and the industry would profit from a more focused research effort in domain-specific topics.

Architecture-specific DL research at fundamental levels exists, including for example topics like floor plan generation through diffusion models[6] or surrogate models for environmental or structural simulations.[7] This research domain merits expansion, as general models appear unlikely to adequately address highly specialized architectural requirements anytime soon.

But substantial potential remains for further integration, particularly regarding LLMs as context-aware agents—either through general-purpose systems or domain-specific training or fine-tuning. This approach could leverage the emergent intelligence of AI systems in ways the architecture–engineering–construction industry and academic research have yet to explore and effectively utilize.

---

6   Amin Shabani Mohammad, Hosseini Sepidehsadat and Furukawa Yasutaka, "House-Diffusion: Vector Floorplan Generation via a Diffusion Model with Discrete and Continuous Denoising," *arXiv*, November 23, 2022, https://arxiv.org/pdf/2211.13287.

7   T. Wortmann, A. Costa, G. Nannicini, and T. Schroepfer, "Advantages of surrogate models for architectural design optimization," *Artificial Intelligence for Engineering Design, Analysis and Manufacturing* 29 (2015): 471–81.

Fig. 38: Zaha Hadid Architects, Image generation controlled by a segmented guidance image

Towards Architectural Intelligence?

The following considerations are predominantly speculative; however, architectural discourse regarding AI-enhanced planning potential appears essential. As automation within the planning industry potentially accelerates—whether beneficially or detrimentally—architects must neither overestimate the technologies' capabilities nor dismiss their possibilities. Developing influential perspectives on tool development could help to ensure benefits extend beyond real estate developers and clients to creative practitioners.

Recent implementations of LLMs as context-aware agents for decision-making and content generation suggest potential integration as planning and design software assistants, comparable to the programming environment's "copilots." Given the impressive capabilities—and substantial market valuation—of code-generating models, numerous tools have emerged embedded directly within integrated development environments as programmer assistants.

With comprehensive project context, language models receive substantial code segments and provide informed development suggestions. While architectural software integration as design, drawing, and modeling copilots offering continuous suggestions and natural language interaction appears conceptually straightforward, implementation presents significant challenges.

Primary obstacles include insufficient structured and labeled datasets and the absence of a unified architectural framework. Each challenge describes different approaches to architectural data utilization for generative DL methods, with distinct problems, limitations, and potentials.

Comparing architectural data to software engineering easily reveals the fundamental disparities. While the Internet provides abundant code for LLM training—a volume incomprehensible to human cognition—architectural data exists under different conditions. Unlike software engineering's structured, collaborative, annotated, and cloud-stored codebases, architectural plans and 3D models lack standardized formats or consistent data structures across projects or practices, with no centralized repository for sharing and potential training utilization.

Despite efforts toward data interoperability and format standardization—particularly through Building Information Modeling (BIM) with Industry Foundation Classes (IFC)—and dataset generation for machine learning research, effective utilization for generative design assistance remains uncertain.

Whether existing architectural data could at all support emergent intelligence comparable to code-generating language models represents an open research question—potentially answerable only by major CAD software developers with access to substantial cloud datasets.

Beyond challenges in data collection lies the absence of a unified computational framework capturing essential design information. Current project data files often omit critical contextual knowledge that humans implicitly incorporate. While BIMs provide extensive detail on the elements and geometry of a building, they frequently lack more fundamental information for informed decision-making, including basic things such as interior–exterior differentiation, spatial connectivity, area utilization metrics, or environmental factors.

Generative models would consequently lack crucial context information for intelligent design progression—information architects typically acquire through site research, constant visual interpretation during the design, and drawing from their education-based intuition. Even assuming inherent emergent architectural intelligence, DL models would require comprehensive contextual data access for informed generation and decision-making and therefore frameworks providing this as partial snapshots for effectively guided generation.

This approach could demonstrate particular value for complex or large-scale design decisions, often found in urban planning or complex public buildings, where requirement, regulation, and constraint volumes challenge even human cognitive capacity.

The idea and proposal of a unified framework concept aligns partly with a recent research strain in computational architecture utilizing gamified systems.[8] Architectural configurator games are constantly tracking key information such as spatial layout and connectivity, area sizes, simplified environmental considerations, and basic structural calculations. These projects can be seen as representing simplified approaches to such frameworks, potentially serving as experimental platforms for testing generative or agent-based approaches.

Well-thought-out, comprehensive, and structured frameworks for architectural data, ideally complemented with standardized formats, could be a big

---

8   José Luis Sánchez. "Block'hood—Developing an Architectural Simulation Video Game," eCAADe 33 (2015): 89–97; A. Peacock, "Zaha Hadid Architects creates parametric London for Fortnite game," Dezeen, September 23, 2024, https://www.dezeen.com/2024/0 9/23/parametric-london-zaha-hadid-architects-fornite/.

step towards establishing extendable and common foundations for automation-focused architectural research.

Fig. 39: Zaha Hadid Architects, Gamification as design exploration

Final Thoughts

As Generative AI continues its rapid evolution, architectural DL applications in the end may manifest differently than anticipated in this article. But given potential impacts on core architectural competencies, the discipline should actively participate in technological development alongside data and computer scientists.

While this text has assumed progression toward increased automation and co-piloting systems, this trajectory is neither inevitable nor likely to manifest in the immediate future.

Nevertheless, the profession's engagement with these technologies seems crucial, particularly considering global urbanization trends and migration patterns necessitating substantial built environment expansion. Research into automation tools that could enhance qualitative mass production of buildings and urban quarters warrants serious consideration.

Generative DL presents significant opportunities for architectural research, requiring a technically grounded exploration. Ideally, a robust academic research community will investigate these possibilities in collaboration with data scientists, engineers, and programmers—similar to developments following parametric modeling tools' emergence. Establishing an independent architectural research ecosystem with common frameworks is essential for maintaining both academic rigor and professional autonomy from computer-aided design (CAD) software developers and full-fledged AI corporations.

Despite the delayed engagement of the profession on a more foundational level with these technologies, meaningful participation remains possible and undoubtedly necessary—also to ensure a future implementation that ultimately benefits the occupants of buildings and urban environments and not only their financiers.

D: Teaching in times of AI

The Power of Interpretation: A Reflection on the Application of Parametric Programs and Artificial Intelligence (AI) in Teaching

Giulio Bettini, Ron Edelaar

How does architecture relate to technology?

Architecture is conservative. On the one hand, it follows a deliberate, slow, and traditional development process. This is directly related to the fact that construction itself and the durability of a building are long-term. On the other hand, the economic investments and risks are high in relation to the resulting returns—there is a certain caution and a need for the tried and tested. Other influences in architecture are the conventions of utilization[1] and the nostalgic view that architects have of their world. We look to old models and use references from examples built in the past.

Perhaps because the profession has existed for thousands of years, architects are very conscious of tradition. The tried and tested is good. We can only combine things in new ways. Experimentation is the exception rather than the rule.

To a certain extent, the circumstances of this profession shape the structure of thinking. Innovations or even technical revolutions are observed and followed with interest. However, they are not widely applied until years or decades later. For example, while the first CAD systems were developed in the mechanical engineering industry at the end of the 1950s, with the first applications appearing in the 1960s and a breakthrough in the 1980s, CAD

---

1   In housing, for example, the convention is still based on the petit bourgeois family apartment, which was common in the middle of the twentieth century. It is used in scaled variations for single and couple households (They make up around sixty percent of all Swiss households), although the forms of housing are very different.

programs were not widely used in architectural offices until the end of the 1990s.

Fig. 40: Ismaili Abdolrauf/imagine: turn the forest into a cinema crowd, projector light shines through, 2024. Generated with Midjourney.

It is therefore not surprising that architects in general have long been critical of the potential of new technologies. This is currently the case with parametric software and AI. In the Fall 2023 semester, we approached both technologies with students on the Constructive Design master's course as part of a classic design task. In this text, we take a closer look at the AI tools used during the semester.[2]

The value of playing, not learning

The profession of architect is multifaceted, complex, and deeply rooted in its culture. Put simply, it consists of technical and creative requirements. The technical aspect can easily be supported by digital development. Tools such as spreadsheets, CAD, etc. are now widely available. ChatGPT supports architects in their daily work by searching and understanding standards and laws or summarizing the content of meetings. AI-based applications will find their way here, making the profession easier, but not changing it significantly.

In relation to the creative part of our work, the approach and handling of digitalization is somewhat more complex. First, we need to have a rudimentary understanding of where creativity comes from. We need to look at our own perception and thought processes and start with the neurological characteristics of humans. With neuroscientist Prof. Dr. Dario Cazzoli from the University of Lucerne and the artist and architect Nicolas Feldmeyer from London, we ventured to compare so-called AI with human intelligence at the beginning of the semester. According to Cazzoli, there are obviously many differences. Perhaps the most important insight was that AI—despite the information base developed exclusively by humans—will never be able to understand the world in an anthropocentric way: data are processed as objective and not as related to human behavior. Although AI has the task of understanding human needs, it will not act within the human self-image, but will always respond to human perception from "outside." A reciprocal behavior would have to develop between humans and machines, similar to a symbiosis. In connection with his own understanding of creativity, Feldmeyer quotes the French poet and philosopher

---

2   In the context of parametric applications and their programming, we would like to make just one brief comment: the architect Steffen Lemmerzahl showed us in an exercise at the beginning of the semester that parametric programming with Grasshopper can simplify intellectual and drawing steps. In addition, there are now ways to make the manual part of the design process (floor plan design) much easier with the help of parametric controllers. This development is amazingly powerful and extremely quick to use—if you are prepared to have a certain affinity with programming.

Paul Valéry: "To see is to forget the name of what is seen." This implies that creativity can only come from an unbiased view of the world. Creativity is therefore closely linked to naivety.

Naivety is often successful in our profession, leading us to new, solution-oriented ideas rather than fear- or fulfilment-based ones. Chatbots or image generators are not interested in intellectual or emotional exchange. This makes the exchange one-sided and seemingly pointless for the design process. It is therefore primarily good for a kind of game. The most important difference between human thinking and AI at the moment (and for the foreseeable future) is that humans, as children, learn by playing, by experiencing, without having to learn. AI knowledge, on the other hand, is based on the clear learning task of acquiring as much information as possible.

As Marie-José Kolly observes: "From an evolutionary point of view, children are made to play. Playing means doing something with the environment and seeing how it reacts. Getting to know the world without a goal. Without wanting to learn." By contrast, "the machine lacks experience and therefore the knowledge gained from it. It lacks the context of world knowledge to be able to generalize what it has learnt more easily and more widely."[3]

With this in mind, we also learned from our students that chatbots and image generators are extremely knowledgeable, but can only help to a limited extent in finding and reflecting on ideas, narratives, and strategies for design. The exchange between colleagues is much more fruitful.

Interpretation and analogy

What can "intelligence" mean in the context of architectural design? As noted above, the term is closely linked to specific human characteristics and is difficult to define objectively, especially in the context of the creative activity of design. Dealing with the initial situation of a project can be seen as a fundamental process of contemporary design: location, program, framework conditions, and desires collide and must be synthesized by the architect in a project. Order is created through an (often personal) interpretation of these issues. Interpretation can therefore be understood as a form of intelligence. This process is profoundly human and therefore ambiguous: no theory of interpretation survives

---

3   Marie-José Kolly, "Der Wert des Spielens, des Nicht-Lernens," *Republik*, April 11, 2023. Authors' translation.

when it is enforced in a clearly defined discipline. The inescapable relationship between architecture and reality requires design interpretation to engage with real objects (utilitarian objects, architectures, landscapes)—and this is usually done visually. The image of reality therefore plays a central role, for example in the form of drawings, photographs, collages, or renderings. These means establish a relationship between what is depicted and what exists in reality (or its potential to take on such forms). What is defined in photography as a "trace of the real"[4] forms the basis of design interpretation and is therefore an essential part of architectural "intelligence." AI recognizes images merely as data sets, without understanding the connection to the objects depicted. Its results may seem "real," but they are not. In the words of artist Charlie Engman:

> AI is not intelligence. It does probability calculations. It doesn't understand what a horse is. It can only make inferences about what a horse might be. That's why AI images have these qualities of body horror ... For this reason, the creative process of producing images with AI is more a form of curation than photography.[5]

The question arises: Could these "cracks" in the representation provide new starting points for design interpretation, rather than the depicted, non-realistic images themselves? Engman describes the phenomenon as an "uncanny valley effect"—a gap in acceptance because some elements are correct, while others appear in the wrong context (for us humans).

Beyond the image, AI is already being used to simulate design processes. However, these only seem to parameterize certain aspects of the process and do not (yet) reproduce the creation of designs from scratch. One reason for this is the human way of generating ideas that motivate design. One such process is analogue thinking.

An example of an AI-generated image created with the prompt "Imagine a hotel in Zermatt" illustrates this. Images associated with Zermatt often show sloping roofs and patterns of mountain chalets. So, the AI-generated image will contain these elements in unexpected combinations. Humans, however,

---

4   Philippe Dubois, "Die Fotografie als Spur eines Wirklichen" [1990], in *Texte zur Theorie der Fotografie*, ed. Bernd Stiegler (Reclam, 2010).

5   Adrian Kreye, "Gerade die Fehler sind schön," *Das Magazin*, no. 15 (2023): 20–27. Authors' translation.

work differently: without an immediately recognizable logic, they make personal connections. For example, a human might associate a design for a hotel in Zermatt with the "thin air" of the mountain village: the hotel could emanate a certain lightness through a reflective metal structure. The association could also be more figurative. The Matterhorn near Zermatt is notoriously difficult to climb; the hotel could thus be made up of small units connected at the corners, similar to a rope team of climbers. These striking examples could not be generated (without a data set of a previous human experience) by AI, and demonstrate that it is questionable whether (and how) AI can not only simulate the analogue thinking of individuals, but actually generate it. The psychologist Carl Gustav Jung described analogical thinking as "inexpressible in words,"[6] and the Italian philosopher Giorgio Agamben gets to the heart of the phenomenon when he writes: "In contrast to the classical alternative 'either A or B,' which excludes the third, analogy always asserts the third, its stubborn 'neither A nor B.'"[7] Oswald Mathias Ungers illustrates this in architecture:

> When Le Corbusier compared the building to a machine, he saw an analogy where no one had seen one before. When Aalto compared the design of his organically shaped vases with the Finnish landscape, or his design for a theatre in Germany with a tree stump, he did the same ... The analogy establishes a similarity, or the existence of some similar principles, between two events that are otherwise completely different ... In using the method of analogy, it should be possible to develop new concepts and discover new relationships.[8]

These observations highlight the challenges that AI still faces when it comes to replicating architectural design. It will not be enough to implement these processes in a deep learning model, as design processes are known to be fluid and change over time—a particularly human characteristic.

---

6   "Logical thinking is thinking expressed in words that is directed outwards as discourse. Analogue or imaginative thinking is sensitive, figurative, and silent; it is not a discourse but a regurgitation of material from the past, an inwardly directed act. Logical thinking is thinking in words. Analogical thinking is archaic, unconscious, unspoken, and basically inexpressible through words." Carl Gustav Jung, letter to Sigmund Freud, in Vittorio Savi, *L'architettura di Aldo Rossi* (Franco Angeli, 1976), 112. Authors' translation.

7   Giorgio Agamben, *Signatura rerum. Sul metodo* (Bollati Boringhieri, 2008), 21; Valter Scelsi, *Osservazioni su architettura e analogia* (quodlibet Studio, 2022), 30. Authors' translation.

8   Oswald Mathias Ungers, *Morphologie: City Metaphors* (Walther König, 1982), 12.

Fig. 41: Charlie Flotho /imagine: abstract and hand-crafted architectural scale model of a BIG HOUSE, flying basketball yards, a public shower, and a hidden theater, black background, 2024. Generated with Midjourney

Generica and curation

Chatbots and image generators get their information exclusively from the web. They therefore have direct access to an unimaginable amount of existing, non-curated data. These programs are able to organize, filter, and categorize this knowledge in a very short time. The result is an answer to a question that is highly likely to be the right one. Answers from today's AI are therefore always "compliant" and never bold or daring. This programmed characteristic is ideal for scientific purposes, for example. By "calculating" answers from probabilities (with negligible variations) that always come from the same pool, they create a limited, controlled reality. As Joseph Weizenbaum pointed out in the 1970s: "There is a danger of reducing reality to those aspects that can be processed by computers."[9]

Generic answers are not helpful to a creative activity because they do not produce "ideas." For example, if we look at oral histories, they never claim to be an exact account of what happened. They are retold and adapted according to each teller's view of the world. In the process, the stories are "polished," losing more and more of their temporality and gaining general meaning and relevance. In contrast to "static" information science, this state is dynamic. A dynamic always creates an imbalance.

So, progress is born of an imbalance, a dream, a hunch, a need. We call this an "idea." The realized idea always continues to write our cultural history. In the assignment for the semester, we wrote:

> An idea often overlaps various familiar or common themes. Looking at this overlap is crucial! What may at first seem like a mistake or something useless has potential. The important thing is not to shy away from these discoveries or simply dismiss them as mistakes, but to be brave and go down this road.

Image generators such as Midjourney also produce such "overlays"—as described above—when sufficiently contradictory or surreal conditions are formulated in an assignment. When asked by a student to visualize proposals for "a school complex in Zurich used as a community center with a gym as a theater," the image generator responded with a series of images with collage-like overlapping typologies. It seemed as if the AI was desperately trying to create a convention out of the brief. Reflecting on this collage in the studio was more productive for further design than the generated proposal. It is quite possible to create surprising images with AI. In contrast to the search for architectural references, the generated images function more metaphorically. However, the metaphor itself is part of the playfully learning human.

---

9   Joseph Weizenbaum, *Computer Power and Human Reason: From Judgment to Calculation* (W. H. Freeman and Co., 1976).

AI Architecture Studio Without Architects

Immanuel Koh

Then: Paperless Studios

The "paperless" studios of the mid-1990s stood out as a revolutionary experiment in the annals of architecture pedagogy, and their impact has remained exemplary in both academia and practice today. Initiated by Bernard Tschumi during his deanship at Columbia University's Graduate School of Architecture, Planning and Preservation (GSAPP), the studios were taught by a team of then-young faculty who are now world-renowned architects, such as Greg Lynn, Hani Rashid, Jesse Reiser, Stan Allen, Alejandro Zaera-Polo, and Ben van Berkel. In fact, Lynn curated the 2013 exhibition "Archaeology of the Digital,"[1] held at Montréal Canadian Center for Architecture (CCA) and organized a two-week summer seminar called "Toolkit for Today" with lectures by Tschumi, Allen, and Rashid, retelling the history of the paperless studios. In Tschumi's account, the story of the paperless studios was not simply the inclusion of computers in the studios, but more fundamentally, preceded by a deliberate shift in pedagogical vision, change in curriculum structure, sourcing of a large sum of funding (USD$1.5 million), and renovation of existing studio spaces at the university to accommodate the newly purchased computing infrastructure. In Allen's account, the interest in the computer was first and foremost intellectual, rather than practical, and was preceded by the theoretical transition from Derrida's deconstruction to Deleuze's difference which, in turn, was also a formal transition from the language of rupture to that of continuity. The paperless studio served predominantly to accelerate the pace of manifesting "the language and the operations ... theorized before the actual

---

1   Greg Lynn, *Archaeology of the Digital* (Sternberg Press, 2013).

use of the computer."[2] It was not so much about the general use of computers for architectural designs, as was the case for most architecture schools that had introduced computers prior to the paperless studio at GSAPP such as at MIT or the AA, but very much about the specific use of computers for an a priori set of philosophically driven and materially visualized concepts to generate a new architectural language. For example, Lynn's 1992 model of the Stranded Sears Tower was made of cut and twisted foam, expressing his philosophical concept of the supple with material suppleness prior to the use of computers.

In this light, it is thus not surprising that the studios were called neither "digital studios" nor "computer studios," but "paperless studios"—a negation of what went before (i.e., "paper") rather than a proposition of what was to come. Strictly speaking, "paperless" need not mean digital, nor even the computer. The "−less" in "paperless" should therefore be understood as a conceptual provocation rather than a literal pronouncement. In fact, Tschumi himself confessed that the use of paper in the studio projects did not end with the introduction of the computers but instead continued to support the digital exploration in parallel. In his text, "Building with Geometry, Drawing with Numbers,"[3] when comparing the text–geometry approach of Vitruvius/Alberti before the age of printing and the drawings–measurements approach of Palladio/Vignola thereafter, Mario Carpo was in a way recasting the paperless studio as one characterized more by a shift in notation (e.g., spline modelling or animation keyframing). It is a shift in architectural language corroborated by new notational systems resulting in a new conception of architecture. Although Carpo has insisted that there will not be an AI-driven "third digital turn,"[4] this might turn out to be premature. Increasingly, it seems inevitable that there could indeed be a "third digital turn" propelled by today's rapid development and widespread infiltration of AI technology such as ChatGPT and Stable Diffusion. The notation is however different this time round, and its manifestation not necessarily straightforwardly oppositional as seen in the first two turns; namely, the "continuity" of the first digital turn and the "discreteness" of

---

2   Stan Allen, "The Paperless Studios in Context," in *When is the Digital in Architecture?* ed. Andrew Goodhouse (Sternberg Press, 2017), 390.

3   Mario Carpo, "Building with Geometry, Drawing with Numbers", in *When is the Digital in Architecture?* ed. Goodhouse, 35–44.

4   Mario Carpo, *Beyond Digital: Design and Automation at the End of Modernity* (MIT Press, 2023).

the second. In fact, for the very first time in the history of architecture, there may no longer be a need for any notation, whether it is notation as architectural drawings or programming codes. More concretely speaking, "natural language is all you need,"[5] and text-prompting is now the dominant "AI notation." A decade ago in his 2015 book, professor of computer science Pedro Domingos proposed the idea of a "master algorithm"—the ultimate machine-learning algorithm capable of solving all tasks.[6] And, as early as 2017, computer scientist Andrej Karpathy (now director of AI at Tesla) wrote about a paradigm shift in software development with the emergence of deep neural networks from Software 1.0 to Software 2.0.[7] The former refers to software traditionally written in programming languages that explicitly specify human-understandable instructions/algorithms to the computer. The latter instead refers to software written in the form of the weights of a neural network which learns an "algorithm" from its training dataset. As he puts it, "Software (1.0) is eating the world, and now AI (Software 2.0) is eating software."[8] AI is the master algorithm. In early 2024, Jensen Huang, CEO of NVIVDIA, even went as far as to say "don't learn to code" when asked what kids should learn in the age of generative AI. Might a "codeless studio" be indeed the "paperless studio" of the near future in architecture?

Now: Codeless Studios

There are a few important lessons to be learnt from the paperless studio of the 1990s as one begins to formulate a possible form of a codeless studio in the age of AI. First, the "–less" in "codeless" is to be understood in a similar manner whereby coding will not in effect end with the introduction of large language models (LLMs) like ChatGPT, but instead continue to support the AI exploration in parallel. Therefore, current computational design skills in visual programming (e.g., Grasshopper 3D) and text-based programming

5   Here, alluding to the title of the landmark AI research paper. *Ashish Vaswani et al.*, "Attention Is All You Need," in *Advances in Neural Information Processing Systems*, vol. 30, ed. I. Guyon et al. (NIPS, 2017).

6   Pedro Domingos, *The Master Algorithm: How the Quest for the Ultimate Learning Machine Will Remake Our World* (Basic Books, 2015).

7   Andrej Karpathy, "Software 2.0," *Medium* (blog), November 12, 2017, https://karpathy.medium.com/software-2-0-a64152b37c35.

8   Karpathy, "Software 2.0."

(e.g., Python) will serve to support the AI exploration at the codeless studios, especially when integrating AI models with existing CAAD tools and creating specific AI models for the architecture discipline. Second, just like how setting up the paperless studio had incurred significant expenditure on software (e.g., Softimage at USD$9,000) and hardware (e.g., Silicon Graphics IRIS Indigo Extreme R4400 machine at USD$25,000),[9] the codeless studio will need substantial funding for either paid subscriptions in accessing frontier closed-source AI models (e.g., OpenAI's GPT-4o or Midjourney) or purchasing local/cloud GPUs, computers, and data storage (e.g., A100 or AWS) for running open-source AI models (e.g., DeepSeek-R1 or Meta's Llama). Unlike the paperless studio, a codeless studio will also require datasets for training its AI models. Before the current paradigm of pretrained foundation AI models, it was still financially possible to train an AI model from scratch with one's own datasets and workstation. However, today's training cost for models like GPT-4 is in the tens, if not hundreds, of millions.[10] Therefore, the training datasets for the codeless studio will mainly be used for the purposes of fine-tuning such pretrained foundation models or training smaller AI models, in order to adapt or customize the AI models for architecturally specific use cases. Third, it should be noted that the tutors (e.g., Lynn and Rashid) at the first paperless studios in 1994 were mostly non-experts in the technical operations of the computers and had digital assistants (DAs) who were computer-savvy students (e.g., Ed Keller) supporting them. This unusual pedagogical combination turned out to be synergetic in such an experimental studio context. However, unlike the predominantly platform-specific software application tooling the workflow of the paperless studios, AI workflows of the codeless studios can vary greatly in complexity and diversity, ranging from simply using paid online blackbox AI services to implementing one's own AI models. The latter will require a certain level of understanding and expertise in AI. AI models (especially agentic AI) of the codeless studio will also have greater design agency than the animation software of the paperless studio. It would therefore be more strategic to have faculty who are well-versed in AI, not only technically, but even more crucially, theoretically and conceptually, in

9   Endriana Audisho, "Screening Architecture: Architecture, Media, and Conflict since the 1990s" (PhD diss., University of Technology Sydney, 2024), https://opus.lib.uts.edu.au /handle/10453/179447.

10   Ben Cottier et al., "The Rising Costs of Training Frontier AI Models," *arXiv*, last modified February 7, 2025, https://doi.org/10.48550/arXiv.2405.21015.

order to steer studio projects into novel and unknown architectural territories. Instead of DAs, the faculty will ideally be supported by AI student assistants who might not necessarily be from the architecture department. Lastly, to broaden the conception of architecture, Tschumi wanted the paperless studio to borrow notations from other domains such as film and music and combine them with architecture's own axonometric mode. For the codeless studio, it will remain important to encourage relevant conceptual influences from domains outside of architecture. However, such "outside" borrowings will go beyond notations alone to include design briefs that are framed as more generally "architectural" (i.e., not just about making buildings), augmented by new AI processes. In short, coding skills in computational design should still be taught, funding for GPUs and AI-model access should be raised, teaching undertaken by faculty whose works conceptually resonate with the "yet-to-be-defined" language of AI, and AI-augmented concepts and processes should be borrowed from other domains outside architecture. In fact, as evidenced from the impactful career trajectories of the then-faculty and then-students at the paperless studio within academia and practice, the third and last lessons are the most crucial. The codeless studio is about putting in place a pedagogical platform that is theoretically critical, conceptually radical, and technically experimental. Only then could the germination of a new AI x Architecture culture emerge to instigate a third digital turn. In the next section of the text, we will look at how a similar "putting in place" of a codeless studio is beginning to take shape at the Singapore University of Technology and Design (SUTD).

Pedagogical Inversion: An Outside-In Architecture Studio

SUTD has recently announced itself as the world's first Design AI University,[11] with an SGD$50 million investment in AI and design, focusing on "Human–AI interaction." Its vision of AI is to enhance and complement human capabilities through their mutual interactions. At first glance, SUTD might be mistakenly seen as yet another institution riding the current wave of AI hype and doing an AI-washing branding exercise to stay competitive. However, one should

11   Gabrielle Chan, "'Human–AI Interaction' Drives SUTD's $50m Push for New Specialization in Design and AI," *Straits Times*, January 15, 2025, https://www.straitstimes.co m/singapore/human-ai-interaction-drives-sutds-50m-push-for-new-specialisation-i n-design-and-ai.

remember that SUTD was in fact the first university in the world to offer a four-year Bachelor of Science in Design and Artificial intelligence (DAI) degree back in 2020, predating even the late-2022 AI hype triggered by OpenAI's ChatGPT release. In fact, the first cohort of DAI students graduated in May 2024, exactly one and a half years after ChatGPT. In other words, the progression from the world's first Design AI degree to the world's first Design AI university is somewhat natural and convenient for a university of its size where a relatively agile administrative process is an advantage. Just as the paperless studio grew out of a convergence of theory, technology, media, and culture in the 1990s, SUTD's Design AI trajectories also grew out of an AI-First Nation[12] backdrop that consisted of Smart Nation 1.0 (2014), AI Singapore (2017), National AI Strategy (2019), and Smart Nation 2.0 (2024). These government-initiated strategic policies and multi-million-dollar fundings involving industry and academia to prepare an AI-trained competitive future workforce provided a very unique context which eventually propelled SUTD's rapidly focused adoption of AI in its university technology and design curriculum. SUTD's Architecture and Sustainable Design (ASD) degree program is no exception to this university-wide AI pivoting. Being the lead AI faculty jointly appointed at ASD and DAI degree programs, I have been responsible for designing and teaching all existing AI x Architecture courses offered at SUTD, namely, 20.318 Creative Machine Learning (2019–) and 20.224 Artificial & Architectural Intelligence in Design (2020–) at ASD, and 60.006 Spatial Design Studio (2023–) at DAI. Beyond the undergraduate level, through my own research laboratory, Artificial-Architecture, at SUTD, I have also been supervising AI x Architecture theses at both the MArch and PhD levels since 2020. In the following section, to shed light on the emergence of the so-called "codeless studio" at SUTD, the pedagogical structures developed for 60.006 Spatial Design Studio at DAI and the design research work produced at Artificial-Architecture shall be discussed.

A key pedagogical innovation of 60.006 Spatial Design Studio is the inversion of the standard architecture design studios. First, the students are not actually architecture students from ASD, but design and AI students from DAI. Second, there is no single architecture studio project brief enforced by a studio lead, but multiple problem statements that are inherently "architectural" and solicited from diverse industry partners curated by the studio lead (i.e., me). Third, specific AI approaches are not predetermined at the onset and can vary

---

12   Laurence Liew, *AI-First Nation: A Blueprint for Policy Makers and Organisation Leaders* (AI-First Nation, 2024).

greatly from project to project throughout the duration of the studio. Thus, the creative exploration and critical evaluation of the appropriate AI techniques play an important role in the success of each project. Last, the final project outcome is not the design of a building, but the design of an AI prototype addressing existing gaps in architecture's conception and use of AI. In short, the pedagogical inversion here is the generation of a new AI x Architecture discourse from outside-in, rather than inside-out. That is, renewing existing architectural concepts with AI's notations through the production of the "architectural," instead of simply "adding" AI as a tool into the business-as-usual architecture design briefs and studios. In fact, the DAI Spatial Design Studio is designed to be a codeless studio prototype potentially paving the way to a future School of Architecture that must accept a transdisciplinary stance in the age of generative AI, especially when the architecture practice is at risk of de-professionalizing[13] and the discipline losing its intellectual autonomy.[14]

The Brain-Perception Encoding project (or "Waves") at the DAI Spatial Design Studio in Fall 2024 built on the existing research work done at Artificial-Architecture to explore 3D architectural perception with neuroscientific and AI techniques.[15]

---

13   Richard E. Susskind and Daniel Susskind, *The Future of the Professions: How Technology Will Transform the Work of Human Experts* (Oxford University Press, 2022).

14   Patrik Schumacher, "The End of Architecture," *Khōrein: Journal for Architecture and Philosophy* 2, no. 2 (2024): 3–40.

15   Immanuel Koh and Ashley Chen, "Your Memory Palace in the Metaverse with AI," *Proceedings of the AAAI Symposium Series* 1, no. 1 (October 3, 2023): 19–22, https://doi .org/10.1609/aaaiss.v1i1.27469; Elissa Hartanto, "Empirical Insights into Architectural Aesthetics: A Neuroscientific Perspective," in *Accelerated Design—Proceedings of the 29th CAADRIA Conference, Singapore, 20–26 April 2024*, vol. 3, ed. Nicole Gardner et al. (CUMINCAD, 2024), 69–78, https://papers.cumincad.org/cgi-bin/works/paper/caadria 2024_486.

Fig. 42: Immanuel Koh, Brain-Perception Encoding, 2024. Electroencephalogram (EEG) and eye-tracking (ET) signals triggered when observing an architectural model in 3D via VR/AR are computed in parallel to generate a corresponding 3D saliency point cloud, where black-to-grey = high-to-low saliency and transparent = no saliency; A DGCNN AI model is trained to predict (with limited accuracy for now) the likely personal preference and attention distributions of any given unseen 3D CAD models.

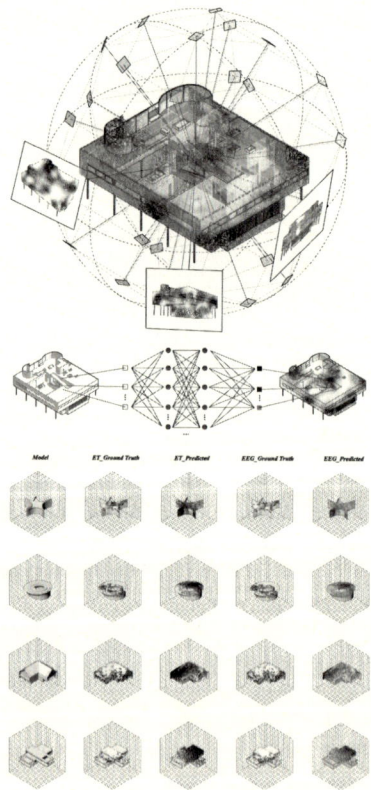

The industry partner was HKS, Inc. which mainly supported the project by providing an initial dataset of 3D CAD models. In light of the increasingly prevalent, yet often conceptually superficial and technically simplistic, use of text-to-image generation models (e.g., Midjourney) among architects and architecture students, the project explores the potential of non-linguistic perceptions and generative designs. Six AI models were trained from scratch on electroencephalogram (EEG) and eye-tracking datasets recorded from human subjects (i.e., architecture and non-architecture students) interacting with 3D CAD architectural models in an AR environment. The trained AI models (specifically, a modified version of the dynamic graph convolutional neural network / DGCNN) were able to predict implicit attention and preference maps in the form of 3D saliency point cloud outputs given any new 3D model inputs. The project critically questions the affordances of today's generic text-to-image generation models while proposing an alternative form of the "non-generic" through the deep learning of brainwave and eye-tracking signals of individuals, thus potentially turning AI perception-predictive models into AI generative models. In short, a brain-to-architecture generation model.

The earliest conception of the ReGen City Design Brain project was seeded at the DAI Spatial Design Studio in Fall 2023 as the ArchitectMind.ai project, and is now a much larger ongoing research project at Artificial-Architecture. The then-industry partners were Autodesk and SAA Architects (a member of the Surbana Jurong Group). The former provided support and access to their Autodesk Forma API for the studio's development of custom add-ons, and the latter supported the project by granting the studio a glimpse of their existing non-AI workflows when conducting feasibility massing studies. The project leveraged LLMs to ingest design development planning guidelines from the online portal of the Urban Redevelopment Authority (URA) and trained a deep reinforcement learning model to generate feasible massing design solutions that ensure compliances such as building setbacks, while optimizing the maximum allowable building height and gross floor area (GFA). This project illustrates how a term-long studio could function as a prototyping platform for a subsequent in-depth lab research project, especially when the brief does not concern the design of a building, but the design of a system.

Fig. 43: Immanuel Koh, ReGen City Design Brain, 2024. An agentic multimodal large language model (MLLMs) prototype that generates 3D design massing models compliant with urban development planning guidelines and other relevant regenerative city design principles, while reasoning its own generative design processes in yielding optimal and explainable solutions.

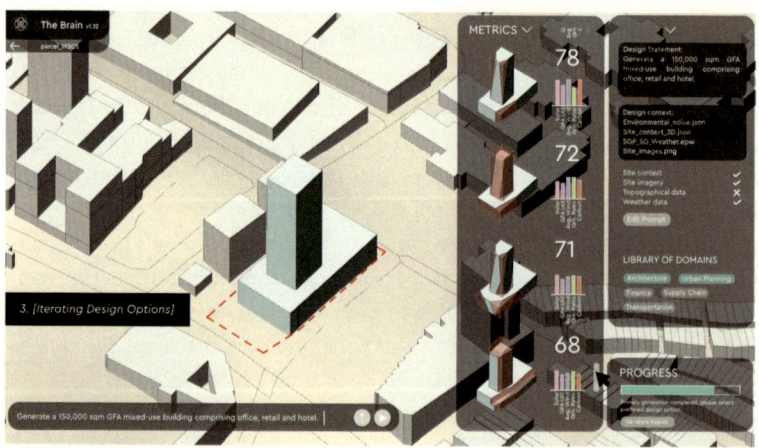

The Curatorial AI Triangulator project was developed with the curators at the Singapore Art Museum (SAM) during Fall 2024 of the DAI Spatial Design Studio to explore ways in which artworks' semantics learnt by AI models could inform curators' own existing techniques of narrative spatialization. SAM's curators often use a linear circulation path embedded with a successive series of artworks' spatial triangulation to unfold an intended narrative/itinerary. In view of this curatorial practice, the project used an LLM to first generate a taxonomy for the artworks that included their physical attributes (e.g., dimensions and viewing distances), conservation requirements (e.g., lighting and humidity guidelines), and formal similarities (e.g., colors, materials, and figurations). The Curatorial AI Triangulator then computes the visual and narrative scores among all triads of artworks in order to construct a spatial network that adaptively adjusts itself with the generative placement of wall partitions, according to the given constraints of a linear path and gallery space. Using the 3D layout of an existing ongoing exhibition, "Everyday Practices,"[16] the iterative outputs of the newly generated layouts were then evaluated as design options.

---

16   "Everyday Practices," Singapore Art Museum, accessed February 10, 2025, https://www .singaporeartmuseum.sg/en/art-events/exhibitions/everyday-practices.

Fig. 44: Immanuel Koh, Curatorial AI Triangulator, 2024. (LEFT) AI-encoding the individual artworks being displayed at the "Everyday Practices" exhibition held at the Singapore Art Museum; (RIGHT) New spatial configuration iteratively generated using LLMs for visual-narrative triangulations within the given gallery space.

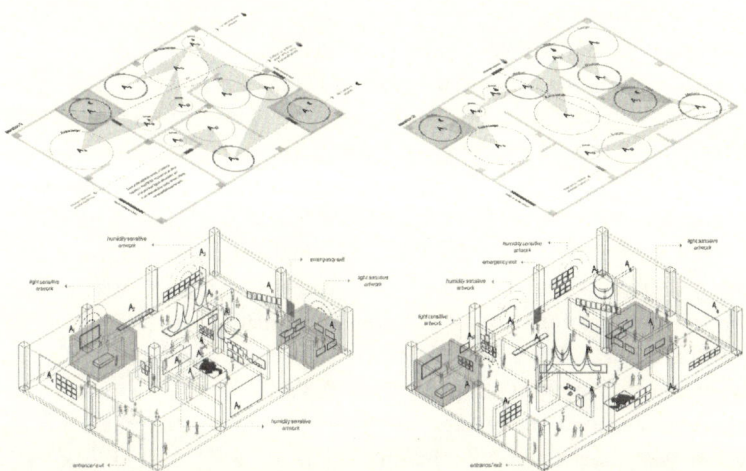

Despite having only conducted the Spatial Design Studio twice thus far (Fall 2023 and Fall 2024), much can already be learnt from the students themselves when evaluating the effects of such pedagogical inversion. In substituting a common architecture design brief with a multitude of vastly different industry-informed "architectural" problem statements, students had first to overcome the immediate unfamiliarity of their chosen spatial domains, alongside the domain-specificity of workflows and tools, before even being able to articulate and then formulate an AI design prototype. It was both a technical and conceptual challenge. However, it was precisely the messiness of such pedagogical reconfiguration that students found not only exhilarating, but also liberating, because none of them had to act like architects in delivering building designs. It was like doing architecture without architects.

Neural Tectonics: An AI-Native Architectural Language

If the success of the paperless studios was measured by the intellectual impact of their faculty in manifesting a new architectural conception, language, or theory, it is only fair to reflect on my own architectural development in the concluding section of the text. Indeed, a new language has emerged alongside a new theory called "neural tectonics." It is a search for an AI-native architectural language for a third digital turn. Similar to how Prensky coined the terms "digital-immigrants" and "digital-natives" to differentiate two generations of human learners—those that were born into the digital age and those born prior[17]—the term "AI-native" of the third digital turn is to signal its difference from the first (digital-immigrants) and second (digital-natives) digital turns. An AI-native language is the language of the codeless studios and Artificial-Architecture. Neural Artefact Black (2023) and Neural Monobloc Black (2024) are perhaps most illustrative of this new language of the artificial. It is not the language of any particular "AI-simulated styles," but that of AI's very own "style of simulating" any styles. Both projects deliberately express the "Janus problem" as a form of AI aesthetics embedded in today's text-to-3D diffusion models. This commonly generated computational glitch refers to the presence of an object's canonical view (typically the front view) in several other non-canonical views (e.g., the side and back views), thus resulting in a 3D-generated object with multiple fronts or faces, much like the two-faced Janus, Roman god of beginnings. This glitch is a direct consequence of the inherent non-3D-aware behavior found in such 3D-generative models. Neural Artefact Black is the world's first built physical public art-bench that is generated directly in 3D with a custom fine-tuned text-to-3D model and fabricated in an artisanal way with 100 percent upcycled wood. Sited in front of the Asian Civilisations Museum and along the historic Singapore River, it formally blends the learnt features from the antique Peranakan wooden furniture collection in the former and the long-disappeared small wooden boats (sampans) on the latter. The Neural Monobloc Black is a series of eight furniture pieces generated and fabricated in a similar way, except that it uses the generic white plastic Monobloc chairs as the learnt features to critique notions of optimized machine production and human consumption. The first project concerns an archival AI-reading of history while the second concerns an AI-critique of everyday design.

---

17   Marc Prensky, "Digital Natives, Digital Immigrants Part 1," *On the Horizon* 9, no. 5 (2001): 1–6, https://doi.org/10.1108/10748120110424816.

Fig. 45: Immanuel Koh, Neural Artefact Black, 2023. Medium: Partially charred teak. Dimensions: 220cm x 108cm x 121cm. The "Janus" effect inherent in current non-3D aware text-to-3D diffusion models can be observed from the formal ambiguity of the bench's "two-faced" seating configuration, which resulted in a two-way bifurcation at the leftmost end of the seat. 1 Express Place, Singapore. Photograph courtesy of Arts House Limited.

While AI researchers would call neural tectonics an undesirable hallucination problem, it is here a creatively desirable AI weirdness[18] and formal subversion. After all, the paperless studios were not using the animation software to make movies, but as a new language to subvert then-existing modes of form-making in architecture. On a pessimistic note, however, when all creative AI hallucinations are resolved, and when all architectural ambiguities cease to exist, the notational space between academic studio experimentation and professional architecture practice might also dissolve, signaling the end of architecture studio culture, even the codeless studios themselves.

---

18   Mark Fisher, *The Weird and the Eerie* (Watkins Media Limited, 2017).

Fig. 46: Immanuel Koh, Neural Monobloc Black, 2024. Medium: Fully charred teak. On exhibition display at the National Design Centre in Singapore. Each of the eight functional chairs was generated with a custom fine-tuned non-3D aware text-to-3D diffusion model. The AI-driven "Janus" effect is even more pronounced here as observed from the multiple doubling/repetition of smoothly synthesized monobloc-like fragments.

Annex

Authors

Oya Atalay Franck is an architect, historian of architecture and urbanism, and a Professor of Architecture. She is the Dean of the School of Architecture, Design, and Civil Engineering at Zurich University of Applied Sciences (ZHAW) in Winterthur, Switzerland. She is a past president and honorary member of the European Association for Architectural Education (EAAE), the network and lobbying body for architecture, design, and urban planning schools in Europe. She holds the Special Recognition Award 2024 from the Association of Collegiate Schools of Architecture (ACSA), the association of architectural schools in the USA and Canada. Atalay Franck has taught architecture and construction, urban design, and architecture theory at Rensselaer Polytechnic Institute (RPI) in Troy, NY, the Swiss Federal Institute of Technology (ETH) in Zurich, and ZHAW. Her research areas include design research methods with a focus on research by design at all scales, design-driven doctoral research in artistic fields, and higher education policymaking. She acts as an expert for various international scientific bodies and funding agencies in the fields of architecture, design, urbanism, planning, and civil engineering. These include, among others, the Swiss National Science Foundation (SNF), the Fundação para a Ciência e a Tecnologia of Portugal (FCT), and the Research Foundation Flanders (FWO) of Belgium. She is a regular member of international peer review committees, scientific conferences, quality assessment audits, and professional competitions. She is dedicated to education, research, and professional practice that promote social responsibility and a high-quality built environment at all scales.

Cem Ataman is a postdoctoral researcher in the Information Systems in the Built Environment (ISBE) group at Eindhoven University of Technology (TU/e) in the Netherlands. He is an architect and a researcher specializing in sustainable cities, AI-based methods, and digital participation processes that support human-centric urban environments. He was awarded his PhD in Architecture and Sustainable Design by the Singapore University of Technology and Design (SUTD), where he was affiliated with the Informed Design Lab. Prior to that, he completed his Bachelor (2016) and Master of Architecture (2018) at Middle East Technical University in Ankara, Turkey, focusing on architectural research methods, alternative housing strategies, performative architecture, and computational design processes. To pursue his doctoral studies, he was awarded the Singapore International Graduate Award (SINGA), which supported his research at the intersection of technology and design. His research interests include urban (big) data, information and knowledge management, computational linguistics, and AI-driven approaches for informed architectural and urban design processes. Throughout his career, he has collaborated with city administrations and government agencies in Germany, Spain, Singapore, and the Netherlands, in addition to leading research institutions including Politecnico di Torino, RWTH Aachen, TU Delft, and École Polytechnique Fédérale de Lausanne (EPFL). His work explores collaborative and co-creative processes among architects, urban researchers, city makers, and communities, aiming to design inclusive, sustainable, and digitally-oriented urban systems.

Giulio Bettini is a Swiss architect who leads the Zurich-based office PENZIS-BETTINI. Architekten together with Daniel Penzis. Their architectural practice focuses on public buildings and spatial potentials of structures. Their experience has been synthetized in the book *Typostruktur* (Park Books, 2025). After studying at ETH Zurich, he worked in Milan, Lisbon, and Zurich. He won the BSA fellowship in 2014 and published the book *La città animata. Milano und die Architektur von Asnago Vender* (gta Verlag, 2016). Bettini has written articles for different magazines, including *Werk, Bauen+Wohnen, Hochparterre,* and *Archi.* He taught as an assistant of Professor Martin Boesch at the Accademia di architettura di Mendrisio, and has taught at the ZHAW Institute of Constructive Design since 2021.

Roberto Bottazzi is an architect, researcher, and educator based in London. He studied in Italy and Canada before moving to London. He is currently Programme Director of the Masters in Urban Design at the Bartlett School of Architecture, University College London (UCL). He is the author of *Digital Architecture beyond Computers: Fragments of a Cultural History of Computational Design* (Bloomsbury, 2018) and co-editor of *Walking Cities: London* (Camberwell Press, 2017). Bottazzi's research analyzes the impact of computational technologies on architecture and urbanism, and has been exhibited internationally at venues including the Centre Pompidou, Venice Architecture Biennale, FACT Liverpool, and Future Places Porto.

Mario Carpo is the Reyner Banham Professor of Architectural Theory and History at the Bartlett School of Architecture, UCL. He was a Guggenheim Fellow in 2022–23, Vincent Scully Visiting Professor of Architectural History at the Yale School of Architecture from 2010 to 2014, Head of the Study Centre at the Canadian Centre for Architecture in Montréal from 2002 to 2006, Resident at the American Academy in Rome in 2004, and Senior Scholar in Residence at the Getty Research Institute from 2000 to 2001, among others. Carpo's research and publications focus on the history of early modern architecture and on the theory and criticism of contemporary design and technology. His award-winning *Architecture in the Age of Printing* (MIT Press, 2001) has been translated into several languages. His most recent books are *The Alphabet and the Algorithm* (2011), *The Second Digital Turn: Design Beyond Intelligence* (2017), and *Beyond Digital: Design and Automation at the End of Modernity* (2023), all published by MIT Press.

Ron Edelaar is a Swiss architect whose career has been marked by a search for experimental practice and teaching. After training as an architectural draughtsman, he studied at the Kunstgewerbeschule Zurich from 1997 to 1999. After working as a carpenter and graphic designer, he studied architecture as a visiting student at ETH Zurich from 2001 to 2003. He then worked for a short time with Peter Märkli and Bétrix Consolascio. Since 2004, he has run the Zurich-based architecture studio Edelaar Mosayebi Inderbitzin together with Elli Mosayebi and Christian Inderbitzin (EMI). Having won numerous competitions, housing and urban development have a special place in their work. After a short teaching assignment at the ZHAW Institute of Constructive Design in 2010, he headed the "Ruins and Machines" design studio at ETH Zurich together with Elli Mosayebi and Christian Inderbitzin in 2017. He has taught at the ZHAW Institute of Constructive Design since 2020. Housing and its current changes are an essential part of his practice and teaching.

EMI Architects has won several awards and prizes, including the Swiss Art Award for Anthropomorphic Form in 2019, the Prix Lignum 2024 for the school building Chliriet, and Die Besten 'Gold' for the Performative House in Zurich. In 2023, the Japanese magazine a+u dedicated an issue to their work. Ron Edelaar is co-editor of several publications such as Performanz (Park Books 2025), Signau Haus und Garten (Park Books 2019) and Garten (Park Books 2017).

Lidia Gasperoni is associate professor, co-director of design, and member of the Just Environments Cluster at the Bartlett School of Architecture, UCL. She is a philosopher and architectural theorist specializing in the transformative function of architectural theory, practice, and pedagogy. Before her role at The Bartlett, she was a postdoctoral researcher and lecturer in the Department of Architectural Theory at TU Berlin between 2018 and 2024. Her publications include *Versinnlichung* (De Gruyter, 2016), *Media Agency*, with Christophe Barlieb (Transcript, 2020), *Construction and Design Manual: Experimental Diagrams in Architecture* (DOM publishers, 2022), and *Epistemic Artefacts: A Dialogical Reflection on Design Research in Architecture*, with Matthias Ballestrem (AADR, 2023).

Elena Gavagnin is an Italian–Swiss researcher and lecturer specializing in AI, data science, and computational astrophysics. She holds a PhD in Computational Sciences from the University of Zurich, with a focus on numerical astrophysics and hydrodynamical simulations, following degrees in Physics and Astrophysics from the University of Bologna. She is currently co-head of the Information Systems and Technologies Group and a senior lecturer at the Institute of Business Information Technology, both at ZHAW. Previously, she worked as a data scientist at Swiss International Air Lines and a postdoctoral researcher at the University of Zurich. Since 2023, she has also been an Associate Fellow at the ZHAW Centre for Artificial Intelligence. Her research focuses on machine learning, computer vision, and natural language processing, with particular emphasis on multimodal AI and human–machine interaction. She has secured funding for projects ranging from generative deep learning for astronomical data to the development of intelligent systems for assistive technologies. Her work has been published in peer-reviewed journals and presented at international conferences, covering topics from astrophysical simulations to AI-driven human–computer interaction. She actively contributes to scientific advisory roles, serving on the SRCNet Advisory Committee for the Square Kilometre Array Observatory and as a board member of SKACH.

Christoph Geiger is a researcher for Computation & Design at Zaha Hadid Architects. Having studied in Stuttgart, Istanbul, and Tokyo, he joined the firm in 2022 as part of the CODE and Analytics and Insights (ZH A+I) team.

His work there focuses on data-driven design and procedural and generative methods. He is responsible for developing and maintaining a computational framework for evaluating and comparing spatial layouts and he has contributed to a variety of projects by providing consultation to design teams, delivering additional insights for optioneering, and creating buildings and interior layouts with computationally-optimized performance. Additionally, he is involved in developing concepts for data-driven building environments. In addition to his expertise in spatial analytics and the collection and maintenance of large, structured datasets, Geiger's research interests extend to generative deep learning for architectural design. Recently, he has focused on building workflows and customizing tools and integrations to effectively utilize AI, particularly text-to-image systems and large language models, as an emerging technology within architectural practice. Geiger also teaches technology modules at the B-Pro program at UCL, where he collaborates with students to explore building and training deep learning models for applied design purposes.

Andri Gerber is an architect and co-head of the Institute of Constructive Design at ZHAW in Winterthur. He studied architecture at ETH Zurich and worked for Peter Eisenman in New York. He holds a PhD (awarded with an ETH medal) and a habilitation (founded by an SNF Ambizione grant) from ETH. His recent interests revolve around the potential of analogue and digital games to address and convey architectural and urban subjects connected to sustainability. He is the author of several games, such as *Dichtestress* (a game on the COVID-19 Pandemic and the perceived density of urban environments), *Where am I* (a game for Ukrainian Refugees in Zurich), and the tabletop *Re-Use Game* (with Michelle Schneider). He is currently designing a computer simulation game on sustainable construction—*Net Zero*—and a game for training spatial abilities (with Ulrich Götz). He is also the co-editor, alongside Ulrich Götz, of *The Architectonics of Game Spaces* (transcript, 2019). He recently finished work on an SNF-founded project on leftist architects in Milan (1960–1990) and is currently working on an SNF-founded project on the history of ecological architecture in Switzerland.

Adam Kiryk is a Swiss-based architect and researcher specializing in the intersection of architecture, art, and emerging technologies. His work explores extended reality and AI-driven design, integrating 3D scanning and 3D printing into contemporary architectural and artistic practices. Alongside his architectural background, he has contributed to art exhibitions, providing technical solutions and visual content for the art industry. As an educator, he has taught immersive technologies at ETH Zurich, prior to which he studied architecture in Warsaw (TU Warsaw, Bachelor's), Tampere (TU Tampere), and Zurich (ETH Zurich, Master's). From 2017 to 2025, he worked at ETH Zurich, initially at the Chair of Architecture and Art under Professor Karin Sander, where he focused on 3D scanning, modeling, and immersive design, while also teaching courses such as "360° Reality to Virtuality" and "3D Scanning and Freeform Modelling." He later joined the Chair for Digital Building Technologies under Professor Dillenburger, where he expanded his research into AI-based design solutions. Between 2020 and 2023, he was an architect at Burkard Meyer Architekten, developing virtual reality workflows for the competition team. In 2022, he co-founded Hybrid Reality Research at ETH Zurich with Adi Grüninger, Nicolas Rolle, and Nico Stutz, a group focused on hybrid digital design solutions in architecture. Since 2023, he has been working at Penzel Valier, initially as an architect in the cost management team, and subsequently as a Project Manager for Landscape and Infrastructure. In 2024, he took on the role of Head of the AI Unit within the firm's technology department, focusing on the integration of AI in architectural workflows.

Immanuel Koh is an Assistant Professor in Design & Artificial Intelligence (DAI) and Architecture & Sustainable Design (ASD) at the Singapore University of Technology & Design (SUTD). Trained at the Architectural Association (AA) in London and holds a PhD from the School of Computer Sciences and Institute of Architecture at the École polytechnique fédérale de Lausanne (EPFL), he is an international pioneer in AI x Architecture. He directs Artificial-Architecture and is the Principal Investigator for several AI research projects, such as those supported by the National Research Foundation, AI Singapore, DesignSingapore, Urban Redevelopment Authority, Ministry of Defence, and National Supercomputing Centre. Internationally, he conducts research for high-profile architecture practices such as Zaha Hadid Architects (London) and MVRDV (Rotterdam) in developing custom state-of-the-art deep learning models. His work has been featured at premium AI conferences (e.g., CVPR, ICCV, NeurIPS, AAAI), published in top architecture journals (e.g., Architectural Intelligence, AD, Design Computing and Cognition), awarded with prestigious architectural design prizes (e.g., BLT, WAF, IDA, SG Mark, A'Design, ADC), and exhibited at international biennales and museums (e.g.,

Venice Architecture Biennales, V&A Museum, National Design Centre). Immanuel is the author of the book 'Artificial & Architectural Intelligence in Design' (2020) and guest-editor of IJAC special issue 'Artificial Architecture: Accelerated 3D Forms with Generative Artificial Intelligence' (2025). He is the conference chair of CAADRIA 2024 and co-curator of the Singapore Pavilion at the Venice Architecture Biennale 2025.

Julia Krasselt is a linguist and professor for methods of language data analysis at ZHAW. She studied German linguistics, medieval and modern history, and psychology at the University of Leipzig and received her PhD in linguistics from the Ruhr-Universität Bochum in 2016 with a corpus-linguistic study on the serialization of verb complexes in Early New High German. She worked as a research associate at Ruhr University Bochum from 2011 to 2016 before joining ZHAW in 2017, where she focuses on digital linguistics, corpus-based discourse analysis, and open research data. Her research includes large-scale projects such as Swiss-AL, a language data platform for analyzing multilingual discourse in Switzerland, as well as studies on media discourse, language technologies, and quantitative text analysis. Krasselt is co-founder of the ZHAW Digital Discourse Lab. Her research has been published in peer-reviewed journals such as the Journal of Cultural Analytics, Journal of Communication Management, Publizistik, and Zeitschrift für Diskursforschung, and she has contributed to edited volumes on corpus linguistics and digital discourse analysis. Krasselt is a strong advocate of Open Science in linguistic research.

Stefan Kurath is a Swiss architect, urbanist, lecturer, and writer whose work centers on the production of urban landscapes, the role of architects, and the future of architectural practice. After studying architecture in Switzerland and the Netherlands, Kurath read for a PhD at HCU Hamburg in the field of urban planning. Since 2010 Kurath has been co-director of the Institute of Urban Landscape at ZHAW School of Architecture, Design and Civil Engineering. Together with Peter Jenni he was awarded the 2013 Credit Suisse Award for Best Teaching for his Master Studio Urban Project. Alongside his academic work, Kurath works as an architect in his offices in Zurich and Grison. His projects, "Viamala Raststätte Thusis" and "Besucherzentrum Viamalaschlucht," were published in architecture journals internationally. He is also the author of many well-known books on architecture and urbanism, most recently *Baukultur mit Bestand* (Triest Verlag, 2025).

Clemens Lindner is a Designer at Zaha Hadid Architects, which he joined in 2021. He studied at TU Munich and the Tongji University in Shanghai. At Zara Hadid Architects, he is involved in innovative design projects, notably the Forest Green Rovers Eco-Stadium in England, a soccer stadium which features a pioneering timber frame structure—the first of its kind globally—as part of a broader zero-carbon campus initiative. Clemens specializes in the integration of Generative AI into contemporary design practices, focusing on systematic AI-assisted workflows and the development of custom AI models tailored to architectural applications. He organizes and leads forums such as the AI Round Table, which promotes knowledge exchange and explores the implementation of AI tools within diverse design projects and competitions. Additionally, Clemens has experience teaching and leading workshops at TU Munich and at various conferences in Germany and China. His research interests span the customization and application of Generative AI in design, with an emphasis on practical integration of AI technologies within professional architectural contexts. His work and contributions have been recognized by awards including the University Prize of the Bavarian Construction Industry Association and the Student Award for Excellence in Architecture from Tongji University.

Christian Georg Martin is professor of philosophy at the University of Stuttgart. He has also been a visiting professor at the University of Chicago, the Panthéon-Sorbonne in Paris, and the University of Leipzig. In his philosophical work he focuses on post-Kantian metaphysics, philosophy of logic and language, aesthetics, and the philosophy of nature. He is the author of three monographs entitled *Ontologie der Selbstbestimmung. Eine operationale Rekonstruktion von Hegels 'Wissenschaft der Logik'* (Mohr Siebeck, 2012), *Die Einheit des Sinns. Untersuchungen zur Form des Sprechens und Denkens* (Brill | Mentis, 2020) and *Hegel's Philosophy of Nature* (Cambridge University Press, forthcoming). Among others, he has edited *Language, Form(s) of Life, and Logic. Investigations after Wittgenstein* (de Gruyter, 2018) and *Naturästhetik im Zeitalter der ökologischen Krise* (Brill | Mentis, 2022).

Dieter Mersch, Prof. Dr. Emeritus, is a German philosopher and former Director of the Institute for Critical Theory at the Zurich University of the Arts (ZHdK). His work focuses on aesthetics, media and art theory, the philosophy of images and music, and the philosophical foundation of artistic research, and most recently on a critique of algorithmic rationality with a special link to the relation between art and AI. His main publications include *Posthermeneutik*

(De Gruyter, 2010), *Epistemologies of Aesthetics* (Diaphenes, 2015), *Kein Würfelwurf bringt den Zufall zu Fall. Spiel Kunst Zufall* (Willms Neuhaus Stiftung, 2023), *Actor & Avatar: A Scientific and Artistic Catalog*, edited with Anton Rey and Thomas Grunewald (transcript, 2023), *Humanismen und Antihumanismen. Studien zur Gegenwartsphilosophie* (Diaphenes, 2024), and *Kann KI Kunst?* (Herbert von Halem, forthcoming).

Michael Mieskes is an artist working in sculpture, painting, and digital modelling. He works as a lecturer at the architecture department of ZHAW and TU Munich. He holds a Bachelor of Arts in Industrial Design (Pforzheim University), a Diploma in Fine Arts (ADBK Munich), and a Master of Arts in Aesthetics (Goethe University Frankfurt/M.), focusing on philosophical aesthetics, media theory, and theory of the fine arts and architecture. He has recently submitted his PhD dissertation at Goethe University's Faculty of Philosophy, focusing on the effects of the digital and AI in artistic practice. His practical and theoretical interests include the influence of (digital) technologies on the arts, mimetic practices, and artistic material. He has received scholarships from the Digitalization Initiative of the Zurich Higher Education Institutions (DIZH), Bauhaus Stiftung Dessau, and Stiftung Kunstfonds, among others.

Darío Negueruela del Castillo has led the Center for Digital Visual Studies at the Max Planck Institute, University of Zurich since January 2020. From 2017 to 2019, he was Head of Research at the ALICE lab at EPFL, where he earned his PhD in 2017 with a dissertation entitled "The City of Extended Emotions." Negueruela del Castillo's current research focuses on the implicit urban theory of Foundation Multimodal Deep Learning Models, examining how to leverage these models' general learner capacities for urban analysis. He is also actively involved in the critical spatial curation of large collections using AI, demonstrated in his project "Newly Formed City" for the Helsinki Biennial. His research spans architecture, urbanism, affect, and spatial and visual perception with an emphasis on imagination and spatial agency. Among others, his current projects "On the Urbanity of Images" and "Multimodality and Digital Apophenia" explore the processes of machinic imagination, mimesis, and love and artificial desire. In addition to his research, Negueruela del Castillo is the co-founder, along with Shin Koseki, of Data Think, a research and educational platform dedicated to critical and creative approaches to data and its methodologies. Data Think has successfully organized three summer and winter schools to date. Negueruela del Castillo recently co-organized the symposium and upcoming edited volume "Digital Double—AI & Cities: Situating and Troubling AI Technologies for Architectural De/Reconstruction and Urban Simulation," as well as the "Uncertainty & Aesthetics Symposium 2025." He is the co-editor, alongside Eva Cetinic, of From Hype to Reality: Artificial Intelligence in the Study of Art and Culture (Hertziana Studies in Art History, 2024).

Iacopo Neri researches at the intersection of architecture, computer science, and the humanities. Engaged in both theoretical and applied research, he is passionate about the implications of machine learning for architecture and city studies and more generally the way we interact with the digital, and the way the digital interacts with us. He serves as Computational Lead at MUPD, and scientific collaborator for the Center for Digital Visual Studies (Max Planck – University of Zurich). He received an Msc in Architecture & Arch. engineering – Polytechnic University of Milan in 2019, and a Master degree in City and Technology, MaCT – Institute for Advanced Architecture of Catalonia – IAAC in 2017

Philipp Schaerer is a Swiss artist and lecturer whose work critically engages with digital image processing and examines the increasingly blurred boundaries in the representation of virtual and physical worlds. After studying architecture at EPFL, Philipp Schaerer worked from the year 2000 as an architect and knowledge manager at Herzog & de Meuron in Basel. He is the author of many well-known architectural visualizations for the same firm and has significantly contributed to new digital imagery standards in the architectural context through his work. Between 2003 and 2007, he directed the postgraduate program in CAAD under Prof. Dr. Ludger Hovestadt at the Department of Architecture at ETH Zurich. Since 2010, alongside his freelance artistic work, Philipp Schaerer has lectured at various universities in Switzerland, and since 2014 as a visiting professor at the School of Architecture at EPFL. Schaerer's works are continuously published and exhibited, and represented in several private and public collections including the Museum of Modern Art (MoMA) in New York, the Centre Pompidou in Paris, the National Museum of Norway in Oslo, the Museum of Contemporary Photography (MoCP) in Chicago, the Center for Art and Media Karlsruhe (ZKM), and the Fotomuseum in Winterthur. In 2023, Schaerer was honored with the Art Prize of the City of Thun.

Bige Tunçer is a Professor and Chair of Information Systems in the Built Environment at TU/e in the Netherlands. She is an architect and researcher specializing in data-driven AI methodologies for design and decision support in the built environment. Her chair's work focuses on the interplay between urban spaces, user behavior, and perception, as well as the role of physical attributes in shaping spatial experiences. She holds a PhD in Architecture (Design Informatics) from TU Delft, an MSc in Computational Design from Carnegie Mellon University, and a BArch from Middle East Technical University. Before joining TU/e, she was an Associate Professor at SUTD, an Assistant Professor at TU Delft, and a Junior Faculty member at ETH Zurich. She has also held visiting positions at ETH Zurich, MIT, and the University of Pavia. Her research centers on data collection, information and knowledge modeling, and visualization to support architectural and urban design, energy transition, urban resilience, digital construction, and nature-based solutions. As an established leader in evidence-based design and urban science, she leads and collaborates on large-scale, multidisciplinary research projects spanning AI, IoT, big data, and smart cities. She frequently delivers keynote speeches at academic, governmental, and industry events and serves on various expert panels and advisory boards. Her work has been widely published in leading academic journals and conference proceedings and has received international recognition through exhibitions and awards.

Image Copyrights

Introduction
Fig. 1: © Werner Hofmann
Fig. 2: Gottfried Semper, *Entwurf eines Systemes der vergleichenden Stillehre*, 1884
Fig. 3: © Midjourney

Elena Gavagnin
Fig. 4: © Giorgia Lupi and Stefanie Posavec
Fig. 5: Wikipedia

Dieter Mersch
Fig. 6: Wikipedia
Fig. 7: Wikipedia

Christian Georg Martin
Fig. 8: © Christian Georg Martin
Fig. 9: © Christian Georg Martin
Fig. 10: © Christian Georg Martin
Fig. 11: Fliegende Blätter, 23. 10. 1892

Mario Carpo
Fig. 12: Leonbattista Alberti, *Della Architettura. Della Pittura e Della Statua*, Traduzione di Cosimo Bartoli (Bologna, 1782)

Philipp Schaerer
Fig. 13: © Philipp Schaerer
Fig. 14: © Philipp Schaerer
Fig. 15: © Philipp Schaerer/Midjourney
Fig. 16: © Philipp Schaerer/Midjourney

Fig. 17: © Philipp Schaerer/Midjourney
Fig. 19: © Philipp Schaerer

Julia Krasselt
Fig. 19: © Julia Krasselt
Fig. 20: © Julia Krasselt

Bige Tunçer, Cem Ataman
Fig. 21: © Bige Tunçer
Fig. 22: © Bige Tunçer
Fig. 23: © Bige Tunçer
Fig. 24: © Bige Tunçer
Fig. 25: © Bige Tunçer
Fig. 26: © Bige Tunçer, Cem Ataman

Darío Negueruela del Castillo, Iacopo Neri
Fig. 27: © Darío Negueruela del Castillo, Iacopo Neri
Fig. 28: © Darío Negueruela del Castillo, Iacopo Neri
Fig. 29: © Darío Negueruela del Castillo, Iacopo Neri
Fig. 30: © Darío Negueruela del Castillo, Iacopo Neri
Fig. 31: © Darío Negueruela del Castillo, Iacopo Neri

Roberto Bottazzi
Fig. 32: © Xuming Cai, Muskaan Mardia, Yiwen Qian, Yiheng Xu, Accent Diffusion, B-Pro Urban Design RC14, Bartlett School of Architecture, University College London (UCL), 2023
Fig. 33: © Credits: Liu Jie, Wu Yu, Wang Huiye, Ping Yuan, Sensory Balance, B-Pro Urban Design RC14, Bartlett School of Architecture, University College London (UCL), 2024
Fig. 34: © Credits: Manan Hingoo, Qiutong Huang, Flip Meijaard, Jiahui Xu, B-Pro Urban Design RC14, Bartlett School of Architecture, University College London (UCL), 2023
Fig. 35: © Credits: Sharima Achmad, Ananya Pandey, Shiyun Yang, Ebb and Evolve, B-Pro Urban Design RC14, Bartlett School of Architecture, University College London (UCL), 2024

Adam Kiryk
Fig. 36: © Penzel Valier

Christoph Geiger, Clemens Lindner
Fig. 37: The images are courtesy of Zaha Hadid Architects.
Fig. 38: The images are courtesy of Zaha Hadid Architects.
Fig. 39: The images are courtesy of Zaha Hadid Architects.

Giulio Bettini, Ron Edelaar
Fig. 40: © Midjourney
Fig. 41: © Midjoiurney

Immanuel Koh
Fig. 42: © Immanuel Koh
Fig. 43: © Immanuel Koh
Fig. 44: © Immanuel Koh
Fig. 45: © Immanuel Koh
Fig. 46: © Immanuel Koh